NEW COLLECTED POEMS

W. S. GRAHAM

New Collected Poems

edited by Matthew Francis

faber and faber

First published in 2004
by Faber and Faber Limited
3 Queen Square London WC1N 3AU
Published in the United States by Faber and Faber Inc.
an affiliate of Farrar, Straus and Giroux LLC, New York

Photoset by Wilmaset Ltd, Birkenhead, Wirral
Printed in England by T.J. International Ltd, Padstow, Cornwall

A CIP record for this book
is available from the British Library

ISBN 0–571–21015–5

2 4 6 8 10 9 7 5 3 1

Contents

THE NIGHTFISHING (1955)

Foreword

Greenock is where what used to be industrial Clydeside gives in to the grander, more permanent theatre of the Firth of Clyde, after, that is, its own drama of once-busy shipyards, ropeworks and sugar refineries. To that extent, as in many places in the British Isles, it can be seen as a border country – waterscapes, hills, mountains, proud industry and robust, stone-built settlements, and none of them far from agriculture, song, and legend. John Galt was raised in Greenock, and John Davidson also was brought up there and wrote about the place in his 'A Ballad in Blank Verse on the Growth of a Poet'. Travelling west along the south bank of the Clyde, Greenock comes immediately after Port Glasgow, where James ('City of Dreadful Night') Thomson was born. More recently it figures in Bill Bryden's plays and Alan Sharp's fiction as well as Peter McDougall's tough TV scripts.

W. S. Graham's early background was in engineering. Much of what has been criticized as his 'rhetoric' might be better understood as a joy taken in the design and joining of words, cadences and images, all within what seems a concept of sonic draughtsmanship. It is an approach to poetry which he intuited from how he was immersed in his home town. Dylan Thomas is frequently mentioned as an immediate source of Graham's poetic habits. While that is true to some extent (if you add Hopkins, Joyce, Eliot, Hart Crane, and others) it should be equally clear that Thomas, too, was a writer affectionately and expertly involved with an immediate community. It is more conspicuous in Thomas's work through his short stories and *Under Milk Wood*, but present in the poems too. Graham, though, reserved prose almost entirely for his correspondence, and his fiction-making prowess for myth-building through imagination. Graham's work as a whole creates the remarkable impression of a poet determined to be proseless. He was relatively untouched by the commerce in poetic argument, or by the anxieties of critical debate, as if they might have contaminated a purity of

xiii

response to what his instincts and convictions demanded he try to achieve. He seems a poet who was immune to changing fashion and who possessed an effortless knack of digging his heels in and defending his own gift. Instead of the tiresome footwork of reputation-making, with which readers of new poetry have become more than familiar, he preferred a remoter existence, in Cornwall, with forays to the U.S.A. and London and elsewhere such as Iceland and Crete. In a relatively late poem, 'The Night City', he wrote of London, 'the golden city' (that phrase being an echo of a children's song, usually sung by girls when skipping rope):

> Between the big buildings
> I sat like a flea crouched
> In the stopped works of a watch.

Cornwall provided him with a community, of wife, friends, some of them artists, if not relatives and family friends, even if it was far from the

> unwitnessed town
> Set where my making and collected surnames wrangle
> To landmark the sudden garden past the latch.

Famously, perhaps notoriously, readers and critics since the 1950s and the emergence of the journalistically invented Movement have found trouble appreciating Graham's poetry, although there were those who followed his work admiringly throughout his career, while after the publication of *Malcolm Mooney's Land* in 1970 he attracted loyal and younger readers. It could be more truthful to suggest that opposers of his work and its principles have simply found them harder to understand than they actually are in a context of poetry less inventive in diction, less challenging in subject matter, more given to a clearer narrative, and infatuated with ordinary existence. It is as if many readers find Graham a sort of throwback to the 1940s, a relic of that stream and sound of poetry allegedly obliterated by the Movement, which is what a simplified canonical belief in literary history invites us to believe. Simplified literary history can be a comfort to some, but to those whom it omits, or slanders, it can be injurious. As Ian Hamilton pointed out in the introduction to his *Oxford Companion to Twentieth-Century Poetry*, a damaged reputation may not necessarily be rectified through a process of 'passage-of-time school of literary judgement'. 'It isn't true that "if it's good, it will survive"; someone, somewhere, has to keep saying that it's good – or if not good, exactly, then at least worthy of a small piece of the historical jigsaw, the map.' Steadfastness of supporters (and the steadfastness, the indestructibility of the work) have led to Graham's reappearance in this necessary and excellent volume. And if anyone needs a canonical crutch to help them recognize Graham's value, then let them attend to T. S. Eliot's opinion. Writing of *The Nightfishing*, Eliot said that 'some of these poems – by their sustained power, their emotional depth and maturity and their superb technical skill – may well be among the more important poetical achievements of our time' (quoted in *NFM*, p. ix).[*] Eliot was Graham's editor and publisher and his opinions carry weight. Yet they are not entirely full-throated – 'some', 'may well be'. But I believe that Eliot has been proved right.

Graham is a poet of place, or, rather, places – Greenock, Cornwall, and imaginary or 'constructed' spaces such as the sea when converted by the application of the poet's experience and intellect, or the Arctic/Antarctic, the icy and glacial, the remotest, loneliest spaces on the planet. He is also a poet who writes out of an early working-class experience of life but from whose work self-conscious proletarianizing is absent. Simultaneously, in Joyce's oft-quoted expression in *Portrait of the Artist*, he flew 'by the nets' devised in this case by Hugh MacDiarmid and cast by him in order to confine Scottish poets to manifestly Scottish purposes and language. Graham's relations with MacDiarmid were cordial enough, however, although from early on, and despite some conspicuous Scots diction, and always a Scots voice, Graham had no time for the Nationalist prescriptions for poetry laid down by the older poet. What connects them is a concern for language.

[*]For abbreviations used in the Foreword, Introduction and Notes, see Bibliography, p. 379.

In MacDiarmid's case it was a matter of historical re-enactment, a battle of retrieved words lined like a regiment of the Sealed Knot Society (and there are equivalents in Scotland) and fighting a war in the distant past which MacDiarmid's linguistic gestures sought to bring back into the present. MacDiarmid was also the erudite author of *In Memoriam James Joyce* (1955), written in 'synthetic English' and subtitled 'from *A Vision of World Language*'. Graham was more interested in, more obsessed with, communication itself, with the imperatives of listening and reading, and the improbability of being entirely heard or understood. It is his major subject, and, like a songbird's, it has no nationality unless one is imposed on it arbitrarily.

What Graham's poetry is about is illuminated by remarks scattered through his correspondence. For example, in 1943 he wrote to Edwin Morgan that 'A poet doesn't write what he knows but what he doesn't know' (*NFM*, p. 14). Quotidian, autobiographical reality formed far less of Graham's poetic than that of a poet like Philip Larkin. When it dawned on Larkin that he could write straight from his own life, it proved a liberation. Such a notion never so much as crossed Graham's mind. In one of his rare prose pieces, Graham wrote,

> The most difficult thing for me to remember is that a poem is made of words and not of the expanding heart, the overflowing soul, or the sensitive observer. A poem is made of words. It is words in a certain order, good or bad by the significance of its addition to life and not to be judged by any other value put upon it by imagining how or why or by what kind of man it was made. (*Poetry Scotland*, No. 3, July 1946; reprinted in *NFM*, pp. 379–83).

These were early convictions, but he stuck by them throughout his life and career. That they diverged from how poetry tended after the 1950s seems not to have caused him the slightest anxiety. An exhilarating fact of that career is his dedication and independence of mind, despite the penury which he was obliged to endure as a consequence. For years he was sidelined, or neglected, even ignored, but he proved himself durable and dogged. He underwent that determined, suffering silence which turned out to be a touchstone or proof of his subjects and the artistry through which he presented them. It can sometimes seem that a poet's value in society is the perseverance with which he or she cleaves to instinctive choices made early on and which in the course of time become identifying matters of faith or principle.

Literary history invites us to *choose* between Graham and Larkin, or Larkin and Hughes, or who and who . . . It's the owl-cry of bores attempting to make a name for themselves by 'revising the canon'. God rot them. In doing what they do they show that literary history is often wrong, its fallibility caused by a self-interested heave of opinion, much of it academic, and most of it guilty of ignoring the possibility that poetry can emerge from mysterious sources, both secular and spiritual at the same time, and address itself mysteriously to mysterious subjects. There are different kinds of poetry and they are all indispensable. My first encounter with Graham's work was *The Nightfishing* (1955), which I bought secondhand from a book-barrow in a lane off Renfield Street in Glasgow over forty years ago in 1960. Thoroughly jolted by local references which spoke to me of the Firth of Clyde, which I knew well, from the water and not just 'views' from the land, I was obliged to shudder with an acknowledgement to myself that I'd never before heard of this poet.

> Very gently struck
> The quay night bell.

Could these opening lines of *The Nightfishing* be any more evocative, authoritative, exact, and as wonderful as they are? The impression is as beautiful as the green light that Jay Gatsby sees on a pier on the other side of his Firth, except that here we do not see it so much as listen to it. Graham can oblige you to listen to light. His poetry permits you to listen to what is not normally audible.

> I am befriended by
> This sea which utters me.

He is a poet who surrenders to the impulses and wisdoms offered by his subjects. Although the 'voice' in his poems is strong, and there is much first-person singular, there is hardly any presence of an ego, of a personality and its grievances, although there is regret embodied in his recollections of the past. Much of his achievement stems from this. Graham's is a poetry very much of voice or sound, but with doses of self kept to a minimum, although there can be heard an audible force of character. 'These words take place', he writes in *The Nightfishing*. He saw his poems as *events* that would 'disturb the language'.

If *The Nightfishing* represents the height of his ambition by the mid-1950s, it was to be fifteen years before his next collection finally appeared. *Malcolm Mooney's Land* (1970) was worth the wait. The title poem contains one of his crucial images, perhaps one of the most arresting moments in twentieth-century poetry as a whole. Here he has no need to mention the word 'language'. Instead, the image says it all, and appeals to the five senses with uncanny force.

> Yesterday
> I heard the telephone ringing deep
> Down in a blue crevasse.
> I did not answer it and could
> Hardly bear to pass.

The repetition of 'language' and communication as obsessive, unfinished subjects can at times feel overdone. But they sit at the core of his work in a context of the sea, aloneness, love, friendships, memories, of speaking into a haunted and haunting void. It is as if his meanings exist on a table by lamplight, dropped there from a questing mind, in a place where solitude and silence were possible. He is a nocturnal poet, a poet of 'the small hours' who can perceive the poetic momentousness of what are practically non-events.

> Yet somewhere a stone
> Speaks and maybe a leaf
> In the dark turns over.

Implements in Their Places appeared in 1977, just two years before *Collected Poems 1942–1977*. Simple bibliographical fact illustrates how Graham's reputation and readers' interest in his work had become consolidated after years of relative neglect. *Implements* included 'Johann Joachim Quantz's Five Lessons', which I consider one of his finest poems. Quantz, an eighteenth-century virtuoso flautist, speaks on five occasions to a pupil, Karl, 'a lout from the canal/ With big ears but an angel's tread on the flute.' I feel tempted to read it as the closest we get to a manifesto on art-making by Graham, the least abstract of cerebral, contemplative poets. It ends:

> What can I say more?
> Do not be sentimental or in your Art.
> I will miss you. Do not expect applause.

Douglas Dunn
Dairsie, October 2003

Introduction

Admirers of W. S. Graham have long felt that his *Collected Poems* is due for revision. It is not, in fact a collected volume at all: while the last three collections, *The Nightfishing* (1955), *Malcolm Mooney's Land* (1970) and *Implements in their Places* (1977), are included complete, the book contains only a selection of his earlier work. In 1979, this omission was understandable; the poetry of the neo-romantic 1940s, when Graham began his career, was treated by critics as an embarrassment. Unlike some of his contemporaries, however – Tom Scott and Norman MacCaig, for example – who renounced their work of this period, he never regretted his youthful experimentalism, and defended it to the last. Writing to Gavin Saunders, he maintained:

> My early poems are as good as my later poems. They are maybe not as fashionable, but neither are my later poems. The early poems are other objects with their own particular energies. To say I am getting better, or have written myself into a greater clearness, is very much a surface observation. (*NFM*, p. 367.)

Now, with the steady growth of his reputation since his death in 1986, and an increasing interest in the British modernist poetry scene in which he started his career, it is time to make the entire contents of his seven collections available at last.

A more difficult decision is what to do about the material Graham never published in book form. There are the poems published in magazines which he left out of his collections, or which were written too late for the *Collected*, and there are the poems from notebooks or included in letters to friends. Some of this work has already found its way into print, notably in the pamphlet *Uncollected Poems* and the book *Aimed at Nobody*. Nevertheless, it has a different status from 'the official canon', as the editors of *Aimed at Nobody* acknowledge in their introduction. Graham himself was quite clear about the distinction; when one of his off-the-cuff poems was printed in the *Times Literary Supplement* without his permission, his reaction was indignant (*NFM*, p. 189). I have therefore decided to segregate uncollected and manuscript poems in an appendix. *Uncollected Poems* and *Aimed at Nobody* are included complete, as well as a few other poems which have not yet appeared in book form. The present collection makes no claim to be a *Complete Poems*, but I believe it does contain his best and most representative work.

In making the notes for this collection I have been astonished all over again by the richness of Graham's vocabulary (including many words drawn from Scots), by the breadth of his knowledge of myth, history, art and popular culture, and by the ease with which he slips between the real world and one peopled by the creatures of his imagination. It is not always easy to tell the latter two categories apart (and no doubt it is not meant to be). The references in these poems leave plenty of scope for scholars of the future. In particular there are many minor characters for whom I have not been able to provide supplementary information, and who may be either fictional or untraced real figures. To avoid too much repetition or cross-referencing between notes, I have created separate sections for people and places mentioned in the poems, and a glossary. Readers seeking help with a particular poem are advised to read the notes to that poem first, then turn to one or more of the other sections if necessary.

Graham's spelling and punctuation often appear eccentric. While this may sometimes be attributable to simple error, he was also fascinated by the transformations that could be achieved by breaching the conventional boundaries of words and sentences. Words are run together (*gloworm, lamblood*) or split apart (*child / Hood, home / Ing*), or their spelling changed to create new meanings (*nighthead* instead of *knighthead*). Syntax is given similar treatment: 'Gently disintegrate me / Said nothing at all.' This approach, liberating for the poet, can cause problems for the editor. In the end, the only consistent policy is to resist the temptation to make corrections, and follow the text of the *Collected Poems*, or best published source. The only changes made are corrections of known typographical errors, and the replacement of double inverted commas, as used in the *Collected Poems*, with the less intrusive single ones, as found in the original volumes. Unpublished poems follow the manuscript, even to the extent of reproducing an obvious (but not authenticated) typo like 'the the' in 'With the Dulle Griet in Canada'. Readers should note that the names of people and places are also subject to Graham's playful transgressions. A misspelled name may be the marker of a shift into a parallel universe, as in the poem 'A Walk to the Gulvas' where the poet and his wife vainly search the Cornish landscape for a place transformed by his imagination from its real-world equivalent, the Galvers. The originals of proper nouns can be found in the glosses of the People and Places sections.

MATTHEW FRANCIS

Acknowledgements

I should like to thank the following people for their help with this book: Paul Keegan, for offering his own enthusiastic support along with that of Graham's publishers; Anthony Astbury, Ronnie Duncan, Geoffrey Godbert and Malcolm Mackintosh for assistance in compiling materials; Susan Gillespie, Eddie Dowds, 'Uncle Bernie' and members of Sue's Blether Board for information on Greenock and Scottish life in general; Tony Lopez, whose pioneering scholarship I have drawn on freely for the notes; and my wife Creina for living with all of it. Most of all, I should like to thank Michael and Margaret Snow, whose ceaseless and devoted work has surely been the biggest single factor in the steady growth of Graham's reputation since his death, and who have lent their knowledge and experience to this project as to so many others.

THE SEVEN JOURNEYS
(1944)

.

THE NARRATOR

I am the hawk-heart braced in the epic's hero
Hollow and lit in a single follyless zone
Twinned with a dawn and a dark.
Graceless in gardens I hear my unvisited care
Squawk back at the sculptured cuckoo's nursery rhyme
Chimed in the dandelion tower.
Eyelashed and petald alone in the shepherd season
I walk heaved high from the earth confessing the voice
That runs ever over the hour
Confessing the death without space for the laying of dead
The rudder and rocket stem and the murder swerve
At the tender right-wrong heart.

The hiccuping hero the narrator lindenward
Reels at the waltz with diaphanous water fronds
Telling his ribbed in vanity.
I worship a skylift of Narnain blaeberry globed
Priestlike sealed in a tensile sac in a nerve
In the vein-geared bubble of vision.
While whisper the tethered anemones under the grave
And the narrative sprouts from the bone-sweet skull
Telling a blossom to its bulb
And spins in a hollow of sound in the emerald dome
Tinctured vermilion and told in the glacier heart
That trades the unmapped spell along the blood.

The raven at larch time dwarfed in the calyxed chronicle
In my head's helmet weathers no wheeling sky.
The banished bird spins no horizon.
Yet my eye webs the word. History in a bowl
Spreads out a firth for ptarmigan and the pedlar's moth
And anarchy within a cage.

3

Who knows the rose or quotes her holy somersaults
Preached from a dangled spinner on a maypole thread.
What summer eyes perched deep within a dream
Could bring the god the child and the rose to speak.
What tongue like a stamen stemmed on a kiss or a grave
Is yet enchanted into form.

THE FIRST JOURNEY

Launched three windy neptunes high from a gargoyle scree
My birth in a spittle of glass like the death of a lark
In a settling largo falls from the crucified height
Or in motion fearfully loves the rainbow waterspout
And climbs the myth, the tented miracle.
Born in a diamond screeched from a mountain pap
My faith with a hoof in myrtle considers the jig
Of the rowans and brambles rocked in the beanstalked moon.
Amen to the dark medusa freezing in air
With the plough in sparstone like the eyes of idols.
Without a song backward since spring bleeds the peat at my shin
My balancing giant so strideful of farewell words
Leads the tenderly mimicing feet of my wormward heart
On a weaving hair path gouged by a roving seal
Through mauve seas tasselled and trellissed in emerald.

Each eye has a maidenhead set for a crimson cry
That will swim from the oak of my human ghost
Or flow in a troutless day from Sgurr nan Gillian
The crumple of waking wind at my winter's edge
Peers over the prance of my shoulder in air
At the last erupted second, feeding my dance
Through Helen's eyes down through the prayers of fingers.
The sponge of stone holds cold my cinder of striding
Holds my earth's map of journeys like a toadstool owl.
Now my young shouldering east radiant in quartz

Spins on a pilgrim compass through the dawn
Stranding the stars on waking shoals of light.
My flourishing prophet on cockhorse scatters the sun
Through dragonfly graves dark on my pith of travel.
SHEER I break AGAINST those EVERMORE GLITTERING SEASONS.

THE SECOND JOURNEY

Even this woman to her lover woven
Inherits my spidering stranger's mile upon mile
Over skeleton fevers of bells that speak
Swung in the shell of her creel-dwelling heart.
In a meadowing ballad my sprit points bliss
To plough in the rivering air of her footpath songs.
And away where forsworn profiles in her eyes
Peak their discovered metaphors through mortal dells
My brogue strikes kingdoms on enduring flints.
My cobbler's innocence breaks too fondly sprigged
Across her estuary of oyster-speaking womb.

Even the harlequin at blithe meridian
Snared at her elbow furred with a driven frost
Takes my wind's feathering dagger of crystal North
Over his legendary silt of brain.
His twelfth day dies. He herds peninsulas of dark
Brings round his sky the straying seeds of stars.
They roost in minnow-crossing circuses above his land.
And I move under climbing the coral sins
Their charmed way branching from his clown-bonny cairns
And stitch my floral spectre on his proud cataract
That spins the cascade-turning mills on his moral glade
And drains to farthest outlines of his vaulted fable.

Even this landscape piled in a level of love
Wrecks a rich filament of roads across my heel.
Three rivers rinse a desert from my prow.

A mountain's wiseman covers with perfect joy
The brow of a tumult of splendours hung in midamber.
Under my threading demon, direction in a gland
Throws round her dream's device a hermit's oval.
Over my hair in a gale of geese
The clown's volcano and the echoing girl's plateau.
And this saint's bridge that decorates with lightning
My shadow's perpetual visit, excels my birth.

THE THIRD JOURNEY

Later through a million fells the tempest in my spine
Lays a strath-serpent engraved on the roseate earth
From my wakened head's young verdict of the year
To seasons sluiced in a paradise of pinions
In carillioned regions hung with a vow of stars.
Were you in this land with the clutch of a poet's sleeve
With the venturing rill of my scarlet spraying marvel
Crossing more luminous margins than April.
For I am a genius of rivers. My muse is a ship
Exalted and rigged on the spray that your worlds present
To my hazards of spate, like a nebulae-misted child
Lonely of lullabys pelted on aerial plains
And sailing on deltas endeared in the wizard's head.

My mast in pearly latitudes of ploughman's skies
Dredges the rooks from under simpler keels
Than score their dusk-endented wakes in divers' ears.
I build an iliad in a limpet dome.
I lay my tributary words in lovers' lakes
Tangled and tied in a knot of eels
Melodiously patterned in a pitch-black shell
That whorls my ruddering heaven in grammars of tide.
Charted on leaves the crucified river in veins
Harks with a bridebell speaking on far canals

To the drunken bow of a foreign sailor's knell
That swims on the foam of your whale in a gland of blood.

I am a scholar of seas. My alphabet steers
The mull of a kettledrummed villagers' land of choirs
And swings from the elbow of friends at a fair of peaks
To the untillered islandless reasons of tide
That spill in a seanight's cave behind the eyes.
Still I pass fathom-voyaged in a volted thread
Rigged with a stay of justice devised in fables
Differently learning an avalanche of kin.
Here at this leapfrog place learning laws
Building an infant's alchemy of mermaid wests,
My craft with leopards at the lonely bow
Swings a long shadowed jib of proud alarms
And wakens villages and larks in scalloped cells.

THE FOURTH JOURNEY

There are no certain miles in ice-invented vales
Yet look where my saint's value pads in snow turrets
Like down a polar spiral in a berg of bone
And scrawls on keels of glaciers governed in glass
The sign of a nervous leglong crucifixion.
This is a pod of creeds, an architecture
Towered with needles, rung with a peal of seeds
That veer on infant-levered winds over pale ranges
Nailed to the gyring victories of North and South.
Yet all in ice-constructed fruit in glass orchards.

Answering the abstract annals of unhero'd floes
The chimes of sweet Elizabethan turtled air
Guide their soul cirrus monuments of azure
Round the skull's thundery cathedral adored in ice.
Let this head's unsearched gorge gird a fool's Philomel.
Let this bird's moon bleach a swain's velvet bed.

Let me from a Celtic sex with granite my costume
Rise like a bangled Messiah in a saga's beak
And break the Arctic girl with no seal's barrier
And set her madrigals round my flint wrists.

There are no sheer frontiers of bliss in astral prisms
The crystal pastures unsure with spectral foals
The stallions stamping rainbows on unbridged graves.
And under icy garments of the waves and plains
The barriers lay a maze athwart exchanging battles.
I see the new summer-dreamed arc in the master sky
And juggle with highroads of precious eyes
For my next step's harbour further than perfection
Or any ceiling's rubies barbaric in halls of love.

My eyes with no landmark tangle in towns.
My toe displays its blizzard to curious accordians.
Foals crop on wise gentians and scare to stalls.
And rats to watchtower ruins run in eternal fear.
This is no tinkling entrance bridged through gems
But eyes derived from mangers in Northern stables
Enter their polar globes for my socket's luggage
And carry all this town's transparent grace
Scored and graded on a glaze of frost
That spheres the jingling fingernail of Christ.

THE FIFTH JOURNEY

Becoming a swan let my sailing sperm relate
The ruthless chorus in a fen of swerving queens
As through a sound my chaos wading the capsized stain
Wins from the varnished loch's awakened runnels
An intimate prologue to a babbling flock of heads.
If only a dish in a cradle of quarries would hear
My sailing song of rituals coiled in willow worms
My water round of fame divining the foam in a womb

And load the fenian idiot's ear and plunge his eye
Where millwakes rob a parliament of ponds.
For this cast swan-mark becoming reality
Speaks with a word of webs in suicides of foam
And finds this history based on level lakes
Where morning unwinds a woman to a cripple.

Becoming the shame on a spilling virgin's mask
My limbs erect a hovering roof of birds
To shelter this unfenced river-couch of dams
Where gardeners prune the glow-worm coasts in breasts
And screen her vault's vagina with tormenting rakes.
As I in solitary distortion on enamelled weirs
Veer through a wave on a girl's diagonal joy
Flesh sings a law of years from grief to grave
And hangs a rebel from a theory's watershed.
So between parallel cliffs walling the seed's minch
I pass in the soil of a bed-sinning venus
And hear the archaic crimes on shore gardens
The cries of the lame sexdealer on nipples of rock
And the flashing funeral of night in anchored knees.

Becoming a dhow from the reign of a finial phallus
My deity buoyed on the lake of a basin of bone
Unreefs a windy code across the gruff season
And twines a linen language on tilting acres.
The lame girl pegged on the daughter's bitter sheet
Marks out in sanskrit her love-broke bible
Lays out a legend on her heart-built pebble
And turns her winter's manuscript to face the wall.
If words in a woman of silk hold a wand's wound
Then this bell singing duties to the mandrake vandal
Unfastens Magdalen to love and leads her guilt
On morning shores where stamens are bound in stooks.

THE SIXTH JOURNEY

A hundred heavens and west on every pinnacle
Tent with a geography of gannets my trinket skerry
And wheel the fish in piper's gales of vine
Round the surf spun in a cherry in mangers of dulse.
With Judas my head, the thunderclapping hub
The joywheel ring of tempest-engendered wrack
Peels round my Crusoe sky a drunken almanac
Lights on this Galway inish my island's negro
And swings the wrinkling sea on a servant hinge.
Here inland the goat on felsite galleries
Diseased with the bleat of a brain's nightingale
On crevice altars crops the briny grape
And crops the burning bush with shrivelled heart.
I am the spindle of the equator's garland
Signed with the intellectual bruise from agate.

My cavalcade of druids that hoop the island's guts
In miraculous dykes from pineal elements
Expose the otter in the insect's flying sea
Weaving a dead rudder in hemispheres of milt.
Here is the navigating beetle that quenches Jesus
And stings a cauterising reel in gaelic kilns.
But I, although the bonfire in my blackthorn ribs
Translates my reasonable church to ladled kelp,
Spin out on fertile kyles a footprint wake
Fictitious as the telescope's terrain of torrents.
As salt as glittering gratitude this testament
Heaves in a trend of rock-betrothing darlings.
I call the ocean my faith. I write my breath
On bright unpunishable minds where pentacles
Singe the winged flamen's pelt and branded loin
And jerk an earring's carol as he milks the stars.

Who times my deity, defines my walking sin
In curfew inches on a chain of printed chimes?
What text is my breath on resurrected reefs
Where west records my teething bliss of helms?
Lulled in a mould the main dead land replies.
A collar-bone of moor recites a pine's history
Building a silent lintel on the curlew's parish.
In the main grave where resin fountains and fiddles
Beetles cast peacocks. A Mary blesses worms
Still as unhunted wires folded in ticking fossils.
And all the continent of season-bottled kings
Where climates rule the coursing heaven cat
Translate the burning strata of this clay sermon
And hang a heather harvest from a tomb-cold gravity.
I am the frosty prophet of a grasshopping summer.

THE SEVENTH JOURNEY

Time and again a Mayscape's botany shapes
My weathering heart that shakes and marks a door.

Forerunning the rose and climbing swans and skies
My anvil hill (who tells what a faith will forge?)
Makes trim a law-landmark for summer's instrument
Makes sure example of the skinflint spring
That fires a country foreword to my spinal stair
And fashions a journey's flora in my liveoak sense.
Cock of the season-printed North, with a name of litmus
Testing the pollen scales and scotfree crimson lyns,
My ceaseless trespass steps a bridge-swung formula.
With wonder towards, expecting only, prophecy
From any pedestrian ocean or fisherman,
I, in the rills and eddy of a wreck's triton scream
Gesture a harbour in morning for a beggar finch.
An easter tree of crosses, green sin by sin

Sprouts a long spite of inches on my stepping zodiac
That whets a young moon in the tightrope ruffian dusk
To screech cut water from Christ's walking feet.

It has been dialogue and garden's answer
In my nightfalling heart, delving a valley.

Beyond my dawnrung footgems tilts a stellar phrase
Preaching a discovered hallow to my world's toe-stars
Till my truth's accident builds a sealed tropic of love
Girt with a cage of latitudes no gauge destroys
And exiled in a molecule no liberty selects.
Here is the midwife anarchy of longedfor summer.
Here is the husband hearseman in the enchanted meter.
And I am the eyelashed son with a private proverb
Dreaming a glenman's library under Cruachan.
Count out the thunderlimits of the exquisite step
Through the griefless arcade of this median spring.
Count out the distant seasons. The towns lie under.
Hear the far face and voice as though of winter.
Somewhere in distilled harmonies a tumult spins
One for each human constellation in a skull,
And blows a world of faculties in a watched bubble
And ribs my magpie comet in a cage without grievance.

History has run along my heart's boundaries
And webbed a creature, so making noisy war.

Time takes my hand. Here, as the headland fosters joy
Caverned in foreheads, outlawed in whinstone fists,
The calendar calls diagrams down dinging wells.
The nighthead tells my simple destination
With the unstinted wailing signs of encirclement
That break upon the shores of my deserves.
The earth, braced as a steed to draw the prince
With spear of joy between the cockroach spires
Revolves in each ingredient and flower,

Turns with the meadow's gentle acrobat.
I fall not here nor ever when beetles clock blood
That flows in a crimson aqueduct on the green heartside,
Can fear suggest my lover in a puppet sexton
Dangling a wilderness of love from her fond ceiling.
I fill the chart but the heart is a changing ground.
The eye is a lake. The sky is Neptune hovering.
May was my law. Nineteen fortytwo.

CAGE WITHOUT GRIEVANCE
(1942)

OVER THE APPARATUS OF
THE SPRING IS DRAWN

Over the apparatus of the Spring is drawn
A constructed festival of pulleys from sky.
A dormouse swindled from numbers into wisdom
Trades truth with bluebells. The result unknown
Fades in the sandy beetle-song that martyrs hear
Who longingly for violetcells prospect the meads.

As luck would testify, the trend for logic's sake
Takes place on pleasant landscapes within graves
That flesh, the sun's minister, in jealous agonies
Seeks out in choral vagaries with bird and blood.
Those funnels of fever (but melody to gales)
Tenant the spiral answer of a scarecrow daisy.

The country crimes are doctrines on the grass
Preaching a book of veins. The answer is order.
A derrick in flower swings evening values in
And wildernight or garden day frames government
For thieves in a prison of guilt. Birches erect
The ephemeral mechanism of welcoming.
And Spring conquests the law in a cuckoo's school.

OF THE RESONANT RUMOUR OF SUN,
IMPULSE OF SUMMER

Of the resonant rumour of sun, impulse of summer
My bride is born. Love finds not here ambition.
I am the dunce of sacrifice yet at the sun's table
With vein after vein unmaking the cadence of blood

My hope is wildly heaven's, certain of conflict.
Who, with a heart bound to his writing battle
Would sign humanity and index legendary bliss?

Questions ring bells and thistles blow the time.
Chime speaks in silken floaters. The answer settles.
Blood builds its platform on a love-me-not
And calculates from exile the seed's dominion.
Love cascades myrtle gospels from the nipple's hill.
Who, with a nettle forefinger sparking covenants
Will sting humanity and point the docken ground?

How shall I deal her the shock of summer?
Well the Spring knows and the hovering ram
That prances the long black gunwale of days.
Questions bud arteries and tribunals cast berries.
The weasel prints lust in a palace of maggots.
Who, with a map of picnics primed for April
Could probe humanity and hoist a sign of veins?

O GENTLE QUEEN OF THE AFTERNOON

O gentle queen of the afternoon
Wave the last orient of tears.
No daylight comet ever breaks
On so sweet an archipelago
As love on love.

The fundamental negress built
In a cloudy descant of the stars
Surveys no sorrow, invents no limits
Till laughter the watcher of accident
Sways off to God.

O gentle queen of the afternoon
The dawn is rescued dead and risen.
Promise, O bush of blushing joy,

No daylight comet ever breaks
On so sweet an archipelago
As love on love.

AS IF IN AN INSTANT PARAPETS OF PLANTS

As if in an instant parapets of plants
Would squander the tricks of summer
And sprout in a madman's enterprise,
My leashed pigeon in theatres of hawks
Creeps down the bow-back rafters to my hair.

Should I be here in this rare scaffolding
Clutching the promise of primrose?
You with a yokel handful of blight
Pitching your jacket on gowan,
Conceal the hollow in the core of love
For fear will fast after it move.

This lyrical contrivance feeds the grain
That feeds not you or astragal
Crisscross on air to perch a bird.
But nourishes the nest enclosed
Three ways by bone and one by blood.

Here is a garland for this neck of fear
That never from heaven's joist dropped feather.
Time to be safe from every Spring.
Creep down a stanchion of the ark.
Time is not here to chime a harvest brooch.

19

Right break your tooth on faith. Climb up the sea.
Saw you my noose of flowers, my world's anemones
Punish her playground in the children's trees?
I also climb theories in so shallow a burn
As Calder, restless for trout and a genius
That life wears out on a ladder of water.
What wakens in rivers where couples glimmer
Keeping to park paths of landscape glamour
Babbles through rooks, the people of my blood
Who sing through evenings in my wood of worlds.

Offer me summer to speak from at my hand
With fingers sipping the rose of a blouse of bush
And the right to raise across my ceiling
More than her smile to rent to the martyr,
And what this festival would tell forgive.
For I see slanting through her sex's heaven
Love walled in petals with a choice of planets,
A face for death with a will for faith.
Offer me centre of the winter's parish
That I might sweep or weep the snow away.

And sure enough fences are everywhere.
Behind me science advances and you see me walk
Parallel to the same canal where she as a swan
Swims round the pastoral and camouflage of wars.
If tides have a minute the denying harbour
May land rebellion for her struggling cargo,
So in you my costume walks trying your trestles
Telling her wound and woman-found circle of sea
Her will in a family of waves in a circle of sea
To the host of your head, to your hoisted heart.

When over your firth my volcanic sorrow
Falls in a cinder of never-cooling birds

Gather the words like a scholar of coral
And build up hordes in your brain for burial.
With chorus and carol of blood for ceremony
Sink deep in veins those birds for bridges.
She must sigh and walk for her heart is hers
To take with a rigged perspective on the sea
All lashed with the never-wreck of night and day
That buoys her rung will and obeys her faith.

HERE NEXT THE CHAIR I WAS WHEN WINTER WENT

Here next the chair I was when winter went
Down looking for distant bothies of love
And met birch-bright and by the blows of March
The farm bolder under and the din of burning.

I was what the whinfire works on towns
An orator from hill to kitchen dances.
In booths below bridges that spanned the crowds
Tinkers tricked glasses on lips and saw my eyes.

Like making a hut of fingers cupped for tears
Love burned my bush that was my burning mother.
The hoodiecrow in smoke in a wobbling wind
If a look is told for fortune saw my death.

So still going out in the morning of ash and air
My shovel swings. My tongue is a sick device.
Fear evening my boot says. The chair sees iceward
In the bitter hour so visible to death.

THERE WAS WHEN MORNING FELL

There was when morning fell
No rest for ghosts or the hosts that feed my days.
Webs nourished no alarm.
At green partitions the serene infusion of eyes
Discovered resorts crossbeamed for journeymen.
Through a scale of classics on tilting planes
Crowds behind giggling masks calculated trade
And alone by the seaside's fury.

My flag on a shipyard's truss
Grappled with eyes on spinning lathes under frames
With a cornice of rust and Spring.
Proof needs no faith. This bedstead for my lung
Tethered no grasses from her traffic's transom.
For my devotion craftsmen lined out death.
Time's cable or serpent wound round winch or reel
And squealed sin's question.

Day through my prison walked.
Cockles submerged their flower-exploding cells
And climbed my weedy wall.
And here the structure's lawful artist showed
Bound in the description of a staircase pier.
This beamwork in jigsaw apexes displayed
A scene made three and whirling chairoplanes
On architectured slopes.

After, when who I was
Stands rarer and as fair as natural hawk
My death will need no roof
To trellis Spring's horizon from my head.
Laid out with bloodshot pennies on my mind
My dead discovery in evening corridors
Shall bring this crossbeamed sycamore of steel
To brace my crowded heart.

SAY THAT IN LOVERS WITH
STONES FOR FAMILY

Say that in lovers with stones for family
A railway runs on limestone viaducts.
In him the blood will arm an iron monk.
In her the tear will forge a metal law.

Where walk in lovers, ploughmen with drunk feet
A wood shouts up, bends round the nostril rock.
In him she speaks beside a boatless sea
To minnow children milling cliff to sand.

Where bridal rivers fuse a prison's plain
A hill carves up a husband in a tor.
In her he tries a plumbline from a tree
That guards her serpent grave with pleasant roots.

Say that in lovers with laws for family
A seedway streams in rocky viaducts.
In him the night sends up a crop of peaks.
In her the day heaves up the idle groves.

THIS FOND EVENT MY ORIGIN KNOWS WELL

This fond event my origin knows well
How this nativity the young twig's editor
Sees progress down
At a bone-depth bore the grave's gravel
And squabble for April's blessing.

My heart is headhung on a peartree girl
Whirled from the season's pollen flume.
The maiden fiddle
Fresh from the dogslept dawn fanfares the flesh
That crushed a clover fleece and a wing's wall.

Being bound all sworn ways when fable in flood
Treads on the holy heel, to lay out green
The earthy eyes
That tread the iris-cobbled park of wonders,
I pluck a lexicon of May-locked riddles.

This I can better love than tell in virgins
How this philosophy the mind's ambition
Sees parliament down
At a bone-depth bore the grave's gravel
And squabble for April's blessing.

LET ME MEASURE MY PRAYER WITH SLEEP

Let me measure my prayer with sleep as an
Infant of story in the stronghold eyelid
Left by a hedge with a badge of campions
Beats thunder for moles in the cheek of Spring.

Stronghold till squall robs holiday within
This wonder where twin hills back the eyes
Holds weeds and geometry in a girdered hive.

God will hear all that pastoral can tell
Where this throe this offence to where I walk
Propels in hemispheres through rook and rowan.

So to go counter magnify my dress.
Let swimmers tussle fatal as the fools
That all the bones of anarchy can tell.

And inland sleeps the sorrel and silverweed
Not less in gardens where the bliss is heard
Climbing the well of unrecurring cures.

Let me measure my trade with a tented sleep
Where none shall in heart's ease landlord love.

Leave me for child's sake hubbed in harebells
Where planets in pasture magnify my face.

ENDURE NO CONFLICT.
CROSSES ARE KEEPSAKES

Endure no conflict. Crosses are keepsakes.
Guilt gathers no beginnings on Goatfell.
Let mountains answer when no curlew wakes
The anvilling moral to its prophet peal.
A mound of plaything-sermons comfort the braes
Like the wreck of a rock in a river's love.
Let the head's volume, the valve of a speaking rose
Take Cruachan for kernel. Not guilt shall give.
Not out of pressure whirled in a pool of fear
Shall gush the wound-well's dealer of leading.
No fonder father have you in tear and fire,
In brier pities for the self-nailed feeding,
Than ptarmigan rocked in a rod of battles
Than blaeberries swung in a womb of beetles.

Cruel to myself my nicknamed heart, named Rock
Dams here now next and every time Time's burn
That from height's hell or heaven cracks the stick
On Cruachan quartz and splits the long trough quern.
Keepsakes are crosses for the sake of nails
Keeping the kirkyard's gardener. Guilt gives.
Is reared to be heard and adored in bells.
Gives government to dead in granite grooves.
Peaks are the parables or pity man born
With house too rocked discovering with April
The holy brackets of the mountain's morn.
Pity not spilling law from my heart's gable.
Here this rock forefinger nails wrist to cairn.
This heart named Rock dams guilt to joke and mourn.

TO GIRLS AT THE TURN OF NIGHT
LOVE GOES ON KNOCKING

To girls at the turn of night love goes on knocking.
For each daylight turns hero and gravity spins
Through each her animal eyes love's hollow mast.
I in the charted Eden of this my great heart
Today see sorrow from no hill of mourning
See Hell with no reply save student's tongue
At where her breast gives suck to island roots.
Study can teach to know her resting place.
Where shall it lie long? Where it shall shelter keep,
Grove for the visible darling of showers.
And deep under ground and grave her season
Follows new flowers and her ointment lingers.

Scotland or my own seaboard outlined heart
Lying in subterranean summertimes
Each storytime with struts of oak and willow
Brings in the heroine calling her holy.
Her home I love. All heaven climbs her towers.
I in a spire of circles begin the womb
Which is my risk, my logic's vertical.
Deep is the place. Stay still in a ball of peace
And wind and wonder dress this history
That naked for grief goes growing through my stem.
And ice, my father, in the beds of winter,
Blow through my limbs' design the North of sin.

NO, LISTEN, FOR THIS I TELL

No, listen, for this I tell
Till song becomes my home.
This drop no man descends
To death or depth of meaning if there's day.

His gouged initials fixed in stone and bone
Make up no allegory.
He has no prophecy
To hatch or harass your mind.

Clouds he can recognise
As hair of children dead
And kept alive in air
To make committees of eternal peace.

The air winds round his wheels
And all the creatures know
How I the pirate come
And stand inside his cylinder to watch.

God as the day is good can tell no fraud.
I let my hat go sly
As I see my day keel
To the fall of peace and pleasure.

The sky holds stars and lice
In the disk of the chimney eye.
They have no prophecy
To hatch or harass your mind.

We fall down darkness in a line of words.

2ND LETTER

Nevertheless this livelong day I grieve
My own day measured by each one alive
That puts God mildly to the heart I own.
Wherever this leaving lover hearing wires
Goes drawing through the dome my morning ram
You are not loved, my lived-in welcome boy.
From the dark I make I veer with the miles.
Not the hand not the end of years shall grasp

27

The lips my girl with seas along her face
Took through my word and crucified to snow.

Shall I once I have quickened from the window
Take a new highroad for my flying nature?
Or shall the law of shape stroke the pale hill
With one long chord of terrible years?
Over my death Christ weeps not a moment.
First on the footpath round my grave
Cries 'She is the only livelong girl
To take this death according to her tree
That shakes his fruit no life can understand.'
'Bleed on the simple grass' my breath cries.
And where the wires and worms of all my kin
Tell in my jailing basket the drive of rivers
My hung dumb head swings out a bell for weevils.

Above me the whistling world that joy can stop
Makes up my law-printing weather and wears
A hood for heaven and a lamp that cages
My head in heliotrope and my heart in Hell.
Look there O where tear has never told
Its perfect decoration on her sleeping moor
How the walk of the trees that roof her windy heart
Steps through this conversation in a shell.

Lastly I am the sea in a brow with crowds
And I hear all the fair of a thousand heads
In my dawn in the wash of the sky
In my night in the wish of the sea.
And close on my falling filling sieve of drowning
The whirlpool follows in a screw farewell.
My cap is the ocean and my hair floating
In a map of bells and a moral tide.
And her own lip is lived on with weeds and words.

I, no more real than evil in my roof
Speak at the bliss I pass I can endure
Crowding the glen my lintel marks,
Speak in this room this traffic builds
About my chair and table for my nature.
I feel the glass collide with light and day.

Outside this lull is happening the young
Who cough their stories in the curving siding.
I, no more real than my enclosure
Devise my eye to irrigate my love
For where the slates slew down my roof
The sky tilts back its shingle with no sign.

From inward through my window's needle eye
Children cartwheel from prison in procession
And stage their fear on mulls of rock
And build boundaries with ochre bricks.
Thunder falls round the fieldmice and the house.
Through all the suburbs children trundle cries.

I, no more real than when my hill of head
Finds evil in my dredged up heart,
Press down my padding question on the floor.
What things the young will take for song or grief.
The flagstone under sky is canopy
For other air where other thunder falls.

2ND POEMS
(1945)

EXPLANATION OF A MAP

Near farms and property of bright night-time
By mileaway dogbark how there is means to say
What unseen bargain makes heavier where I walk
The meanwhile word here of this neighbourhood.
Mileaway for answer tilling the fertile sky
Direction's breakdown assembles my own heaven
Builds up, breaks the dead quarter into miles
With towering tongue of each discovering hour.
Some loud means in the dark for my sake tells
My journey manned and sailed but none so man,
Bullhorned, treehorned from the heads of huntsmen.

As man sets out under his roof of lanterns
Joisted hawthorn and a thousand fabled bonfires
I take the starry whiphand quick with means
Blood, maid, and man, as they set out to be
Fruitful in each house and fulfil all seas.
By side of trespass under this same roof
What further tests knock under lock and keep,
Catapult famously as I have worn my fires
Curled in the scoop of fear? The shell to weep
Back simple seas, eyewitness to hell and heaven,
Is now for man's sake manfully the measuring watchman.

Good stars above you, night pedestrian.
How do you pleasure and approach the prize?
By side of canted sin set in my zones
I strip the crimes of west from my flat palm.
As man breaks flight alone in a blue disguise
Love scarlet on its axis of gone days
Tilts a new measure for pain in a crush of pleasure.

I am parliament in a roaring way. My word
Knows mister and missus, measure and live feature,
So fume and jet of the floor and all its towns
Wording the world awake and all its suns.

Under the bright ventriloquist the quiet
Animal raises and knocks the years to war.
Under the process of the flooding sky
Deeps in the desert know no rising up.
Near gates and fences astronomy's possessions
On whinny fields creep through the precious pools.
I cast, before peace grips my world's stoked womb,
High my bled ground. O over me the cambered
Wave, motive to all to tell the untold room,
Tells fable and fire. My eyes drown where they lie.
Grief with a silent oar circles to say.

SOON TO BE DISTANCES

Soon to be distances locked sound
In the day of travel my passing knows
The place across which I slowly move
With ease and the lonely stumble
Feeds day with dark and fastens me
Meaning no hurt or comfort
To parallels barbed in the brake and bramble.

What I learn turns barrier to voice.
Sea nurses rock. Down dwindles land.
The curving thorn swims through the grass
Goes through each water-broke sentinel.
The river main talks word and world
Sea-marching with no man
Talks with no man's device to shingle.

All that I hold to water breaks
With that in me my foam holds rigid
Bound salt in sand and roped in roots.
Held better before the time of burial
Soon grapples in mornings more calm my day,
My weight on sea and sand
Prints my own screeve in the oblong wood.

And through the lochan of my eye
The horning fish bound between stems
See the sand ballet-pit on summits.
I see the man I made for land
From where the fake pitch unrolls levels
High over green parades,
Drown in the sudden sounding trees.

THE SERVING INHABITERS

Wonder struck one inhabitant of me
Which server in his riot house
Becomes for joy my own spectator
That threads to thundering faculties
The whalehailed alphabet of hills he sees.

Crowbar struck light becomes the hooligan
Hearing my nation's windows break
Letting light in. Day through the courts
Walks on the thoroughfare to wake
A method my hunch knows under the look.

I am my womb or man for woman fetched
By strict ambition. I my shepherd am
And feed a million harmonies.
The roar they fall in is my home
And all the serving distance is my room.

Flowers shook off me and the blood he sees
Becomes the rain and every drop
I fall in is the air I live in.
Can blood admit a people's map
Together district to a common shape?

Can I before the lizard in my throat
Strikes my country with a dark tongue
Become what they say, who inherit
All contraries I kneel among
Kneecapped with gravity upward heaving?

NEXT MY SPADE'S GOING

Next my spade's going the pivoting beetle
Overthrows windier masters than
My mountain scaffold.
What simple miracle, my mile to topple,
My words leave hold
On oystercatching birds that settle
On aquarium clouds above my field.
My eyes leave hold on cattle.

Silence that makes each grain spin thunder
Litters rebellious whispers down
On the roof of soil.
And the acting pyramid bleeding under
Holds up the tragic gland of summer
For reason in my foot to kill
For the spike of my vertical to spoil.
I sing in each cave in cinder.

All faster histories trace the acrobat
Turning with pockets of myrtle
In under the tongue of the tempest
Sung under the walls of the water-rat.

A war falls past.
No wing on the worm. No clouds create.
My youth will build quick to hoist
The bulb through the snare of the athlete.

Matters the moon to beetles in thunder?
Who sees how silently the mist
Begins ascent
Through gut and keel of each moving cancer?
O see how fastly
The splaying anchor holds the swept flower
Safe off the squalling shoal sent windily
Over the scalp of the whisper.

HIS COMPANIONS BURIED HIM

Always by beams of stars (and they disclose
India Africa China Asia then that furry queen)
I see Earth's operator within his glade
Gloved in the fox of his gigantic hour.

The first ship cast to perish wintered blood
Found beachbergs on the flesh. Another tongue
Flooded what law the planet's bowline hung
Where sun and moon go up the blinded shipping.

The second ship cast to perish bruised on brain
Tethered to hydrogen, explored the island.
Popular as are its people, the land they found
Disguised its landscape with a wagtailed sand.

The third ship cast to perish perished hard
On land rigged round with sea on speaking sea.
Each word was word and end of it away
With all its travels for almost ever O.

Always by beams of stars (and they disclose
That furry queen who saunters on night's boards)
I see Earth swing within its own explorer
Who dangles each star lighting up his map.

THE NAME LIKE A RIVER

The gean trees drive me to love
To the landwave wearing the shipwreck down
To observing flint-seed through seesaw eyes
From my loss of level in the to-fro bone.
Not resting I look by my seas
In each twin lovewave eye at the gowan
Where over summer the spinning turnstiles
Flower the girl from the green-dyked town.

Let nothing through love's way leave
But the ringing through hawthorn disciple's name
That ever by my bellstrong mouth I scold
On the grindwheel gale that draws me to calm.
Let the young of her tasted and tongued
Ear bite on the voice of her knuckled alarum
Making loud the wrecked lad on her rippling door
Making sure and sharing the lad I am.

The shoremark draws me through love
As drew the womanlaid deadman under
The lettering sand that she walks and reads.
With five seas down the arm-clenched air
Speaks over the skidding seaskin
The picture of ballast and the bunched water.
The load that I fling from the bird-perched ben
Young climbs the sand-laid warrior.

This voice is nothing yet holding
Where love is all ash, a pasture for stone
A wreck for the spar-honing breath to dress
With red at the lips, with red on the fin
In the seesaw scupper beds.
The shore aslant as the host comes in
Lets nothing through love's way but words
Bird-printed, sharing the lad I am.

The buttercups drive me to love
Yet the sea on the atlas-sided boulder
Wrecks many a blood-dressed stem.
The comeback prow yet holding flower
Crows through the weather's barrack
The true disciple's name like a river.
The womanlaid drives me to love
With the brightshaped wreck of love on my shoulder.

ALLOW SILK BIRDS THAT SEE

Allow the local morning make fire.
Silk bars the road, a spider rope.
Birds trail the slippery harbourer
That steers from what eye builds its blinder deep.

See light on man devise the best collision.
See man on word devise the best collision.

Now call the newt with river eyes.
Call brook and girl, the bower sunshine.
And call each drop. The early boys
See word on God devise the best collision.

Many without elegy interpret a famous heart
Held with a searoped saviour to direct
The land. This morning moves aside
Sucking disaster and my bread
On the hooped fields of Eden's mountain
Over the crews of wrecked seagrain.

There they employ me. I rise to the weed that harps
More shipmark to capsizing, more to lament
Under the whitewashed quenched skerries
The washed-away dead. Hullo you mercies
Morning drowns tail and all and bells
Bubble up rigging as the saint falls.

Many dig deeper in joy and are shored with
A profit clasped in a furious swan-necked prow
To sail against spout of this monumental loss
That jibles with no great nobility its cause.
That I can gather, this parched offering
Of a dry hut out of wrong weeping

Saying 'there's my bleached-in-tears opponent
Prone on his brothering bolster in the week
Of love for unbandaged unprayed-for men.'
          Gone to no end but each man's own.
So far they are, creation's whole memory
Now never fears their death or day.

Many out of the shades project a heart
Famous for love and only what they are
To each self's landmark marked among
The dumb scenery of weeping.
I come in sight and duty of these
For food and fuel of a talking blaze.

Here as the morning moves my eyes achieve
Further through elegy. There is the dolphin
Reined with searopes stitching a heart
To swim through blight. No I'll inherit
No keening in my mountainhead or sea
Nor fret for few who die before I do.

THE BRIGHT BUILDING

Then holier than innocence, like ten infant commandments
Any workman in these seas
The man and his labour no man can say.
In lilt some are sped innocently back
On dead feet on a footpath in the noise
Where I have been alive in a rare wave.
My emblem in this sealogged man of fifty
Skyrung and chimed along his vulgar fingers
At land and headland, upward goes for weight's
Hundred seas for good against the ironwork.
So I everywhere where winter meets the ark
Float my table, my books, my precious object
Towards shore and a cairn like a fastened star.

In any workman the harbour and the market
Saying here is the haven delightfully again
Is an even only child in the scared seas
Of the salt trouble and the prizefought argument.
This is to shout not for comfort or comfort ye,
Seaman of the houseboat in everfretting seas,
You in a squad of dead pecked by the tides
Speak as likely as the sea rolls its stones.
Then greater than grief and the fortnight-drowned men
The building in my live ropes and rigged island
With sheepsbit buttonhole and fireworks over
The rough water between Gigha and Jura,

Baits woodshell and rowlocks and all I am
Under guillemots of fire and untethered rockets.

A LETTER MORE LIKELY TO MYSELF

Elsewhere then midnight. It is my head's lost home
Lit with a poor prayer. I am within to outside
Held forward and subjected
To its most violent wing and last grand childhood.
A darkener to threshold a generous dome.
Is it, splintered to majesty in a crowded sky
Always to bear accident's happy appetite
With pity-glutted sight
You move at the ringing window? What lantern's caught
Your head in its precious space and boundary?
This night those fairer flocks, the lock and bright keys
Over the pitheads, is much to take for making
Some dialogues that spring
Past tempest. It is mirth moving there, tongue
Tied to a million halls and errand pities

Out of my single help to what saves hardly
Directing down what luck spoke out as poor,
Asking summer and winter,
Night and noon, east maddened to west, which door.
Then I, world as in need, I am to say gently,
Stain nothing, to dip the goose not in sick dye
But burn with owl-hushed oils the flower of them all.
Is it not sailed to tumble
On this platform so little sealed and us pale all
Below, illshone-on by luck's intricate eye.
This is why this night my keel from a word-lit shell
Drops into frantic allegories and benefactors
The still unFlooded creatures

First hooped, not wholly unvisited, and my star's
Onlooking extremities of moral goods.

MY GLASS WORD TELLS OF ITSELF

Writing this so quietly writes of itself.
So serving only cities falling in words
Round the dead guessed at fifty
In the petrol passover and the dribbling ink
Down hills of quick rubble,
I watch through a medal the drowning Noah sink.

Flood's animal calls each lifesize hill
A shoal, and the panorama of news
Floats man on cork.
Poor like a scribble my crime on a diamond
Is a gannet I am made in,
Not by your head but the beak of my diving hand.

Writing this so quietly writes of itself.
So saving only the seaport in a bottle
With a history of threads
On a told ship under the sky's green grave
On the sea's coloured oval,
I pour round glass the sand my rivers have.

THE DUAL PRIVILEGE

Certify by this, the once-ruins
Restored to cheering. Two skies of praise
Bend over where my head returns
To see this masonry of a mad house.
I'll read the fingersalts and thorns
After thunder and rubble lies
Killed from two rivals' horns.

I'll shoot the seasons' bolts green through the town
But not helpless in ice cut forgiving down.

    Certify by this, the once-grave
    Grown to spires indoors in words
    Marked upon me, to see my wave
    Savagely over the meek birds.
    I'll take up all time's towns that have
    Knowledge of two creatures. The swords
    Of ancient eyes bloodbell above.
They ask the playgrounds and proud gargoyles for bread.
With what reply can I hang my singing head?

Not altogether powdered from one privilege
Of outside meats picked by enormous ways
Through browbeat senses between cower and rage
Of ears and tunnels caved-in and overcome,
But all wrecked not from only one sea under
The wrinkling thunder of a from-overhead-peering face,
    (Looked off Heaven and saw
    Creelsmashed headlong in sacred poles and cages
    Different not lawlessly retraced to warfare
    On furious maps farfetched below the sky
    Perpendicular to bugleing towns that flare
    In turns in the blue eye of a Sunday.)
But from sunkdown smiles and filled seavessels
Daily sucked through the moment and many seas,
Fetched miracles marked alone to blessed herb,
Elderberry, earlier eyesights between those rivals
The wicked and counterpart angers in whose darks
We burn bright in, under the lovely and spilled
Towsack of numerous bright instruments
Careless at any moment across the skies.

Not by further flowing can that single seed
Sow any loud value to guide man's silent gesture.

So should more double the elemental ceremony
Tell me to destroy and up-roar singlehanded
Into what was so merry, the galleries around
Celebrating whipdogday and a choice of law,
Spite's famine bright erect within each one,
Openly miles of daybreaks breaking to dusk.
Equal to question and to allow to tread
In me the serpent rivers twin from two angels
Rivals over my head as nightfall magnified
From people, has of me a very dual fill;
I suffer cries, the snares and charmed faculties
Of captive rivers, hunted and chased replies
To fork under my eyelid's natural heavens.
So fetched together, scattered not only plague
To one bird chirped, but fault of all random
Nailbred kneeling behind the countenance.
Not till I call come to rescue me slowly down
From blackthorns and sloe to meet my whiter ghost,
The rim heaped on the wedding floor and built
Out of the skeleton of my fife and days.

Not by anymore bleeding can a single gospel
Return to dress the oracle of a man's duty.

CONTINUAL SEA AND AIR

So does the sea
If answer take save men from death in air
Does nurse the liveman's trade and God's flare
Feature to be.

Catastrophe
Slapped tinbox on my element put down
By falling, fills the sea with tumbled men
For saving me.

Afloat yes Venus goddess over fair,
Seafriend to progress, she and airlight there
By eyes wheelwrighting wreck the garrison.
Hark, we, experiment to progress, on
Sealaw and emerald and pitched maintainer
Latch summer in the whale. From death in air,
From wing ribbed in a char of childish skin,
From landbreath, animal on earth of brain.

Catastrophe
Tinbox afloat in damage where I hear
All livemen in the dusk along the shore
Floats men in me.

So does the sea
Save men their breath in air. The long outline
Leans over waving houses, new marine
Green man to be.

WARNING NOT PRAYER ENOUGH

Again not to lean with words my tower counted out
I near inchtape the shire with autumn strides
Shake past the rowan, shrivel the hawthorn brat
His haw unseated from the ribbed and ruby tree.
This flying house where somewhere houses war
World of the winding world hands me away
Hauls at my tugging blood for words to wear
Like rose of rising in the mercury counting sky.

Through asking my head how through the season runs
Each fancy feeling that my measure walks
Till leaves will tell me all the law-mapped sins,
I, lost in driving a wheel of prayer and warning
Hear my white cronies cheat the riding frost.
Dice comes on flower down each side swithering

Yells luck with a yellow medicine fist.
He strikes my lovely matter with a fertile burning.

You, the talked relic blowing the trick away
Blow the green down together with my strides.
The simple leapfrog simon of my country
Hurried and capsized from the sulky land
Hears the redrobin trees. The song's hunter
Calls bear and beaver, autumn and squirrel to hand
Plucks at the fences and sclims the starling lether.
He sets the made year loudly with land and legend.

A murmured dragonfly, a trumpet from the coast
They are all pitched. The long crying of spring
No more I hear tabletiming Time's grassy host.
Asleep I answer good day and night to serve us
Pinned with the rascal suburbs through the town.
Autumn shall rob and winter side the seas
With iceberg argument diamond for reason.
I ask the good season, Will Time Give Up Us?

THE CROWD OF BIRDS AND CHILDREN

Beginning to be very still
I know the country puffed green through the glens.
I see the tree's folly appleing into angels
Dress up the sun as my brother
And climb slow branches and religious miracles.
On the deck of the doved woods
Upward unhappy and holy breaks voice of the crowd
That has in my body built shape and its enemy.
Through each harmonic orchard onewhere bloody
With all that my choice chooses in Genesis
The overhead rooks laugh up in a dark borough
With fury making fear to the daybreaking mavis.

Never shudder this day that grins
For fear has saved so many set for climbing
To fear of quenching their own in their each vein's wilderness.
The too-late lovely anger of danger
Begins in my slang gland of drunken areas
Fenced in the cunning legend of the fruit.
The young of the climbing behind their lyrical mother
High over split stones plagued with a tongue of feet
Over cobbles and horse and man says the milking bleeder
Pass each ever sowing a starved handful of bread
On the crowd where the rut and the creaking pin go through
With the carted meat of stories and a whipping youngster.

Flashed over roads said the baillie
Broke price with wrinkles with the grace of beggars
Under the mallet in dizzy townclock squares.
And the monster was rainy with stars
Each watchlight fisherman-tied in the cattlesteep dusk
And a sunk sea noise in the roosting forest house.
Every flying thing the sky gives to a child
To feed his wild crowd and to share his deed,
How the wind can wear him town and village through
And sort out wallspikes round the baiting worm
And resting and rising, he, whose brow is bed
For angles, traces the apples burned in a storm.

Each child is the spit of the parable.
Each child on the trot in the street of choruses
With the eye of the pinning thistle through his hand
Walks on the watercourse of roads
Down hillocks burly with all Time squeezed in a wound.
I am the passenger on cords
Stretched over millions, each to the ceiling a vision
Of sprouting country faces tied on sky.
From my hand's prize the climbing crumbs of words
Engendered in torrents, jagged with a pouring thorn
Ferry the cut straws twisted into birds.

BY LAW OF EXILE

He who has been in exile
By law of words left in a long field
Ganged into stone and fierce foot still
Against place and den of dug creatures,
Who, hauled off love too into trial,
Heard cry the voices waked blind
As he lay white in a carriage of blood;
Suddenly with mouth from the long deck
Thundered stockstill on the keykept mile.
All hot estate and the fall to shelter
Fell to beginning gardens beyond blown call.
By act of cannonshot words manned
The silent cry's drenched trifle of joy.
Lay ending. On quiet cloth I see
Scrawled like first of angel's april
The tide with hooks on grassy script
Sloped and written in the trepanned hill.
All ocean's echoes deal into stone
This law of where I lie fertile
By spouted rock, manrise and law of exile.

THE HALFTELLING SIGHT

Why so notbright, the comets and magpies rocket?

The certain sight enormous from the snow
Tells chiefly drawn in myriads only halfway,
Unlike heaven concealed, breaks into boatloads
By watched example brighter than my voyage.
Peasant to fame my throngs endure their wall
Leaders of all in a staring wagon of frost.

Always the sea, the stagging sluices tell
Tomorrow's transport and of discovery

To beyond where must end the seed we say.
The certain sight enormous from the snow
Tells chiefly only halfway on the land
Tells out afloat the moving hull of planets.

That one sleepsound the sea made, then stopped.

EXCEPT NESSIE DUNSMUIR

Smiling locked round with calling that she is
Over fallen firstfelt nothing so sad is said
As white-killed cunning over her stained eye.
For she grew richly up singing weedwater high
As wallflowers round her shy child her fairest
April and prodigal tongue that looped in a spray
Wades the three wounds from Calder's precious home.
The hall and the hay-hat where she lay dashed
From Dechmont Hill meant for my iron fingers,
Lay knit as the golden mother in a field
And folded more heart than my discovered bird.

We all must, you as my hill and heart and dead
Dark weight of seas turned load behind my eye,
Die and burn down sin from the child's gean tree.
Easily women welcome in their tombs
With pointed tongues the pearl in the vein,
And once encountered, laid with a lid of eyes
Marry the rain-knocked sandstone for the child
That in the chill eye counts the kindling crows.

Except my tongue dipped in the weeding girl
Except her arrival over the sour grass blessed
With the red word out of her cried-out enemies.
And she by the beggar of a common sake
Speaks through her licking joy with a drop of grief.
Call what the earth is quiet on her equal face

That has a mouth of flowers for the naked grave
Sucking my thumb and the mill of my pinched words
In the dumb snecked room chiming dead in my ear.
Now time sooner than love grows up so high
Is now my warfare wife locked round with making.

AT HER BECK AND MIRACLE

At her beck and miracle this living dress
Fashions from ultimately a stranger calibre
Than tonight's procession of my lifetime
And as an entire angel bred never
So fair in blood's crimson tons and calm;
He strikes the broken piers of love.
At her calling, the floored, forest years
Risen to a hill through Dechmont's side
Is all her anchored, and cast to Calder tears.

Ready to do well on tonight's gangway
Through cinder hills and burning opposites
That turn glittering among the times
In Lanarkshire's merry parts, my jacket's
Empire scarletly on the field's crushed chimes,
Makes up the proudly unwinding, whole house.
Which is the alive rag of love to shriek
On the blind barb in the trodden womb.
Which is the blown, new room we make and break.

Under September and the loud moving
Of mountain writing and words in ruin
A red nerve runs in a globe of dew
Related forever to this river
Past the imperfect world and iron
Of bright estates and a quelled shire.
At her faintly history of webbed perishing

I, under dusk and caw-witted smouldering
Wear the western doors and angel on my tongue.

ONE IS ONE

Towards that other, the dim, the one queen
How left alone she lies, my own blindfold
Forgotten, fair ingredients of progress rise
In outlook's public dust and Ascending Light,
Rise where her blood bright out across the deafness
Whales somewhere far my pale originals.
And yet much more the occupied disasters
All kept at hand this long time in myself
Go after to wear evermore her undiscovered body
With beauty under eyelid. She and but one
Surely when night fell for a long time lay.

She and but one utterly unfailing to ferry
Discovery across this longtime-destroyed sky
Served to the leaving and faintly arriving companies
Farewell engraved on a map. No road to lead
Where she upon this monster outlook lies
In watch of grief climbed luminous about,
Unless those workmen in half the moon's light.
I see as though always sailing far out of hand
Is more the prophecy. Much more somewhere hear
The invented seaman alone after far discovery
Near the lips of that nearby, almost one other.

Like never at all live roads ran to her womb
Towards her I'm more led across the deep
Happenings behind the blindfold than I can appoint.
Though I stop now or strike back to the highroads
Where she under shouting dwindles to the future,
Her whisper sails out of all blown direction.
Much more in you hear how she lives blessed

More lookedout-on by moving lamp and footfall
In all distress and sharp eyes of built release.
More one has good of me and bad breaks way.
More to walk out of home to her, that other.

REMARKABLE REPORT BY
SOME POETIC AGENTS

There was from March 3rd to April 3rd the appearance of reality.

Jake said welcome. Perceived by lyrical action
All's leader. Amen to all. Doves conquer all.
In the vivid convention of an old harmony
A man shouted out, involved in outcry.

Man is a third class road. (Which I myself,
Problem of task subterranean to fact,
Perceive and show by means of grievous survey.)
A man shouted out, involved in outcry.

Chiefly by accident (which I myself prefer)
Freedom is reached continually. The king
Paid tribute to rebellion and astronomy.
A man shouted out, involved in outcry.

Death (its apparatus through the anxious rafters)
Appoints the Spring. Relate, by means of grief
Your own fled court to its once-pleasant country.
A man shouted out, involved in outcry.

Where animals sheltered in a high houseboat
A man shouted out, involved in outcry.

Anyhow here's highroad's man's unwitnessed town
Set where my making and collected surnames wrangle
To landmark the sudden garden past the latch.
Wellfared love-right and lettered, the founded sparks
Stoor of the brightsmith and my hammermen,
Strike up the praise that never wrings destruction
One ding of worth through the municipal vein.
Struck from the watershedding words, the tinker
Sets up the unbundled spires shamefacing ruin.

Here's flame as dark as falling and ascension
Native to barefoot accident and beast.
Here where I hope and happen on a cindered hill
Late round me stranger villages and journeymen
And time's bonesetter, chart sleigh of beast and mile.
Here I broach telling reached to with today,
Speak out the unbroken filament and wholesome
Terrible meantime the upward towns appoint me.

Down the green guilds the children and the season
Press shape in mud and chivvy language down
That I might mean my industry and task
Red through the hands that cup a gay trumpet.
What I make falls round you, a ring of rooftops
That tilt the landing birds in a loud market
Into what wordfall strikes from you the marvel.
Under your answer the tower is turned to cinder.
The contented flesh turns truant to a stone.

Here where the quick quays lie along the veins
Arriving others, madmen to my tongue
Cry crimson through the warehouse and the squares,
How black the dark is in the innocent day,
How white the space under the sea's window.
Always they drum the planks, patrol the furlong

Jet through the meadows as they say the season
Over and ever arriving, giving the rising
Seizure to summon the town, anyway fountain.

Now hermit that fox trotting the raftered alp
To stare on the shouting bone and bloody town
Lets down his jewelled jaw a comet bleed
Across the foolscap floors and fostered gangs.
Further through other gables the dead take heed
Laid out on frames along spring's fingertips.
The anyhow highroad's man's householding height
The catherine whirligig, the goodnight sky
Turns with its countrymen slowly about.

THE WHITE THRESHOLD
(1949)

SINCE ALL MY STEPS TAKEN

Since all my steps taken
Are audience of my last
With hobnail on Ben Narnain
Or mind on the word's crest
I'll walk the kyleside shingle
With scarcely a hark back
To the step dying from my heel
Or the creak of the rucksack.
All journey, since the first
Step from my father and mother
Towards the word's crest
Or walking towards that other,
The new step arrives out
Of all my steps taken
And out of to-day's light.
Day long I've listened for,
Like the cry of a rare bird
Blown into life in the ear,
The speech to that dead horde
Since all my steps taken
Are audience of my last
With hobnail on Ben Narnain
Or mind on the word's crest.

LISTEN. PUT ON MORNING

Listen. Put on morning.
Waken into falling light.
A man's imagining

Suddenly may inherit
The handclapping centuries
Of his one minute on earth.
And hear the virgin juries
Talk with his own breath
To the corner boys of his street.
And hear the Black Maria
Searching the town at night.
And hear the playropes caa
The sister Mary in.
And hear Willie and Davie
Among bracken of Narnain
Sing in a mist heavy
With myrtle and listeners.
And hear the higher town
Weep a petition of fears
At the poorhouse close upon
The public heartbeat.
And hear the children tig
And run with my own feet
Into the netting drag
Of a suiciding principle.
Listen. Put on lightbreak.
Waken into miracle.
The audience lies awake
Under the tenements
Under the sugar docks
Under the printed moments.
The centuries turn their locks
And open under the hill
Their inherited books and doors
All gathered to distil
Like happy berry pickers
One voice to talk to us.
Yes listen. It carries away
The second and the years

Till the heart's in a jacket of snow
And the head's in a helmet white
And the song sleeps to be wakened
By the morning ear bright.
Listen. Put on morning.
Waken into falling light.

LYING IN CORN

Fought-over by word and word
This day between my heart and brain lies down
Locked into furious outcome of half my life.
This day dies down to tell so never better
Begun than quietly to lie still lowly bragging
Its birds across a common place that once
Told me all day my thousand caves of audience.
Golden to tell, the sky is up and soaring
Wearing my plundered years, my summed welfare
Taken to nothing but to lie down again in season
With greyhaired books and the forgiving grave.
And in the applauding corn this day dies down
To rest to suffer me half the country told
Into life by severe imagination. Silence alone
Answers clean out raiding my speaking fields.

Or there in front of God to lie down sweet
Where rocked back lost into my own closed care
The weeping word calls innocence into rest.

MY FINAL BREAD

The arrival wakes sunstruck from a million men
Gulled on the waters, wilderness of my beginning
Part sailored by my own likeness part maintaining

My continual farewell. I am continual arrival.
My fear my fireshore and the shouting rest
Fare me for lost. The released nightwatching sea
In a seadogged lifesave cabins the boy in joy
From yelping ice and the public crucibles of sacrifice.
I am made into
Sharpeyed a Fergus-driven breaker with a wrecking lamp
Through Polar streets and ministries of glassblindness
Where mad for martyrdom History withers its nettle arm.

Change into grief. Hold me face up to light.
Sunstroked on bible waters all drowned all hands
And the overloaded dead, tidebare and threaded
Change into shepherds led by their quick flocks.
One man's mad million continually floats one man
Facebright to shore to wear on land his sea.
Float me face up, made into words, towards
My perfect hunger's daily changing bread.
I am made into
White up to light by one way certain arriving
At these birdcaging approaches of my own shores
Where my watch-cairns and fires lamp a landed likeness.

WITH ALL MANY MEN LAID DOWN
IN THE BURIAL HEART

With all many men laid down in the burial heart,
Hearing spring fall and the joyfaring weather waken
Another thunder's arrival under my footfall,
I walk well over the hill of my listening dead.
I wear early April blessed in a best innocence
Won from watched wonder and all my called people
Falling behind me into the look in my eyes.
With all my altering men, my messengers ranging
The never-still Aprils heading up from my first

Step started over shelter's threshold and throe,
And put into speed as green kindles into quickly
A flower in a snap of weather; I walk discovered
Up over the shepherd heart and containing hill
Earning the blood of my dead who lie down flowering.
With yes all wishes and my best men well alive,
Eyes turned to whinwork bright in the present time
And the skyward-worded morning, my word breaks way
After the shape of entering and leaving this welcoming
And lives handmouth on bread of the singing springside.

THE HILL OF INTRUSION

The ear the answer
Hears the wrecked cry
Of the one-time
Holiday boy who
Feathered his oars
On a calm firth
Held still by hills.
Now grey rock clenches
Round the rower over-
Taken by rough
White-haired sea-troughs
That ride the foam
Of Time's bare back.
Wrecked pile of past
Events cindered
Into a charcoal
Of kindling power
And constellations
Of united hearts,
These make reply
To the flare flying
Off from the endangered

Watchman wornout.
The winds from a hill
Halfway Ben Narnain
And halfway hill
Of intrusion into
The silence between
My heart and those
Elements of nature
That are my food,
Sound out alarm
Over the baling
Prisoners of water
This night unsheltered.
The ear says more
Than any tongue.
The ear sings better
Than any sound
It hears on earth
Or waters perfect.
The ear the answer
Hears the caged cry
Of those prisoners
Crowded in a gesture
Of homesickness.

THE SEARCH BY A TOWN

This step sails who an ocean crossed
And mountain climbed, who apprenticed
For this while quietly to bearing me
Put forth a rose and my name to die.

Saint Other. Her names ring out in grass
In joy. Her quieter features dress
My eyes. Accident's better pinions
Innocently summered over whins

Hold birds above the shire. Dechmont
From his mad cap makes up his saint.
He makes his mastertask, in his
Ten worlds lifts up a lightstruck face.

This man from woman walks to grave
As flesh from the girlflowering wave
Perished to talking particles.
His head with far child by his eyes

Wakes quietly the affairs of Heaven over
The whirring shire and each winder
Gently who wears a harp of gold
In dayshift's black hill wildly nailed.

He wakes from morning's earthy bed,
Words berried in his longing blood.
Under the suffering beams and suns
His coat of nerves continually turns.

For ever as the seeker turns
His worshipping eyes on prophetic patterns
Of shape arising from all men
He changes through, he shall remain

Continually stripped and clothed again.
The morning loses sound and man.
The glow invents the worm. His saint
Invents his food and feeds his want.

He takes to himself fleetly the morning
And follows a smoky flock to bring
Him to the apple that rivers his life
And her voice under a tempest leaf.

All words, all men, their names ring down
The dew of energy on this man's garden,
Till over Dechmont and under the whole
Flocked prospect of the skies he shall

Be wept back to her wandering voice,
Sounds of her seas to hold his eyes.
Footheld fast in his head's boundaries
He in his fruit entombed reads skies

That fall across the rising sky
Of Blantyre seasons night and day.
He follows the Fall, how search begins
Under the roof's bright sea. The towns

Shine down on chalked men as they lie
Scribbled to tears and crossedout joy.
All day the lark of infant skies,
Child of a look and fists, replies.

Quietly in his eye night sets out.
A pillar of war to lead the night
Puts up the red and the lost choir
Of slagfire across the industrial counter.

Towns shine down round him, near neighbour,
Before a door or headlong bar,
Each night to spill and drink away
To knock them all down to sorrow.

His winged, his feet, drink up his will.
By eyes of sleet and clear candle
Where town and Calder quake the same
He lies, a new prodigal in a new home.

He lies under her call and hill,
A mute harp in an ancient hall.
He lies. Is lost. That hark in air
Under atlantic movement over

The shire, is lost. For ever as
The seeker takes his newborn skies
His step each field is a new man,
His graves are progress, his garden

Is plagued and planted from the dead.
His saint is child of a new head.
His changing coat cries like a sea.
His story invents his following eye.

All words, all men, their names like bells
In grass ring down to talking particles
Over all night and each cinder heap.
A man breaks grave and new step up

The miracle seeded within his apple.
He wakes and holds above the whole
Shire of her names this fable made
His eyes daybreaking overhead.

His step sails who an ocean crossed
And mountain climbed, who apprenticed
For this while quietly to bearing his sky
Put forth a rose and his name to die.

THE CHILDREN OF GREENOCK

Local I'll bright my tale on, how
She rose up white on a Greenock day
Like the one first-of-all morning
On earth, and heard children singing.

She in a listening shape stood still
In a high tenement at Spring's sill
Over the street and chalked lawland
Peevered and lined and fancymanned

On a pavement shouting games and faces
She saw them children of all cries
With everyone's name against them bled
In already the helpless world's bed.

Already above the early town
The smoky government was blown
To cover April. The local orient's
Donkeymen, winches and steel giants

Wound on the sugar docks. Clydeside,
Webbed in its foundries and loud blood,
Binds up the children's cries alive.
Her own red door kept its young native.

Her own window by several sights
Wept and became the shouting streets.
And her window by several sights
Adored the even louder seedbeats.

She leaned at the bright mantle brass
Fairly a mirror of surrounding sorrows,
The sown outcome of always war
Against the wordperfect, public tear.

Brighter drifted upon her the sweet sun
High already over all the children
So chained and happy in Cartsburn Street
Barefoot on authority's alphabet.

Her window watched the woven care
Hang webbed within the branched and heavy
Body. It watched the blind unborn
Copy book after book of sudden

Elements within the morning of her
Own man-locked womb. It saw the neighbour
Fear them housed in her walls of blood.
It saw two towns, but a common brood.

Her window watched the shipyards sail
Their men away. The sparrow sill
Bent grey over the struck town clocks
Striking two towns, and fed its flocks.

THE CHILDREN OF LANARKSHIRE

To put it springtime the green shepherd
Sheepdogging my fertile heel to word
Plants this birthplace with one rebellion
As one place flourished with flute and whin

And royal occurrence of this one empire.
The earth beneath the cloudy floor
Of Heaven creates a local April.
My lifetime treads a rolling ball.

To put to you not so war the serene
Plain of released creatures on the green
Ground by the town chiefly Blantyre
Where the hung harebells hear the lover

Spread out his flowercoat on grass,
I imperfectly lead you on Dechmont face.
Then even locality of this alive scale
Spread out from Indian ink to hill

Lets not alone the louder constellations
Perishing feverwise with wailing signs
And somewhere shining within the agony's
Faint tenements of toppling flowers and days.

To put my footsore fears to you
In all their animal history
That mildly bears me in this time
In fast disguises to my home,

I plant this ceremony this April day.
I plan with spring legality
The meadow maypole within four walls,
Steeples and birds for pits and miles.

A prison presses dandelion and gowan
Down on sore centuries. Tombstone, hailstone
Out of Tibet breaks down me racing,
Ancient banners of stone to bring.

Since on a scaffold of the times,
My ladders lead me from the rooms
Of quiet origin to encounters
On holy parapets and the world's rafters.

The sun and tears of all the Calder
To abler conflict rise to discover
Across the shire's children's whisper
The racehorse metaphor of immense warfare.

Where gulf of stars above the gloworm
Moves bright with open eyes, and bomb
Sent home to die in its idiot bed
Looks down; I lie with lambs beside

Him at his making food to eat.
It's all barren action that throughout
The killed street sees from ruin the bird
Ascend steep silence with a word.

The common weather of the world
Wears every infant in the wild
Rebellions in the noisy streets.
Yet uncommon its king hand writes.

And under waters of a monstrous language
Its glow and game writes on the age
Here loud with beast and flying offices.
And April rising from the laws

Finds in my nosed and fostering pocket
Kingcup myrtle lintroot for my foot.
And a good black thorn for my head.
And a linty to sing at my deathbed.

And finds me by this equal river
The Calder, and Dechmont that hill there
For sceptre standing on the time
And the same flute to turn the storm

To handwriting across Lanarkshire,
Or grow to royal revolution of the hour
Not trapped under the tapped furnaces
But king of the heart's streaming sources.

What adoration, knelt enough,
Can shade the uproared moon's wrath,
Continual skull of all the world
Across its good intentions hurled?

Just last furiously the littered floor
Sprouts men walking in a den of fire
And Lanarkshire's flowers rebelling fly
The smelter's furnace in the sky.

Lanarkshire's children out of quiet
Respective solitudes handwrite delight
With splitcane seeking after kings
In that birthplace April brings.

THE LOST OTHER

For from liberty at hand held for ever
Comes scarcely answer. Is there an end there
Where my name walks not obviously chosen
And is shouted and given away to everyone?

As high as dove you might call me released
Above the ark of the earth's best
My sprig to find and feather down
To truly each hunted home and man.

Or come in hark this fair spring morning
Of her lost cry never herself losing
Even in this place. I'm out within
The walls I endlessly shoulder down.

I'm this time stepping and found of flowers
Long since they pledged my road through tears.
And to inform where I forsake my home.
And to fade on either side where I bloom.

Till even the crimson porch of the bee
The natural guest by night and day
Describes me as the wanderer
Out of my peace this day to find her.

O mavis the pride as of holiday this
Spring morning, sing. It is trilled to my house.
Kind man if so carved before me you stand
Call her delightfully at this hand.

At hand the wind shakes out my voice
Across the companion distances
That in each action surround me always.
Yet I'm alone. At hand, the companies.

This fair spring morning she may be found
By how I call her. The sea makes land.
Shepherds make by and by their sheep.
And New York turns Dechmont in sleep.

Hence the man's call. The labourer
Anchors his calling kite over
Yarrow and slender Tiber towers
In inverted airts baked in bonfires.

The companies lie scattered through
Lanarkshire and vaulted shire of his eye.
The vault of this fair morning holds
The host. The flowers hold up their worlds.

All hills stand me on Dechmont's empire
Higher than some mountain past where
Pressed back on a royal rocky chairback
I've so gone glad, my joy to take.

Hope holds me high. All my days tell.
All palmed my Mays have rambled full.
I'll shout that ferrysong over water.
The Calder hold her. This hill call her.

Question makes measure of the true answer.
Never so dare I'll doubt the murmur.
The turnstone turning Tara up
Hears in the stones the exiles weep.

Nor I'll (by Blantyre and Bothwell go)
Doubt my house cages America.
Beyond my window the land maintains
My flying memory and best of queens.

Instead like us all fast locked here
I end myself continually where
The dead look out as I move by
Between new rudiments involving liberty.

By her hand set to rule and witness,
Beacon to burn with you in the branches'
Graceful carriage of dancing, how she
Is almost nothing more than I

Made into, let it be bullrushing waters
Wearing her flax and floating daughters
Over the rumours and passed enough
Of kin to her to be stone and grief.

This morning the Calder's earliest bells
Below me call her. Lanarkshire's wheels
Unwind men underground and me under
The flowering bings of my own shire

Where continually my first industries
Echo and call and know her rays,
Having from her first forerunning whisper
Kept on quietly burning there.

Forerunning summer and the parks
Come green away. Mad winter works
Sore withered of its beggaring, wailing
Bewildering wretches' ear-ringing song.

There's home and time again called out
Over the towntops and those delicate
Gangways, ways between Hamilton's pastoral
Shellcups and relics of a child's bell.

Quick by my fortunes every day
Through fire and night-speaking pillow
I'm set to rule what I make pleasant
In this place. She so without stint

Suffers the first walk of the east
While Dechmont turns round all the host
That move differently under this sky
Expecting liberally prophecy.

One time she's to stop by my journey
So gentle with a lost answer to my cry,
To mean with gowan by Calder river,
To minstrel all the morning fair.

I'm to hear tell from her own miles
Fairly her wordway child. All bells
Ring pastime above me this far morning.
She, mother, rocks and sea, she's song.

Am I to start, as sound a Bacchus
In travellers' myrtle, citizen of lochs
Day by deep day under Ben Cruachen.
So strike me now, her companies again,

Strike deadly through my piling justices,
Roof of my grave, sky of my histories.
Strike day by diving on the sea,
The brine of sailing to The One Liberty.

I am all name to be seized to her
So high as cairn and the top bonfire
Alight on Dechmont, servant of the kingdom
Of Heaven this day and choosing my name.

Then, lean out, Love, and yearn from the window
That ever you saw from, that far hero,
Some one wandered into imagination
And weed of the way, and word won.

And grief, hunter of sound, what world
Comes drowning me down loud to unbuild
Before surely my industry finds her
Under the principal sky's care.

So listen to answering me, world overhead
Held listening this May morning. Good
To us all yet more and marvellously near.
It's a good wonder. I give good way to her.

For eyes she has my footsteps on water.
For ears she well knows silence my master.
For tongue she storms my time away.
For joy and body she resembles my doorway.

For sights I brother my eye's invention.
For sounds I break the silent law down.
For telling I feed and drink my story.
For prophecy I begin with The One Liberty.

Content with true promise of Indies
Worth every while I'll cool my cries
On runaway waters white and blue
Out of the shell of the pleasant sky.

This rare morning marvellous windmills
Wind her with forms in green miracles
So faint with burns and green furnaces
That blow the shallows of May cries

Into daytime's other direct shape
Where praised kings of the air rise up
In Grace and One Liberty on high.
Kings of the air so always nativity

Rise from the wars and walking flowers
Like angels over ancient disasters
And call and create her hurling answers
Out of my dead and gentle brothers.

And they carry her into my fair day
With ropes out of my sad meadow,
At hand only a Flood away,
At war only an ignorance away.

They rise up through those elements,
So gentle a battle in my encampments.
A thousand fantails over the Calder
Darken the royal scale of this empire.

And their countenance, bread of our eyes
Shines bright to all men in their places
And becomes a furious difference
To each man in his rebelling distance.

For far away towards his dale
He has to travel, and his terrible
Battle surrounded by the dead
Moves nevertheless in public blood.

And she in front of thorny eyes
Kneels beside processions of sorrows
That invade the world and her right.
Am I to put my right foot out

Seeking somewhere under the fanfare's
Broken neighbourhood of heavenly travellers
To find her in the blessed faculties
Of War's One Liberty where ruin glows

But not touches Saint Other of the Athanor,
More valuable floored with fountains or
Our wrecks of rage and custom house,
Daniel of fire and Kingdom of Agonies.

This better morning she times my search.
She chimes in ships the flowering bleach
Of the dead on the bitter wreckageside.
She almost heeds my neighbourhood.

I'm lost in foxes of falling down.
The human at hand makes into a cannon
My mouth. The dead do up my eyes.
My shoulder idiots crowd out my voice.

My arm holds up the clenched joy
As her eye holds the butterfly
Safe from the night behind the lid
In the violet eye to be darkly laid.

So soft this pace across the earth
Goes trailing after on the path
She certainly, intricately takes.
Blackthorn to bar the way, hayricks

To crow alarm and scare the answer,
Mountain to wound ascending, makar
To feed the arrows, to press gridiron
Into bonfires and into vision.

And let us not turn her glance away
That we'll be work of her womanly
Possibilities of The One Liberty.
Thus let us wise ourselves this day.

TO A TEAR

Tear shed on the soon cracking roof
Of the left alive,
Remember the shedder. The leaf
Remembers Heaven.

Come down on to a charcoal joist.
Alight lawgiver
Gentle on troubledeck and earliest
First bird to leave
My Everesting heart creviced fast.

Tear nearer the stopped dead. Near
The various angels
Wept across my eyes in a cool river.
Release reveals
You love your shepherd, the shedder.

Come fall as from dead to the left
Lonely alive
Bright in a girdle of grief. Left
By an undug grave.

TWO LOVE POEMS

1

Since once (livelong the day) my prayer measured
A love along your face, I've raged and variously
Had all smiles and butchery daily acquainting

You of the springing bloodshot and the tear.
Since there (spun into a sudden place to discover)
We first lay down in the nightly body of the year,
Fast wakened up new midnights from our bed,
Moved off to other sweet opposites, I've bled
My look along your heart, my thorns about your head.

Now this life line that sings you rarely out
Flows better tried than my sore heart in irons
And tries that human many, so buried each heartbeat
Alone in deeper wishes of our kissing lives.
Alone along with us each ascension dives
Down from us homing to flower. Our kindred moves
With skyjacked lantern sailored on the sea.
My warfoot foremost crosses to die as you
Lie as this whole meridian pulled as a great bow.

With all lifeblown lifestories of each breath
Brought into flower in us as involved betrayal,
Here certainty's laid on the bed of the world's bewilderment.
Here, gagged in the riding dark, the farseeing servers
Waken in us. O since that prayer's first measures
In a dress of blood moved mad along your fires,
That first stilled time; I've held my whole wilderness,
Its homing bloodbeat and prophetic sands,
Towards wherever promised to love you happen on my kiss.

2

Where you (in this saying) lag in the waving woods
Under climber moon tonight under branching industry
Of all my homing opposites, this paidout saying
Serves us again the upward legging oaks
Heaving in air. This fastened fire awakes,
Filament between us full of the sleeping rooks.
This wood's around us under the curlew's loveweep.

Glowormed in the myrtle beds, under the stoop
Of the starry harrier boughs, we kindle this memory up.

To still lie low together, heart and hand fast,
We hear the windkindling trees around us move.
These words bribe words away. Man and woman
Lie at their best, lifeline crossed on lifeline
And all signs sail in their holygranted garden.
Kept in one element, devoured in an ore of Heaven,
They're lifebled back to this now double night.
So are we bedded burning in our infinite
Immortal filament where continually our dead cry out.

So you (in this flame-fastened saying) beneath
Bullhorned goatbearded oak, look up at the night
Falling away across the staining sky.
Our branching veins remember us and flower
The morning's first bright resins burning over
Our two kissed lives. Our present morning ever
Handing us back to forgiveness lands us back
To under a stiller sky. The daybreak cock
Fixed in the calyx east crows seven bright heavens awake.

OTHER GUILTS AS FAR

Other guilts as far
As a life away turn up to mourn
Me back over into early outworn
Linens of fear.

Over a time
Again gathering up the old sore
Self house and servants, the far
Parts send their name.

I am not that man
Now as I read the rowan and make

A book of a tree. Better I'd make
Some new guilt shine.

THE BIRTHRIGHT TWINS OUTRUN

The birthright twins outrun
The million peopled mountain.
A chill walks through the bone.
The heart unmasks the brain.
Two ways through warfare
And two ways through the flower.
The martyr strapped to fire.
The intellect strapped to ice.
My childhood in its house
In a prison of no choice
Sprouts me a heart and head
From curious courts of the dead
And shouts me out my bread.
I'm poured from serpent fire
And from the cathedral ice
Into one gesture of ascension
Over a mother in stone
And an unknown illumination.

SHIAN BAY

Gulls set the long shore printed
With arrow steps over this morning's
Sands clean of a man's footprint
And set up question and reply
Over the serpentine jetty
And over the early coaches
Of foam noisily in rows
Driven in from the farout banks.

Last gale washed five into the bay's stretched arms,
Four drowned men and a boy drowned into shelter.
The stones roll out to shelter in the sea.

GIGHA

That firewood pale with salt and burning green
Outfloats its men who waved with a sound of drowning
Their saltcut hands over mazes of this rough bay.

Quietly this morning beside the subsided herds
Of water I walk. The children wade the shallows.
The sun with long legs wades into the sea.

MEN SIGN THE SEA

Men sign the sea.
One warbreath more sucked round the roaring veins
Keeping the heart in ark then down loud mountains
After his cry.

This that the sea
Moves through moves over sea-tongued the whole waters
Woven over their breath. So can the floating fires
Blow down on any.

This deep time, scaling broadside the cannoning sea,
Tilting, cast rigged among galloping iron vesselwork,
Snapped wirerope, spitting oil, steam screamed out jets,
Bomb drunkard hero herded by the hammerheaded elements,
Loud raftered foamfloored house, a waved scorched hand
Over final upheaval and the decked combers.
The filling limpet shell's slow gyre round the drowned.
The cairns of foam stand up. The signed sea flowers.

The love-signed sea
Weeded with words and branched with human ores
Lights up. An arm waves off the land. Thunderous
Time mines the sea.

Men sign the sea,
Maintained on memory's emerald over the drowned.
This that the sea moves through drives through the land
Twin to their cry.

NIGHT'S FALL UNLOCKS THE DIRGE OF THE SEA

Night's fall unlocks the dirge of the sea
To pour up from the shore and befriending
Gestures of water waving, to find me
Dressed warm in a coat of land in a house
Held off the drowned by my blood's race
Over the crops of my step to meet some praise.

The surge by day by night turns lament
And by this night falls round the surrounding
Seaside and countryside and I can't
Sleep one word away on my own for that
Grief sea with a purse of pearls and debt
Wading the land away with salt in his throat.

By this loud night traded into evidence
Of a dark church of voices at hand
I lie, work of the gruff sea's innocence
And lie, work of the deaths I find
On the robbed land breathing air and
The friendly thief sea wealthy with the drowned.

At whose sheltering shall the day sea
Captain his ships of foam to save
Them weary of air, their hair gently
Afloat above them on prongs of water?
Now, prince in the seacircling tower,
Emigrant to grief, furious seafarer swept over

The seven wounds and multiple five
Senses of drowning; he fills his voice
With land-dry prayers and the sea above.
His 'help' or 'save me' like a bird
Bore back only the stretched whitefingered
Hand of the swelling sea and found him sheltered,

Sheltered in soon all of us to be
That memory against the scuppering rocks,
The spilling aprons of the sea.
Grief fills the voice with water, building
Ruin on the ruining land. Sheltering
In sea he breathes dry land, dry grave and dwelling.

THREE POEMS OF DROWNING

1

Workmen on the unleashed drowning floors, what can
You make of it so packed round with the king's unruly
Fullfed ministers, the air turned fraud to their lungs
And under the breath-hushed ceiling of the open sea?
So emerald rigged, your gardens hang their Babylons.

So wandered, bowed into a new affection to inhabit,
You'll likely wake white as salt and lean from the sill
Heavy with shoulder-perching waves of the flocking sea

84

To ask me down under the fighting. Far over early
This morning's wide sea you speak at the white threshold.

Over the early sea-show the speaking ceremonies
Wave me a word of warning and rescue's gesture
By my eyes landmarked in a prison of breathing my crowds.
All working hands throw up, raged in dry images,
The time-combing lintel of foam and door of breath.

2

Now endured sea-martyrdom crucified by the soldier sea,
Hoisted high to nails, crowned over the inventing host
And struck through hammering, his all grief well over
The moneychanging, manfed water; he has left me
Changed by the stampede side of foam swept through.

You numbering skylights where the sent light enters
The seadeep heart, can you not hear the music
Still held in the plundered heart far forsaken
All by my ear? The seafared pulses roar.
His settling hair swims longer round his eyes.

Now left, I'm to wear my lifesave slow in air,
Ark set on the crowd maintaining the hideout heart
And loud uneven seas. My ships fill mercifully
At last done down to nothing but locked into under
The grave-mounded sea kept under with a stone.

3

Wakened by drift and drowned words cast in darkness
Loud to the flying shoals and breath of my sleep
I walk out saved into a good family sea-gentled
Into calling me here. The men of the world knock through.
My scaled seawalls call accent to the unwinding voice.

Their bubbled seabelled sky and the rushing shoulders
With screaming bundles of foam over their home fathoms
Lock them shaped under out of their smiling lifestories.
My eyes on shore stare the crying spray to my mind,
Light lost not to build a lament or pay dry prayer.

Now in these seas, my task of the foam-holy voyages
Charted in a bead of blood, I work. I answer
Across the dark sea's raging bridges of exchange
Proclaiming my own fought drowning, as loud laid under.
All arriving seas drift me, at each heartbreak, home.

MICHAEL'S SEA-LAMB
BEFORE MY BREATH THIS DAY

Michael's sea-lamb before my breath this day
Slighting the impure minch makes miling way
Through seaful filaments well into ultimately
The housed farewells of the drowned loud here in my
First sandprints in seaware beside the limekiln Shony.

Seawind and sand as my grandstand, the whole white length
Nine towns on foaming founds, moves through my wealth
Of hoarsalt onlooking men who drew my breath
Once lonely spokesmen over the screeching firth.
Storm as my grandstand. Straw as my hovelled death.

Not least my drowned men making from their fathoms
Make better known their patron from their watercombs
Caved in empowered elegy. I hear the calms
Swim round the glided weed as emerald becomes
Overhead unfurling skylights as their sea-tombs.

THE VOYAGES OF ALFRED WALLIS

Worldhauled, he's grounded on God's great bank,
Keelheaved to Heaven, waved into boatfilled arms,
Falls his homecoming leaving that old sea testament,
Watching the restless land sail rigged alongside
Townful of shallows, gulls on the sailing roofs.
And he's heaved once and for all a high dry packet
Pecked wide by curious years of a ferreting sea,
His poor house blessed by very poverty's religious
Breakwater, his past house hung in foreign galleries.
He's that stone sailor towering out of the cupboarding sea
To watch the black boats rigged by a question quietly
Ghost home and ask right out the jackets of oil
And standing white of the crew 'what hellward harbour
Bows down her seawalls to arriving home at last?'

Falls into home his prayerspray. He's there to lie
Seagreat and small, contrary and rare as sand.
Oils overcome and keep his inward voyage.
An Ararat shore, loud limpet stuck to its terror,
Drags home the bible keel from a returning sea
And four black shouting steerers stationed on movement
Call out arrival over the landgreat houseboat.
The ship of land with birds on seven trees
Calls out farewell like Melville talking down on
Nightfall's devoted barque and the parable whale.
What shipcry falls? The holy families of foam
Fall into wilderness and 'over the jasper sea'.
The gulls wade into silence. What deep seasaint
Whispered this keel out of its element?

THE BRIGHT MIDNIGHT

Beside this church underneath a saintly element
Once rested in my arms another midnight more
Miracled into early years and maze of pathways
Frosted between the grasses of the churchyard.
Once rested on the flying spire earlier eyes
In appearance likely mine but far and elsewhere
Gazing from. Under this midnight, beside this church
What greyhaired measures and infant measures advance
Between the stones and audience the time contains?

Allow for some answer this winter night, the children
Who live in five worshipping stone houses not far
Arranged under those stars, to reply towards me
Some evidence of an early innocence of sleep.
The winter strikes bright on Christ's walls and glass
Stained into saints and lanterned all disciples
Acting the bible ghosts gone wild into fire
At blind dust. I'll be for a struck silence
Fixed as the bell strikes the midnight dead still.

Served with a breath to breathe rarely away.
Beside his death the infant sleeps, which always
Wears generously his journey with a wise fear.
And he sleeps, particle teemed with stars under
Rafter and stone and family light. He sleeps
So always lost to the candle. Or even there
With slow moon on the sill peering him out
Of sleep, he's wandered out that bitter light
Learning his young shade's new lightnings and burials.

There where his head rests on my mind made white
Under wind and riding brilliance of black winter
Bushed into burning skies, his taken breath
Breaks on the nightheld doors keeping my best
Wishes kneeling towards the manger of his word.

Take hand then in the heed of my head's world
By winter roadside pitched under the breasting
Grave-staring moon. Take care. Take careful breath
Out of this scalding freeze in the diamond midnight.

There with his step take step along the nightway
Chained into white under the snowfalling owl
And spoken bell. He's taken by a dead hand
Across the black hillside, that inheritance
Which utters thousands on his lips and keeps
The illforgiving terrors of all the dead.
His birthright leads him blindfold on his sleep.
The clock knocks on the wall. The boy sleeps all
Gathered in a good breast from the blazing frost.

Now wordawake here bowed under the armoured heavens
Bright over the dead stones, I ring the iron road
Cast dazzling before me hearing the striking winter
Through the moor's dykes. The spire across the signs
Flies burning in a saintly breath. I am near neighbour
Always to the gravestoned head and head covered
With still early angels in the all alone one world whole.
I ring my footsteps under my eyes closed, burning
In my white fires and words in the brain's black branches.

DEFINITION OF MY HOUSE

Halfway victim to the many, halfway victorious
Orator of infant earth's all nations all nature's
His halls and heights, weathers and contraries;
My arms my walls fend off, my vaned roof ferries
The fire-armed day.
For a while the hill, the stroller by us all
Shoulders, makes mortal my loaded found, and the angel
Easier thundering, books breadcrumbs at my sill,
More easily wakens wide earth's window from exile.

It's no room lost for less than the whole advance
Into all sides. Dwelling there shelter's innocence
Halfway keeps off my own, halfway keeps once
And changing all, my work and what it fountains.
The foam-armed sea
At each stonerolling corner buoys me higher
From flood to dove, the food of Heaven's flower
That follows, locked in never-ending fire,
Me through the thunder of my surrounding hour.

Each stone has cornered my breath and the flying cave
At once keeps whole in bone my table and the grave.

DEFINITION OF MY BROTHER

Each other we meet but live grief rises early
By far the ghost and surest of all the sea
Making way to within me. My bowed-down holy
Man of the watchman minute begs that reply,
Your voice or mine.
One another I leave into Eden with. I commit
The grave. Poverty takes over where we two meet.
Time talks over the fair boy. His hot heartbeat
Beats joy back over the knellringing till defeat.

It's a contrary son I'm of. My wave-felled kin
Steal out on the worlding waters farback again
Away to the whirling beaches to reach his alone
Lost eyes and sprinkled miracles of destruction.
Turmoil to shine
In once the whalesway wearing the starboard freights,
I promise I'll ship the mad nights to bright benefits
To that seastrolling voice in waves and states
Not mine but what one another contrary creates.

Or do we know a prince bleeding more gently
Away to best the morning at its gates?

AT THAT BRIGHT CRY SET ON
THE HEART'S HEADWATERS

At that bright cry set on the heart's headwaters
I'm handed keys. I'm drifted well away.
Ahoy, shall I shout, emigrant to save me?
A packet of Irish returning to hoist the wars
Rendering wherein the white world they trod.
Bedside to sea I'm kindled by its garments.

At that cupped cry my oak puffs up its hints,
Was mortal-caulked before it fell to the arrived
Contraries and kegs, bedlams of victorious value.
And was before it fell to this formal ash
The manned quarters of my imagination's courage.
Bedside to land and something of a man, I say
And hoist to words this arrival, and make sail
The deadly manroped hearties of a holy seavessel.

FOR THE INMOST LOST

For the inmost lost neither angel nor beguiled evangel,
Or forgiveness catherined ever on the high starry wheel,
Or crossed rowan, those idiot herbs and ointments of
Adam's healer who talks my crowds from under my roof.
But better waked into the intricate busy garment
With all own heaven's briars burning the innocent
Heart's holy followers as they rise differently mine.
I'm better brought home to learn the ropes of my own
Merrymaking christendom giant to outside crucifixion.

All inmost over the intricate crusade further
Unwound through burnished wilderness and the hour
Of death laid whitening, I find the whole delta's bread
Brought bound into treasury dazzling the crumbsharing word.
And fulfilment's ploughbow promising well the land
Further roams here and sows the flowing imagined
Pastures green sprung in their honeyed years. And lost
As I thread my thieves to wound myself into blessed,
I walk as a lonely energy at large through my host.

THE WHITE THRESHOLD

1

Let me all ways from the deep heart
Drowned under behind my brow so ever
Stormed with other wandering, speak
Up famous fathoms well over strongly
The pacing whitehaired kingdoms of the sea.

I walk towards you and you may not walk away.

Always the welcome-roaring threshold
So ever bell worth my exile to
Speaks up to greet me into the hailing
Seabraes seabent with swimming crowds
All cast all mighty water dead away.

I rise up loving and you may not move away.

Let me all ways from these seas
Restore to never forswear my air
Breathed in the lamblood-reddened deep.
For heart and whale's in covenant,
The caaing thresher in his splendid blood.

Very end then of land. What vast is here?

Always the saving seadoors well
Worth salt homecoming speaking up
The heaving hundred weights of water,
Save me down into a homecoming tiding
Worth while and breath here with my smothering farers.

Your while in all your mighty times is here.

Let me all ways from the deep heart
That's put down out of the crowded air
And put to self seawork across
The rudimental waste and maiden-
Headed foamthatch, speak up the watery ladders.

Your fathoms hear the sheerhulk winches wind.

Always these all sea families felled
In diving burial hammocks or toppled
Felled elm back into the waving woods,
Wear me my words. The nettling brine
Stings through the word. The Morven maiden cries.

Your heartlit fathoms hurl their ascending drowned.

Very end then of land. What vast is here?
The drowning saving while, the threshold sea
Always is here. You may not move away.

2

I sow the eye what it should see.
I look well out to land and walk as
Watermaster towards the flecked rhinns,
Wrecked aluminium (what trinket gone
Down out of hounded air to the drowned?)
Bound kerns of spray, loud sweeps of foam
And sea-trapdoors. Five fathoms up
Into nightair I emerge safe.
I see shorefire and needfire burn

Buried far out in island air
So near fanned into answer venust
Or black wind blow their courage out.
Shelled and fabled flying sprayricks
Over the hosters of the lythed water
Under the sky's night widow-weeds
Cry waly over the homecomingless
Stone, turf and seagreen glimmer.

Only one faint waif, the whipend moon
Makes a poor mite of light to swim
The petrel-treaded gale of the landtrawled drowned.

I swim the heart what it should save,
Its waters millionshared with not
A cheap love tried in oil to float
But nothing less than my lifesaved youngest
Gesture across the raging filament.
O exchanging sea imperilling who
Walks midnight on your braes, fleetly
Older stranger by changing stranger
I approach your causeway-flowing land.
O goddess-enamoured oar, fend me
Away the waterdead, the wastefarers
Once of my fearful looking back.
O humancrowded inhuman sea,
Row me well out unwound unscathed
On to sheerly such waterface
As will want me, a voice advanced
To find the seawalker on such a night.

Only my earliest ghosts bold from
Dry land draw near to hear the heart
Beat out its words to the dummy dead of the sea.

3

For him her heart she wore.
Veinhaired kingdoms of the heart.
And as a child on Dechmont side
She looked down her loud seasons
Down on pits and wheels
Unwinding in diving cages
Young kings mad under meadows,
An infant unwound into her own heartbreak
Hearing the beechtop cradles noisily
Below on the burning season's side.
A woman folkhomed by red Lanarkshire's slag
Held in her foster heart
She endured the furnace in the sky
And with her looking young lifetime
Suffered the high perched season.

For her his heart he wore.
Veinhaired kingdoms of the heart.
And as a child in tenement-top
Looked down on his loud Clydeside
Down on derricks donkeymen
Caulkers platers from the blacksoap timbered cradles
And a visiting deepsea uncle,
An infant fairly twigged on heartoak
Hearing the arkyard hammers noisily
Down in the loud seasided town.
A poor Tom Bowling in high tenement aloft
Lifted like a lighthouse over the firth
He fell down his steep life
And with his bloodline in his hand
Followed the fox in his fables.

They walk towards me kindly as I hold
Well into memory drowned in the crowded seanight.
Drowned in my crowded head and singled out

I walk the midnight waters of the heart.
They walk towards me too well suffered from,
Bright opposites in imagination's room,
Voiced on my seachanged lifetime from their home.
These two are other, with my likeness enhungered
And meet me shared in the bed of the listening world.
But I'm cried out loud on the breath of the dead.

4

All this night are answered.
Some move nearer a homecoming
Out of the midnight stirred
And the humancrowded song
Of the lamenting sea.
We've met when on a time
We walked the foggy dew
Or Kevin's song of the time
His young life broke through
The bloodbolts of his heart.
Or burned our whisky town
Dressed in a waste of comfort
By the barsided public
And sung to the listening firth.
Living where I breathe
The air of the blinding dead
And bright air of each death
I die in the reddened second
Dovebent from the deep,
I've met you across a look
In a quick room cropped up
Out of the law I break.
Older stranger by stranger
I move towards you across
The strange sea borne in a gesture
Of the light word and the face

Turned to the heartbroke wall.
Beside and in the shade
Of my encountered arrival
From the caretaking dead,
This night I make my haul
From the twelve-discipled seas,
Filament from brother to brother.
This night the hill bothies
On the windbreak of Kintyre
Hear the downbearing sea
Break on the seashelled door.
Continually I am answered
By the selfseas for ever
Fed by the blinding air.

5

Good not let up for midnight's cheered centurions
Come home again. A thunder stroked my head.
Too well the midnight fastens welcome on
Those briny lips. I'll welcome not my own
But that other wandered seawalker through the dead.
Hark how he clicks love's wards with a skeleton key
As crowds sail in. Look how the squandered fury
Of all the crowds crosses in every sky.

Good Phoebus youth nailed on the bleeding branches.
Polar pastoral. Legend-tuskèd boar.
Fertile daughter, a Venus brought white forth
Out of the crowds and mouth of a cindered breath,
I'll hold you off your sacrifice even for
The martyr in burning cities brother sister
All of the elemental founded churches' error.
I'll love through other measures. Here as man's heir

Weirdly put out as what the night invents me,
I see the crowds. I stand beneath the fires

Wound into the cheering air and furious roof.
The bush I burn in gives me room enough.
A flame in aid of the dead. Or tonight's furies
In galloping aid of the world's angelic bread
Brought into the loud sky there where violence laid
Waste on the crowded natures of every head.

Good now they're drunken home again, further
Come home than ever under the furious airs
To dryland burning. The frigate floes blow away
As arkloads out to the shouting open sea.
The perished piers as reefs. A fallen force
Across the cleft cathedrals in the furnaced city.
Endeavour burns its gases. The sky below
Fills with a terrible tear and a rising cry.

Good voice towards me all ways let me move
Advanced across the kiss filled with a thousand
Crowded seas. And all ways from other geographies,
Dressed in my best of crowds, cry up my families.
This midnight makes, more than the sea its sand,
My daily dead puff up an ambitious dust
Through native pain endured and through my earliest
Gesture towards the first fires of my past.

THREE LETTERS
(In memory of my mother)
Spring 1948

TO MY BROTHER

Alastair approach this thirty
Lines with a homing memory.
Each step speaks out the springtime.
Our Clydeside merges home.

The morning rises up.
The sun's enamoured step
Crosses the ancient firth.
Your breath crosses my breath.

The sun's encouraged step,
The released word's escape,
Enters the bright bright world
Held in the helmet head.

The firth makes light of us
Exchanged on those waters
Between Gareloch and Greenock
Wearing woodshell and rowlock.

All on this emerged morning
Between banks of shipbuilding
The distilled and hurtled out
Industry of mind and heart

Floats us from hammer yards,
Twin measures of these words.
Foreseen secretly by
Violence and strawdeath eye

As the cairns move against
The natural seamist
We sail for ever the authorities
Of a changed firth's waters.

I let thirty lines loose.
These words make light of us.

TO MY FATHER

Yes as alike as entirely
You my father I see
That high Greenock tenement
And whole shipyarded front.

As alike as a memory early
Of 'The Bonny Earl o' Moray'
Fiddled in our high kitchen
Over the sleeping town

These words this one night
Feed us and will not
Leave us without our natures
Inheriting new fires.

The March whinfires let fall
From the high Greenock hill
A word fetched so bright
Out of the forehead that

A fraction's wink and I
And my death change round softly.
My birth and I so softly
Change round the outward journey.

Entirely within the fires
And winter-harried natures
Of your each year, the still
Foundered man is the oracle

Tented within his early
Friendships. And he'll reply
To us locked in our song.
This night this word falling

Across the kindling skies
Takes over over our bodies.

TO MY MOTHER

Under (not ground but the mind's)
Thunder you rest on memory's
Daily aloneness as rest
My steps to a great past.

My memory saves its breath.
Its flowing stronghold with
Crowds of the day and night
Changes them each heartbeat.

In words I change them further
Away from the parent fire.
Look. Into life or out?
What son did you inherit?

The flowing strongheld Clyde
Rests me my earliest word
That has ever matchlessly
Changed me towards the sea.

That deep investment speaks
Over ship-cradles and derricks
And ebbs to a perfection's
Deadly still anatomies.

Sometimes like loneliness
Memory's crowds increase.
Suddenly some man I am
So finds himself endless stream

Of stepping away from his
Last home, I crave my ease
Stopped for a second dead
Out of the speaking flood.

Under (not ground but the words)
You rest with speaking hordes.

THE NIGHTFISHING
(1955)

THE NIGHTFISHING

1

Very gently struck
The quay night bell.

Now within the dead
Of night and the dead
Of my life I hear
My name called from far out.
I'm come to this place
(Come to this place)
Which I'll not pass
Though one shall pass
Wearing seemingly
This look I move as.
This staring second
Breaks my home away
Through always every
Night through every whisper
From the first that once
Named me to the bone.
Yet this place finds me
And forms itself again.
This present place found me.
Owls from on the land.
Gulls cry from the water.
And that wind honing
The roof-ridge is out of
Nine hours west on the main
Ground with likely a full
Gale unwinding it.

Gently the quay bell
Strikes the held air.

Strikes the held air like
Opening a door
So that all the dead
Brought to harmony
Speak out on silence.

I bent to the lamp. I cupped
My hand to the glass chimney.
Yet it was a stranger's breath
From out of my mouth that
Shed the light. I turned out
Into the salt dark
And turned my collar up.

And now again almost
Blindfold with the bright
Hemisphere unprised
Ancient overhead,
I am befriended by
This sea which utters me.

The hull slewed out through
The lucky turn and trembled
Under way then. The twin
Screws spun sweetly alive
Spinning position away.

Far out faintly calls
The continual sea.

Now within the dead
Of night and the dead
Of all my life I go.
I'm one ahead of them
Turned in below.

I'm borne, in their eyes,
Through the staring world.

The present opens its arms.

2

To work at waking. Yet who wakes?
Dream gives awake its look. My death
Already has me clad anew.
We'll move off in this changing grace.
The moon keels and the harbour oil
Looks at the sky through seven colours.

When I fell down into this place
My father drew his whole day's pay,
My mother lay in a set-in bed,
The midwife threw my bundle away.

Here we dress up in a new grave,
The fish-boots with their herring scales
Inlaid as silver of a good week,
The jersey knitted close as nerves
Of the ground under the high bracken.
My eyes let light in on this dark.

When I fell from the hot to the cold
My father drew his whole day's pay,
My mother lay in a set-in bed,
The midwife threw my bundle away.

3

I, in Time's grace, the grace of change, sail surely
Moved off the land and the skilled keel sails
The darkness burning under where I go.
Landvoices and the lights ebb away
Raising the night round us. Unwinding whitely,
My changing motive pays me slowly out.

The sea sails in. The quay opens wide its arms
And waves us loose.

So I would have it, waved from home to out
After that, the continual other offer,
Intellect sung in a garment of innocence.
Here, formal and struck into a dead stillness,
The voyage sails you no more than your own.
And on its wrought epitaph fathers itself
The sea as metaphor of the sea. The boat
Rides in its fires.

And nursed now out on movement as we go,
Running white from the bow, the long keel sheathed
In departure leaving the sucked and slackening water
As mingled in memory; night rises stooped high over
Us as our boat keeps its nets and men and
Engraves its wake. Our bow heaves hung on a likely
Bearing for fish. The Mor Light flashes astern
Dead on its second.

Across our moving local of light the gulls
Go in a wailing slant. I watch, merged
In this and in a like event, as the boat
Takes the mild swell, and each event speaks through.
They speak me thoroughly to my faintest breath.
And for what sake? Each word is but a longing
Set out to break from a difficult home. Yet in
Its meaning I am.

The weather's come round. For us it's better broken.
Changed and shifted above us, the sky is broken
Now into a few light patches brightly ground
With its rough smithers and those swells lengthening
Easy on us, outride us in a slow follow
From stern to stem. The keel in its amorous furrow
Goes through each word. He drowns, who but ill
Resembled me.

In those words through which I move, leaving a cry
Formed in exact degree and set dead at
The mingling flood, I am put forward on to
Live water, clad in oil, burnt by salt
To life. Here, braced, announced on to the slow
Heaving seaboards, almost I am now too
Lulled. And my watch is blear. The early grey
Air is blowing.

It is that first pallor there, broken, running
Back on the sheared water. Now the chill wind
Comes off the shore sharp to find its old mark
Between the shoulderblades. My eyes read in
The fixed and flying signs wound in the light
Which all shall soon lie wound in as it slowly
Approaches rising to break wide up over the
Brow of the sea.

My need reads in light more specially gendered and
Ambitioned by all eyes that wide have been
Me once. The cross-tree light, yellowing now,
Swings clean across Orion. And waned and very
Gently the old signs tilt and somersault
Towards their home. The undertow, come hard round,
Now leans the tiller strongly jammed over
On my hip-bone.

It is us at last sailed into the chance
Of a good take. For there is the water gone
Lit black and wrought like iron into the look
That's right for herring. We dropped to the single motor.
The uneasy and roused gulls slid across us with
Swelled throats screeching. Our eyes sharpened what
Place we made through them. Now almost the light
To shoot the nets,

And keep a slow headway. One last check
To the gear. Our mended newtanned nets, all ropes

Loose and unkinked, tethers and springropes fast,
The tethers generous with floats to ride high,
And the big white bladder floats at hand to heave.
The bow wakes hardly a spark at the black hull.
The night and day both change their flesh about
In merging levels.

No more than merely leaning on the sea
We move. We move on this near-stillness enough
To keep the rudder live and gripped in the keel-wash.
We're well hinted herring plenty for the taking,
About as certain as all those signs falling
Through their appearance. Gulls settle lightly forward
Then scare off wailing as the sea-dusk lessens
Over our stern.

Yes, we're right set, see, see them go down, the best
Fishmarks, the gannets. They wheel high for a moment
Then heel, slip off the bearing air to plummet
Into the schooling sea. It's right for shooting,
Fish breaking the oiled water, the sea still
Holding its fires. Right, easy ahead, we'll run
Them straight out lined to the west. Now they go over,
White float and rope

And the net fed out in arm-lengths over the side.
So we shoot out the slowly diving nets
Like sowing grain. There they drag back their drifting
Weight out astern, a good half-mile of corks
And bladders. The last net's gone and we make fast
And cut the motor. The corks in a gentle wake,
Over curtains of water, tether us stopped, lapped
At far last still.

It is us no more moving, only the mere
Maintaining levels as they mingle together.
Now round the boat, drifting its drowning curtains
A grey of light begins. These words take place.

The petrel dips at the water-fats. And quietly
The stillness makes its way to its ultimate home.
The bilges slap. Gulls wail and settle.
It is us still.

At last it's all so still. We hull to the nets,
And rest back with our shoulders slacked pleasantly.
And I am illusioned out of this flood as
Separate and stopped to trace all grace arriving.
This grace, this movement bled into this place,
Locks the boat still in the grey of the seized sea.
The illuminations of innocence embrace.
What measures gently

Cross in the air to us to fix us so still
In this still brightness by knowledge of
The quick proportions of our intricacies?
What sudden perfection is this the measurement of?
And speaks us thoroughly to the bone and has
The iron sea engraved to our faintest breath,
The spray fretted and fixed at a high temper,
A script of light.

So I have been called by my name and
It was not sound. It is me named upon
The space which I continually move across
Bearing between my courage and my lack
The constant I bleed on. And, put to stillness,
Fixed in this metal and its cutting salts,
It is this instant to exact degree,
And for whose sake?

It is this instant written dead. This instant,
Bounded by its own grace and all Time's grace,
Masters me into its measurement so that
My ghostly constant is articulated.
Then suddenly like struck rock all points unfix.
The whole east breaks and leans at last to us,

Ancient overhead. Yet not a break of light
But mingles into

The whole memory of light, and will not cease
Contributing its exiled quality.
The great morning moves from its equivalent
Still where it lies struck in expressed proportion.
The streaming morning in its tensile light
Leans to us and looks over on the sea.
It's time to haul. The air stirs its faint pressures,
A slat of wind.

We are at the hauling then hoping for it
The hard slow haul of a net white with herring
Meshed hard. I haul, using the boat's cross-heave
We've started, holding fast as we rock back,
Taking slack as we go to. The day rises brighter
Over us and the gulls rise in a wailing scare
From the nearest net-floats. And the unfolding water
Mingles its dead.

Now better white I can say what's better sighted,
The white net flashing under the watched water,
The near net dragging back with the full belly
Of a good take certain, so drifted easy
Slow down on us or us hauled up upon it
Curved in a garment down to thicker fathoms.
The hauling nets come in sawing the gunwale
With herring scales.

The air bunches to a wind and roused sea-cries.
The weather moves and stoops high over us and
There the forked tern, where my look's whetted on distance,
Quarters its hunting sea. I haul slowly
Inboard the drowning flood as into memory,
Braced at the breathside in my net of nerves.
We haul and drift them home. The winds slowly
Turn round on us and

Gather towards us with dragging weights of water
Sleekly swelling across the humming sea
And gather heavier. We haul and hold and haul
Well the bright chirpers home, so drifted whitely
All a blinding garment out of the grey water.
And, hauling hard in the drag, the nets come in,
The headrope a sore pull and feeding its brine
Into our hacked hands.

Over the gunwale over into our deep lap
The herring come in, staring from their scales,
Fruitful as our deserts would have it out of
The deep and shifting seams of water. We haul
Against time fallen ill over the gathering
Rush of the sea together. The calms dive down.
The strident kingforked airs roar in their shell.
We haul the last

Net home and the last tether off the gathering
Run of the started sea. And then was the first
Hand at last lifted getting us swung against
Into the homing quarter, running that white grace
That sails me surely ever away from home.
And we hold into it as it moves down on
Us running white on the hull heeled to light.
Our bow heads home

Into the running blackbacks soaring us loud
High up in open arms of the towering sea.
The steep bow heaves, hung on these words, towards
What words your lonely breath blows out to meet it.
It is the skilled keel itself knowing its own
Fathoms it further moves through, with us there
Kept in its common timbers, yet each of us
Unwound upon

By a lonely behaviour of the all common ocean.
I cried headlong from my dead. The long rollers,

Quick on the crests and shirred with fine foam,
Surge down then sledge their green tons weighing dead
Down on the shuddered deck-boards. And shook off
All that white arrival upon us back to falter
Into the waking spoil and to be lost in
The mingling world.

So we were started back over that sea we
Had worked widely all fish-seasons and over
Its shifting grounds, yet now risen up into
Such humours, I felt like a farmer tricked to sea.
For it sailed sore against us. It grew up
To black banks that crossed us. It stooped, beaked.
Its brine burnt us. I was chosen and given.
It rose as risen

Treachery becomes myself, to clip me amorously
Off from all common breath. Those fires burned
Sprigs of the foam and branching tines of water.
It rose so white, soaring slowly, up
On us, then broke, down on us. It became a mull
Against our going and unfastened under us and
Curdled from the stern. It shipped us at each blow.
The brute weight

Of the living sea wrought us, yet the boat sleeked lean
Into it, upheld by the whole sea-brunt heaved,
And hung on the swivelling tops. The tiller raised
The siding tide to wrench us and took a good
Ready hand to hold it. Yet we made a seaway
And minded all the gear was fast, and took
Our spell at steering. And we went keeled over
The streaming sea.

See how, like an early self, it's loath to leave
And stares from the scuppers as it swirls away
To be clenched up. What a great width stretches
Farsighted away fighting in its white straits

On either bow, but bears up our boat on all
Its plaiting strands. This wedge driven in
To the twisting water, we rode. The bow shores
The long rollers.

The keel climbs and, with screws spinning out of their bite,
We drive down into the roar of the great doorways,
Each time almost to overstay, but start
Up into again the yelling gale and hailing
Shot of the spray. Yet we should have land
Soon marking us out of this thick distance and
How far we're in. Who is that poor sea-scholar,
Braced in his hero,

Lost in his book of storms there? It is myself.
So he who died is announced. This mingling element
Gives up myself. Words travel from what they once
Passed silence with. Here, in this intricate death,
He goes as fixed on silence as ever he'll be.
Leave him, nor cup a hand to shout him out
Of that, his home. Or, if you would, O surely
There is no word,

There is not any to go over that.
It is now as always this difficult air
We look towards each other through. And is there
Some singing look or word or gesture of grace
Or naked wide regard from the encountered face,
Goes ever true through the difficult air?
Each word speaks its own speaker to his death.
And we saw land

At last marked on the tenting mist and we could
Just make out the ridge running from the north
To the Black Rosses, and even mark the dark hint
Of Skeer well starboard. Now inside the bight
The sea was loosening and the screws spun steadier
Beneath us. We still shipped the blown water but

It broke white, not green weight caved in on us.
In out of all

That forming and breaking sea we came on the long
Swell close at last inshore with the day grey
With mewing distances and mist. The rocks rose
Waving their lazy friendly weed. We came in
Moving now by the world's side. And O the land lay
Just as we knew it well all along that shore
Akin to us with each of its dear seamarks. And lay
Like a mother.

We came in, riding steady in the bay water,
A sailing pillar of gulls, past the cockle strand.
And springing teal came out off the long sand. We
Moved under the soaring land sheathed in fair water
In that time's morning grace. I uttered that place
And left each word I was. The quay-heads lift up
To pass us in. These sea-worked measures end now.
And this element

Ends as we move off from its formal instant.
Now he who takes my place continually anew
Speaks me thoroughly perished into another.
And the quay opened its arms. I heard the sea
Close on him gently swinging on oiled hinges.
Moored here, we cut the motor quiet. He that
I'm not lies down. Men shout. Words break. I am
My fruitful share.

4

Only leaned at rest
Where my home is cast
Cannonwise on silence
And the serving distance.

O my love, keep the day
Leaned at rest, leaned at rest.

Only breathed at ease
In that loneliness
Bragged into a voyage
On the maintaining image.

O my love, there we lay
Loved alone, loved alone.

Only graced in my
Changing madman who
Sings but has no time
To divine my room.

O my love, keep the day
Leaned at rest, leaned at rest.

What one place remains
Home as darkness quickens?

5

So this is the place. This
Is the place fastened still with movement,
Movement as calligraphic and formal as
A music burned on copper.

At this place
The eye reads forward as the memory reads back.
At this last word all words change.
All words change in acknowledgement of the last.
Here is their mingling element.
This is myself (who but ill resembles me).
He befriended so many
Disguises to wander in on as many roads
As cross on a ball of wool.
What a stranger he's brought to pass

Who sits here in his place.
What a man arrived breathless
With a look or word to a few
Before he's off again.

Here is this place no more
Certain though the steep streets
And High Street form again and the sea
Swing shut on hinges and the doors all open wide.

6

As leaned at rest in lamplight with
The offered moth and heard breath
By grace of change serving my birth,

And as at hushed called by the owl,
With my chair up to my salt-scrubbed table,
While my endured walls kept me still,

I leaned and with a kind word gently
Struck the held air like a doorway
Bled open to meet another's eye.

   Lie down, my recent madman, hardly
   Drawn into breath than shed to memory,
   For there you'll labour less lonely.

   Lie down and serve. Your death is past.
   There the fishing ground is richest.
   There contribute your sleight of cast.

   The rigged ship in its walls of glass
   Still further forms its perfect seas
   Locked in its past transparences.

   You're come among somewhere the early
   Children at play who govern my way
   And shed each tear which burns my eye.

Thus, shed into the industrious grave
Ever of my life, you serve the love
Whose motive we are energies of.

So quietly my words upon the air
Awoke their harmonies for ever
Contending within the ear they alter.

And as the lamp burned back the silence
And the walls caved to a clear lens,
The room again became my distance.

I sat rested at the grave's table
Saying his epitaph who shall
Be after me to shout farewell.

7

Far out, faintly rocked,
Struck the sea bell.

Home becomes this place,
A bitter night, ill
To labour at dead of.
Within all the dead of
All my life I hear
My name spoken out
On the break of the surf.
I, in Time's grace,
The grace of change, am
Cast into memory.
What a restless grace
To trace stillness on.

Now this place about me
Wakes the night's twin shafts
And sheds the quay slowly.
Very gently the keel
Walks its waters again.

The sea awakes its fires.
White water stares in
From the harbour-mouth.
And we run through well
Held off the black land
Out into the waving
Nerves of the open sea.

My dead in the crew
Have mixed all qualities
That I have been and,
Though ghosted behind
My sides spurred by the spray,
Endure by a further gaze
Pearled behind my eyes.
Far out faintly calls
The mingling sea.

Now again blindfold
With the hemisphere
Unprised and bright
Ancient overhead,

This present place is
Become made into
A breathless still place
Unrolled on a scroll
And turned to face this light.

So I spoke and died.
So within the dead
Of night and the dead
Of all my life those
Words died and awoke.

SEVEN LETTERS

LETTER I

Welcome then anytime. Fare
Well as your skill's worth,
You able-handed sea-blade
Aglint with the inlaid
Scales of the herring host
And hosting light. Good morning
Said that. And that morning
Opened and fairly rose
Keeping sea-pace with us
Sailed out on the long kyle.
Early there I could tell
Under the scaling light
The nerves of each sheared knot
Keelcleft twisting back
Astern to make the wake,
And I saw my death flash
For an instant white like a fish
In the second-sighted sea.

That death is where I lie
In this sea you inherit.
There is no counter to it.

Taken my dear as heir
To yes again the ever
Arriving sea, I wave
Us here out on the move.
May we both fare well through
This difficult element we
Hear welcome in. Farewell
Gives us ever away
To a better host. See, I
Hack steps on the water never

For one lull still but over
Flowing all ways I make
My ways. Always I make
My ways. And as you listen
Here at the felling bow
I'll be myself in vain
Always. Dear you who walk

Your solitude on these
Words, walk their silences
Hearing a morning say
A welcome I have not heard
In words I have not made.

And the good morning rose
Fairly over the bows
And whitely waving fray.
We hauled the nets. And all
That live and silver causeway
Heaving came to our side.

These words said welcome. Fare
Them well from what they are.

LETTER II

Burned in this element
To the bare bone, I am
Trusted on the language.
I am to walk to you
Through the night and through
Each word you make between
Each word I burn bright in
On this wide reach. And you,
Within what arms you lie,
Hear my burning ways
Across these darknesses
That move and merge like foam.

Lie in the world's room,
My dear, and contribute
Here where all dialogues write.

Younger in the towered
Tenement of night he heard
The shipyards with nightshifts
Of lathes turning their shafts.
His voice was a humble ear
Hardly turned to her.
Then in a welding flash
He found his poetry arm
And turned the coat of his trade.
From where I am I hear
Clearly his heart beat over
Clydeside's far hammers
And the nightshipping firth.
What's he to me? Only
Myself I died from into
These present words that move.
In that high tenement
I got a great grave.

Tonight in sadly need
Of you I move inhuman
Across this space of dread
And silence in my mind.
I walk the dead water
Burning language towards
You where you lie in the dark
Ascension of all words.
Yet where? Where do you lie
Lost to my cry and hidden
Away from the world's downfall?
O offer some way tonight
To make your love take place
In every word. Reply.

Time's branches burn to hear.
Take heed. Reply. Here
I am driven burning on
This loneliest element. Break
Break me out of this night,
This silence where you are not,
Nor any within earshot.
Break break me from this high
Helmet of idiocy.

> Water water wallflower
> Growing up so high
> We are all children
> We all must die.
> Except Willie Graham
> The fairest of them all.
> He can dance and he can sing
> And he can turn his face to the wall.
> Fie, fie, fie for shame
> Turn your face to the wall again.

Yes laugh then cloudily laugh
Though he sat there as deaf
And worn to a stop
As the word had given him up.
Stay still. That was the sounding
Sea he moved on burning
His still unending cry.
That night hammered and waved
Its starry shipyard arms,
And it came to inherit
His death where these words merge.
This is his night writ large.
In Greenock the bright breath
Of night's array shone forth
On the nightshifting town.
Thus younger burning in

The best of his puny gear
He early set out
To write him to this death
And to that great breath
Taking of the sea,
The graith of Poetry.
My musing love lie down
Within his arms. He dies
Word by each word into

Myself now at this last
Word I die in. This last.

LETTER III

As Mooney's calls Time this moment
Amazed faces me with that
Face Love lashed and lashed
I love and wend me always
To death with. O my strayed dear,

Find me. I find you fairly
Wandered under every eye
Yet fondly near me among
Them all in all the harp-hung
Tara of the drinking time
And the drink talking. What a dark
Rush goes under it all
Here we inherit. We'll drink
Ourselves here face to face
A one for the road across
More than these words. Here's us,
And may tonight's nets stroll
Where the herring are. We'll see.
Come nearer to hear. He's high
Singing on the top and gallant
Grace-notes of his longing.

O you are tonight as first
As ever you were then I
Set eyes on you one summer
Gazing your younglashed eyes
On me and playing shyness
And torment, and then you even
Made me buttercup your chin.
Clearly it seems no time.

There's nothing. Not anything
More. Love swells my tongue.
Let the signs start and peer
Us into light. We drift
Above fathoms that move
Their friendly thunders through
This breathless thoroughfare.
And never fear here under
The light of the brandished gale
Of Michael risen double
Sworded with the salt word
Reeking his tongue. Who hears?
Who sees us? Surely only
A drop or two of the spray
That the main deep may favour.

Mooney's called Closing and
Three standing men in a sculled
Boat brimming slowly the night
Skinned harbour calms, move out
To the riding port and star
Board of their trade. Now let
The sail creak and talk
Over us and the light
Swing at the slow mast-head.
We shall lie held here
In the moving hull of Love
Face to face making

The perfect couple perfect.
So, under every eye,
Who shall we perish to?
Here it's endlessly us
Face to face across
The nine-waved and the berry-
Stained kiss of the moved sea.
And not one word we merge in
Here shall we unmarvel
From its true home. My dear,

Easy. We'll keep a good
Watch for the fresh on the salt
As the river moves through
In a stain of calm on the sea.

Easy. Move as I move
Through this breathless sea
Rended openly. The deck
Bleeds sudden fire and
The binnacle like a clutch
Of glow-worms glows. See.
This night moves and this language
Moves over slightly
To meet another's need
Or make another's need.

Move here. We'll choose inshore,
But that's not their concern.

LETTER IV

Night winked and endeared
Itself to language. Huge
Over the dark verge sauntered
Half the moon. Then all
Its shoal attending stared
Down on the calm and mewing

Firth and in a bright
Breath that night became
You in these words fondly
Through me. Even becomes
Us now. And casts me always
Through who I thought I was.
May Love not cast us out.

Know me by the voice
That speaks outside my choice
And speaks our double breath
Into this formal death.

My dear, here and happy
We are cast off away
Swanning through the slow
Shallows and shearing into
The first heave of the deep
Sea's lusty founds.
And out. Lie here happy
Here on this bed of nets.
Loosen the blouse of night.
It seems no time since we
Lay down to let Love pass.
Past? For almost I stoop
Backward to pick Love up,
From where? My dear, all
You've had of me is always
Here. Lean here. Listen.
Though it is always going.
Nor does it say even
A part, but something else.
Time lowers it into bookmould
Filled with words that lied
To where they came from and
To where they went. Yet, lean
On your elbow here. Listen.

What a great way. So bright.
O the sea is meadowsweet.
That voice talking? It's from
Some family famous for
The sea. There's drink in it.
Where did he drown from, taken
By the sea's barbaric hooks?
Yet lie here, love. Listen
To that voice on the swell
(Old rogue with a skilful keel).
It is that voice which hears
The dog whelk's whimper
And the cockle's call come up
From the deep beds under
Those breaking prisms of water.
And hears old Mooney call Time
Bogtongued like doomsday over
The bar and hears Mooney's
Hanging lamp lapping
The sweet oil from its bowl.

And each word, 'this' and 'this'
Is that night and your breath
Dying on mine moved out
On always the sea moving
Neither its help nor comfort
Between us. Be held a while.

Old Calum's there. Listen.
This is his song he says,
To pass the time at the tiller.
He's sad drunk. Let him be.
He'll not see, that poor
Harper, bat-blind, stone-daft
(That cough was aconite).
Let him go on. His harp's
Some strung breastbone but sweet.

It's often enough their habit,
The old and answered not.

Then what a fine upstander
I was for the cause of Love.
And what a fine woman's
Man I went sauntering as.

I could sing a tear out of
The drunk or sober or deaf.
My love would lie pleasanter
Than ever she lay before.

Now she who younger lay
Lies lost in the husk of night.
My far my vanished dears
All in your bowers.

Fondly from a beyond
His song moved to my hand
And moves as you move now.
Yet here's the long heave
To move us through. Say
After me here. 'Unto
My person to be peer.'
And all holds us in the hull
That slides between the waving
Gates and the bow drives
Headlong through the salt
Thicket of the maiden sea.

And shall for Christsake always
Bleed down that streaming door.

LETTER V

Lie where you fell and longed
Broken to fall to from
Grace in your maidenhooded

130

Cage. And further fall.
Lie down where in a word
That blinding greying bard,
Earl of an armed uprising,
Lifted his head to you
And made you right of way
To the silence-felling prow.
And tonight listen under
The watch kept by the height
Sailed and its gazing host.
Winter sits on the gable.

From where these words first fell
Fall to me now. Fall through
This high browbeating night
And slowly, my dear, loving
Take breath for both of us
In this poem in this house
Awake. Your name is long
A byword on my tongue.
You long remember me.
This room. The narrow lamp
Casting the net of light
On this element. The table
Scrubbed with salt and become
For me the grave's table.
And that same voice listening
And blindly trying the latch.
And listen, my love, almost
I heard the quay night bell
Strike on the sea wall.

Anyhow tonight here all
Is again almost at one
With us, and no, there's not
The least sorrow to shade
Or fear to fall. Dearly

Make haste now in the sweet
Oil-wending light keeping
Us endless for a moment.
Changing becomes you. Dress
In your loved best. Put on
Your roomy cramasie
And gloves of the wild fox.
Nor fear, you've been undone
By myriads everywhere always.
And here slip on your emerald
Deeps and your frilled shallows.
The dark befrond you. The first
Of light shall know you by
Your snares of the bright dew.
Even wear your herring bells
To ring the changes and your
Jingling sea-charms along
Your tongue. To find your sea-thighs
Sail where the metaphor flies.
To find your best for me
Spring all your maiden locks.
I stand by what I see.
You blush like new. You're shy
The same. What nets and beds
We've drifted on. It's tides
And tides ago. And here,
Here's where you wept the first
Time and me with only
A few words to my name.
Lie longing down, my dear
Again. Cast in this gold
Wicklight this night within
This poem, we two go down
Roaring between the lines
To drown. Who hears? Who listens?

I entered. Enter after
Me here and encounter
Dimensions of a grave.
Sometimes night sinks its shaft
And I am crossed with light
Here where I lie in language
Braced under the immense
Weight of dumb founded silence.

I heard voices within
The empty lines and tenses.

The tiller takes my hand
In a telling grip. We drive
On in the white soaring
Meantime of fair morning.
Happy the threshold-whetted
Blade that lays us low
Each time for ever. My sweet
Sea-singer shearing the wave
Engrave us where we fall.
Under the wanderlusting
Sky of morning waked
And worded beyond itself
By me to you, who leans
Down through the fanfared lists
To listen? A day to gladden.
A sight to unperish us from
The flashing wake unwinding
Us to our end. And quick,
Take hold, the quick foam blooms
And combs to our side. And now
Rounding the Rhinns, keep hold
And watch as the fisher flies
With beaks in the netting gale
That veers to the kill, and now
As you sail here look the word's

Bright garment from your eyes.
Be for me still, steering
Here at my keeling trade
Over the white heathering
Foam of the tide-race.
Who asks to listen? And who
Do these words listen to
In some far equivalent?
Through me they read you through.
Present your world. Reply
Now at the growing end
As words rush to become
You changing at your best.
Stand by me here. The roar
Is rising. The old defender
Towers. His head soars.
He stands like downfall over
The high gables of morning
In kindling light. Under
His eye that blinds us now
We go down dazzled into
The crowded scroll of the wake.
As silence takes me back
Changed to my last word,

Reply. Present your world.
Gannet of God, strike.

LETTER VI

A day the wind was hardly
Shaking the youngest frond
Of April I went on
The high moor we know.
I put my childhood out
Into a cocked hat
And you moving the myrtle

134

Walked slowly over.
A sweet clearness became.
The Clyde sleeved in its firth
Reached and dazzled me.
I moved and caught the sweet
Courtesy of your mouth.
My breath to your breath.
And as you lay fondly
In the crushed smell of the moor
The courageous and just sun
Opened its door.
And there we lay halfway
Your body and my body
On the high moor. Without
A word then we went
Our ways. I heard the moor
Curling its cries far
Across the still loch.

The great verbs of the sea
Come down on us in a roar.
What shall I answer for?

LETTER VII

Blind tide emblazoning
My death forever on
The sheldrake dark, unperish
Me here this night. Unperish
Me burning in these words
Murmured and roared through
The listening brain of silence
To where she listening lies.

Are you awake listening?
Or are you sound? The tide
Slowly turns and slowly

The nets of night swing
Round to face the west.
We drift at the nets under
Continual cries wheeling.
What winging shapes of silence
Are for us? The herring
Have had their run for the night.
Our money is in the net
Or out. And now we'll haul
And run for home. Are you
Awake or sound and deep
In the bolster-buried ear
Adrift? Slip by sleep's gates.
Slip by sleep's gates and out
From your lost shire and over
The shore's long curlewing.
Move through the shallows out.
Never the like of bright
Steerers overhead
Started as now. Wended,
So many lie within
Your musing ear. Orion
Is brightly barbed. Again
The glint inlays the gunwale.
The wind is rising. I would
From the fires of this sea
Waylay the headlong dead.
Come nearer to hear. See,
There they arm themselves
With Love and wave the fray
Nearer us as they rise
Through every word. Through you
This branching sea burns
Me away. What blinded tons
Of water the world contains.
And yet now out of all

Its bellowing deeps and shoals
Let me be fond. Love,
Let me be fond awhile.

Bear these words in mind
As they bear me soundly
Beyond my reach. Through you
They love. But they in time
Do murder in that name.

Yet quick forget. It's all
Only a tale. Slowly
The great dialogues darken
Upon me and all voices
Between us move towards
Their end in this. Silence
Shapes before I draw breath.
Stay still. Listen so still.
There! Did you hear? Some ear
Speaks me by stealth to death.
Call through that time where once
You fondly strayed and a'
The flooer o' Galloway
Wad doon an dee. So soon
She fell under a thorn
And me. So it arose
A lapwing wandered us.
The song is shed and now
I'm minded of Calum, a man
Out of Kintyre or out
Of my tongue spoken and straight
The thirst chimes me back,
And words are a thirsty lot.
I have a hake in my throat.
You'll barely know his voice
Now for his millstoned life
Speaks through the branks of grief.

The unkind iron casts
His meaning out. The mute
Harp hangs with aconite.
Yet not mistake. Let him
Begin in time. Calum,
Come out from that black drouth.
We'll man the bottled barque
In Mooney's. Remember there
You first rendered the sash
Of foam your father wore.
May she be musing there
Tonight. For her I have
The length and breadth of Love
That it shall lusty keep
Her mind and body good.
Her bent is mine. Calum,
My tongue is Opening Time
And my ear is in its prime.
Ahoy Mooney. Draw back
The ancient bacchus bolts.
Stand clear of the gates.
And clear we are. So now
Calum, what will you have?
I'll call the rounds. Remember,
When we fished out of Kinmore
They made their own at the farm.
We drank it dripping hot
Out of an antique worm.
Now, Calum, here's to the keel.
Lift up your drinking arm.
I've waited so long for this,
To meet you in the eye
And in the ear. And now
All time's within our reach.
Drink and these words unperish
Us under the golden drench.

Welcome my dear as heir
To yes again the long
Song of the thorough keel
Moving us through the pitch
Of night in a half gale.
Here at the gunwale farewell
Gives us away this homeward
Night keeled into the final
Breathless element.
Always surely your bent
Is mine. Always surely
My thoroughfare is you.
And that is you by both
The high helmet of light
And by the beast rearing
To sire in the dark kiln.
Watch as you go. Hold
The mizzen there as the sea's
Branches burn and emblazon
Our death under every eye
And burn us into the brain
Of silence in these words.
The lit cardinals swing
Round as we swither off
Our course in a following sea.
Yet the bow climbs back
Shearing the amorous foam
And flourishes in this word
The angel-handed sword.

My love, soon to be held
Still in the last word,
Under out of the spray
Is best. But first, see!
By whose ambition shined
Do the signs arm themselves

So bright tonight to stride
At large for Love? Now where
You once lay lie. We all
Must die and we must all
Lie down in the beast cause.

Language becomes us. The ram
At large moves through this huge
Utterance in which we lie
Homelessly face to face.
Farewell then as your skill's
Worth, you wandering keel.
Make your best wake. Drive
Headlong through the salt
Thicket and thoroughfare
That offers her forever.

My love my love anywhere
Drifted away, listen.
From the dark rush under
Us comes our end. Endure
Each word as it breaks at last
To become our home here.
Who hears us now? Suddenly
In a stark flash the nerves
Of language broke. The sea
Cried out loud under the keel.
Listen. Now as I fall.

Listen. And silence even
Has turned away. Listen.

TWO BALLADS

THE BROAD CLOSE

Come dodge the deathblow if you can
    Between a word or two.
Forget the times we've fallen out
    Or who we've fallen through.
For you are me all over again
    Except where you are new.

I may have hurled my skills away,
    Such as they are, but me,
Well, I'm jackeasy if I slip
    The muse a length for she
Appreciates the starkest man
    Her length and breadth to be.

But there you are. Grandfather whirrs
    And strikes dead on his time.
He was the rude oak of his day
    For the bluenose and the sperm
Till the midnight sun with a flensing spear
    Yelled and struck him dumb.

And there you were by Clydeside clad,
    Heir to a difficult home.
But here we fall as men alive
    Within this very room.
Read me your aid as the word falls
    Or all falls to bedlam.

'Twas on (or shall be on) a black
    Bitter Saturday night.
I sat broke in a black drouth
    And not a dram in sight.
I heard a homeward nightfaller
    Passing his courage out.

I think he was an old man
    By that dribbling pace.
And then he must have followed it
    And fell in the Broad Close,
And as he fell he jingled and
    I never heard him rise.

But that's all by the way. It was
    (As Meg was the first to find)
On such a night as would unman
    (It monkeyed with the gland.)
The best of us or even to freeze
    Them off a brass band.

I fell awake. My forty winks
    Fled as before a ghost.
I rose and looked out and the cobbles
    Looked in with a staring frost.
(Hang your coat on the first word.
    You lift it from the last).

They were my dead burning to catch
    Me up in a time to be.
To think they were once my joke and grief
    As real as this bad knee.
But now they are to the grave gone
    That's digged in memory.

The glass has blinded with a breath.
    All that sight is out.
Why should they stare from the grave again
    At me they died to meet?
The sweet oil walks within the wick
    And gulls on the shore bleat.

Away with them all! Now can you sing
    The Smashing of the Van?
You'll not be in your better form

But I'm an easy man.
Just strike up one with a go and I'll
    Beat out the time till dawn.

O sing my grief as joke through
    All the sad counterparts.
Your voice is mine all over again,
    The voice of a lad of parts,
The voice out of the whisky bush,
    The reek in the breathless arts.

But stop. Allow me time to tell.
    The tongue on the quay told.
And told me it was time my great
    Inheritance was hauled.
(O never have heed of dead folk
    If you find them afield.)

I took my weapons up and went
    With hardly a word to spare.
And I wore my father's error for
    That I'll always wear.
But there was no bad in me
    As I went from that door.

And may he strike me down without
    The turn of a holy hair
If there was any bad in me
    When I went from that door.
And as I went my breath aghast
    Proceeded me before.

I tell it here upon the old
    Voices and the new,
And let them have their fling between
    Meanings out of the true
That they may make a harmony
    That's proper to us two.

And I went out on any word
  Would bring me to myself
And they were cold and hard words
  And cut my truth in half.
But I was blind till the frost blazed
  Me suddenly wakerife.

I heard the blindman's hedge and all
  The white roar of the sea.
I saw the deaf man's bell that struck
  The ice from off the tree.
And then I heard but a thin sound,
  Went straight to where he lay.

And O it is not to ask me by
  The flensing or the spear,
Or the grey table of the grave
  That writes between us here.
But it is enough to ask me by
  His likeness I wear.

'Come dodge the death blow, old man
  For I see you are not fain
To yield me my inheritance,
  But you will feel no pain.
You died to meet me once and now
  You are to die again.

And cock your ears and leave no word
  Unturned that I am in.
For the gale will skelp upon the firth
  And drive the hailing stone,
And you out of the weather where
  There is not flesh or bone.

If I am you all over again
  By the joke and by the grief
Dodge if you can this very word,

For it is the flensing knife.'
And I have put it in his breast
And taken away his life.

I turned it round for all that
Seeing he did not stir.
And the Broad Close was bitter and
Is bitter at this hour.
The sweet oil walks within the wick
And gulls bleat on the shore.

Both wit and weapons must the king
Have over all alive
And over all his dead that they
Do him only love.
And wit and weapons must the king
Have down into the grave.

BALDY BANE

Shrill the fife, kettle the drum,
My Queens my Sluts my Beauties
Show me your rich attention
Among the shower of empties.
And quiet be as it was once
It fell on a night late
The muse has felled me in this bed
That in the wall is set.
Lie over to me from the wall or else
Get up and clean the grate.

On such a night as this behind
McKellar's Tanworks' wall
It seems I put my hand in hers
As we played at the ball.
So began a folly that
I hope will linger late,
Though I am of the kitchen bed

And of the flannel sheet.
Lie over to me from the wall or else
    Get up and clean the grate.

Now pay her no attention now,
    Nor that we keep our bed.
It is yon hoodie on the gate
    Would speak me to the dead.
And though I am embedded here
    The creature to forget
I ask you one and all to come.
    Let us communicate.
Lie over to me from the wall or else
    Get up and clean the grate.

Make yourself at home here.
    My words you move within.
I made them all by hand for you
    To use as your own.
Yet I'll not have it said that they
    Leave my intention out,
Else I, an old man, I will up
    And at that yella-yite.
Lie over to me from the wall or else
    Get up and clean the grate.

You're free to jig your fiddle or let
    It dally on the bow.
Who's he that bums his chat there,
    Drunk as a wheelbarrow?
Hey, you who visit an old man
    That a young wife has got,
Mind your brain on the beam there
    And watch the lentil pot.
Lie over to me from the wall or else
    Get up and clean the grate.

Now pay her no attention.
  I am the big bowbender.
These words shall lie the way I want
  Or she'll blacklead the fender.
No shallop she, her length and depth
  Is Clyde and clinker built.
When I have that one shafted I
  Allow my best to out.
Lie over to me from the wall or else
  Get up and clean the grate.

Full as a whelk, full as a whelk
  And sad when all is done.
The children cry me Baldy Bane
  And the great catches are gone.
But do you know my mother's tune,
  For it is very sweet?
I split my thumb upon the barb
  The last time I heard it.
Lie over to me from the wall or else
  Get up and clean the grate.

Squeeze the box upon the tune
  They call Kate Dalrymple O.
Cock your ears upon it and
  To cock your legs is simple O.
Full as a whelk, full as a whelk
  And all my hooks to bait.
Is that the nightshift knocking off?
  I hear men in the street.
Lie over to me from the wall or else
  Get up and clean the grate.

Move to me as you birl, Meg.
  Your mother was a great whore.
I have not seen such pas de bas
  Since up in Kirriemuir.

I waded in your shallows once,
   Now drink up to that.
It makes the blood go up and down
   And lifts the sneck a bit.
Lie over to me from the wall or else
   Get up and clean the grate.

Through the word and through the word,
   And all is sad and done,
Who are you that these words
   Make this fall upon?
Fair's fair, upon my word,
   And that you shall admit,
Or I will blow your face in glass
   And then I'll shatter it.
Lie over to me from the wall or else
   Get up and clean the grate.

If there's a joke between us
   Let it lie where it fell.
The exact word escapes me
   And that's just as well.
I always have the tune by ear.
   You are an afterthought.
But when the joke and the grief strike
   Your heart beats on the note.
Lie over to me from the wall or else
   Get up and clean the grate.

Full as a whelk, full as a whelk
   My brain is blanketstitched.
It is the drink has floored us
   And Meg lies unlatched.
Lie over to me, my own muse.
   The bed is our estate.
Here's a drink to caulk your seams
   Against the birling spate.

Lie over to me from the wall or else
Get up and clean the grate.

Now pay her no attention, you.
Your gears do not engage.
By and large it's meet you should
Keep to your gelded cage.
My ooze, my merry-making muse,
You're nothing to look at.
But prow is proud and rudder rude
Is the long and short of that.
Lie over to me from the wall or else
Get up and clean the grate.

Think of a word and double it.
Admit my metaphor.
But leave the muscle in the verse,
It is the Skerry Vore.
Can you wash a sailor's shirt
And can you wash it white?
O can you wash a sailor's shirt
The whitest in the fleet?
Lie over to me from the wall or else
Get up and clean the grate.

Full as a whelk and ending,
Surprise me to my lot.
The glint of the great catches
Shall not again be caught.
But the window is catching
The slow mend of light.
Who crossed these words before me
Crossed my meaning out.
Lie over to me from the wall or else
Get up and clean the grate.

Cry me Baldy Bane but cry
The hoodie off the gate,

And before you turn away
  Turn to her last estate.
She lies to fell me on the field
  Of silence I wrote.
By whose endeavour do we fare?
  By the word in her throat.
Lie over to me from the wall or else
  Get up and clean the grate.

She lies to fell me on the field
  That is between us here.
I have but to lift the sneck
  With a few words more.
Take kindly to Baldy Bane, then
  And go your ways about.
Tell it in the Causewayside
  And in Cartsburn Street,
Lie over to me from the wall or else
  Get up and clean the grate.

Love me near, love me far.
  Lie over from the wall.
You have had the best of me
  Since we played at the ball.
I cross the Fingal of my stride
  With you at beauty heat.
And I burn my words behind me.
  Silence is shouted out.
Lie over to me from the wall or else
  Get up and clean the grate.

MALCOLM MOONEY'S LAND
(1970)

MALCOLM MOONEY'S LAND

1

Today, Tuesday, I decided to move on
Although the wind was veering. Better to move
Than have them at my heels, poor friends
I buried earlier under the printed snow.
From wherever it is I urge these words
To find their subtle vents, the northern dazzle
Of silence cranes to watch. Footprint on foot
Print, word on word and each on a fool's errand.
Malcolm Mooney's Land. Elizabeth
Was in my thoughts all morning and the boy.
Wherever I speak from or in what particular
Voice, this is always a record of me in you.
I can record at least out there to the west
The grinding bergs and, listen, further off
Where we are going, the glacier calves
Making its sudden momentary thunder.
This is as good a night, a place as any.

2

From the rimed bag of sleep, Wednesday,
My words crackle in the early air.
Thistles of ice about my chin,
My dreams, my breath a ruff of crystals.
The new ice falls from canvas walls.
O benign creature with the small ear-hole,
Submerger under silence, lead
Me where the unblubbered monster goes
Listening and makes his play.

Make my impediment mean no ill
And be itself a way.

A fox was here last night (Maybe Nansen's,
Reading my instruments.) the prints
All round the tent and not a sound.
Not that I'd have him call my name.
Anyhow how should he know? Enough
Voices are with me here and more
The further I go. Yesterday
I heard the telephone ringing deep
Down in a blue crevasse.
I did not answer it and could
Hardly bear to pass.

Landlice, always my good bedfellows,
Ride with me in my sweaty seams.
Come bonny friendly beasts, brother
To the grammarsow and the word-louse,
Bite me your presence, keep me awake
In the cold with work to do, to remember
To put down something to take back.
I have reached the edge of earshot here
And by the laws of distance
My words go through the smoking air
Changing their tune on silence.

3

My friend who loves owls
Has been with me all day
Walking at my ear
And speaking of old summers
When to speak was easy.
His eyes are almost gone
Which made him hear well.
Under our feet the great

154

Glacier drove its keel.
What is to read there
Scored out in the dark?
Later the north-west distance
Thickened towards us.
The blizzard grew and proved
Too filled with other voices
High and desperate
For me to hear him more.
I turned to see him go
Becoming shapeless into
The shrill swerving snow.

4

Today, Friday, holds the white
Paper up too close to see
Me here in a white-out in this tent of a place
And why is it there has to be
Some place to find, however momentarily
To speak from, some distance to listen to?

Out at the far-off edge I hear
Colliding voices, drifted, yes
To find me through the slowly opening leads.
Tomorrow I'll try the rafted ice.
Have I not been trying to use the obstacle
Of language well? It freezes round us all.

5

Why did you choose this place
For us to meet? Sit
With me between this word
And this, my furry queen.
Yet not mistake this
For the real thing. Here

155

In Malcolm Mooney's Land
I have heard many
Approachers in the distance
Shouting. Early hunters
Skittering across the ice
Full of enthusiasm
And making fly and,
Within the ear, the yelling
Spear steepening to
The real prey, the right
Prey of the moment.
The honking choir in fear
Leave the tilting floe
And enter the sliding water.
Above the bergs the foolish
Voices are lighting lamps
And all their sounds make
This diary of a place
Writing us both in.

Come and sit. Or is
It right to stay here
While, outside the tent
The bearded blinded go
Calming their children
Into the ovens of frost?
And what's the news? What
Brought you here through
The spring leads opening?

Elizabeth, you and the boy
Have been with me often
Especially on those last
Stages. Tell him a story.
Tell him I came across
An old sulphur bear
Sawing his log of sleep

Loud beneath the snow.
He puffed the powdered light
Up on to this page
And here his reek fell
In splinters among
These words. He snored well.
Elizabeth, my furry
Pelted queen of Malcolm
Mooney's Land, I made
You here beside me
For a moment out
Of the correct fatigue.

I have made myself alone now.
Outside the tent endless
Drifting hummock crests.
Words drifting on words.
The real unabstract snow.

THE BEAST IN THE SPACE

Shut up. Shut up. There's nobody here.
If you think you hear somebody knocking
On the other side of the words, pay
No attention. It will be only
The great creature that thumps its tail
On silence on the other side.
If you do not even hear that
I'll give the beast a quick skelp
And through Art you'll hear it yelp.

The beast that lives on silence takes
Its bite out of either side.
It pads and sniffs between us. Now
It comes and laps my meaning up.
Call it over. Call it across

This curious necessary space.
Get off, you terrible inhabiter
Of silence. I'll not have it. Get
Away to whoever it is will have you.

He's gone and if he's gone to you
That's fair enough. For on this side
Of the words it's late. The heavy moth
Bangs on the pane. The whole house
Is sleeping and I remember
I am not here, only the space
I sent the terrible beast across.
Watch. He bites. Listen gently
To any song he snorts or growls
And give him food. He means neither
Well or ill towards you. Above
All, shut up. Give him your love.

THE LYING DEAR

At entrance cried out but not
For me (Should I have needed it?)
Her bitching eyes under
My pressing down shoulder
Looked up to meet the face
In cracks on the flaking ceiling
Descending. The map of damp
Behind me, up, formed
Itself to catch the look
Under the closed (now)
Lids of my lying dear.

Under my pinning arm
I suddenly saw between
The acting flutters, a look
Catch on some image not me.

With a hand across her eyes
I changed my weight of all
Knowledge of her before.
And like a belly sledge
I steered us on the run
Mounting the curves to almost
The high verge. Her breath
Flew out like smoke. Her beauty
Twisted into another
Beauty and we went down
Into the little village
Of a new language.

YOURS TRULY

In reply to your last letter
Which came in too confused
For words saying 'Listen.
And silence even has turned
Away. Listen.' Dear Pen
Pal in the distance, beyond
My means, why do you bring
Your face down so near
To affront me here again
With a new expression out
Of not indifferent eyes?
I know you well alas
From where I sit behind
The Art barrier of ice.

Did you hear me call you across
The dead centre of the night?

Where is your pride I said
To myself calling myself
By my name even pronouncing

It freshly I thought but blushed
At the lonely idea.
I saw myself wearing
A clumping taliped
Disguise I was too shy
To take an answer from.

Am I too loud? I hear
Members of the house stirring
Not able to keep asleep
Not able to keep awake
Nor to be satisfactorily
Between. O by the way
I thought I saw you standing
Older losing yourself in
The changed Mooney's mirrors
Of what is left of Ireland.

DEAR WHO I MEAN

Dear who I mean but more
Than because of the lonely stumble
In the spiked bramble after
The wrecked dragon caught
In the five high singing wires
Its tail twisting the wind
Into visibility, I turn
To where is it you lodge
Now at the other end
Of this letter let out
On the end of its fine string
Across your silent airts.

There is more to it than just
A boy losing his kite
On a young day. My flying

Stem and cooper's hoop
And printed paper bucks
And stalls then leaves the air
I thought I had made it for.

When the word or the word's name
Flies out before us in winter
Beware of the cunning god
Slinking across the tense
Fields ready to pretend
To carry in spittled jaws
The crashed message, this letter
Between us. With two fingers
I give one whistle along
The frozen black sticks
To bring him to heel. He knows
He is better over a distance.

And now when the wind falls
Disentangle the string. Kill
The creature if so you move.
Use the material of
Its artifice. You might even
Reassemble for your own sake
A dragon to live your life with.

But the quick brown pouncing god
Magnifies towards us.
He crunches it up like a bird
And does not leave one word.

THE CONSTRUCTED SPACE

Meanwhile surely there must be something to say,
Maybe not suitable but at least happy
In a sense here between us two whoever

We are. Anyhow here we are and never
Before have we two faced each other who face
Each other now across this abstract scene
Stretching between us. This is a public place
Achieved against subjective odds and then
Mainly an obstacle to what I mean.

It is like that, remember. It is like that
Very often at the beginning till we are met
By some intention risen up out of nothing.
And even then we know what we are saying
Only when it is said and fixed and dead.
Or maybe, surely, of course we never know
What we have said, what lonely meanings are read
Into the space we make. And yet I say
This silence here for in it I might hear you.

I say this silence or, better, construct this space
So that somehow something may move across
The caught habits of language to you and me.
From where we are it is not us we see
And times are hastening yet, disguise is mortal.
The times continually disclose our home.
Here in the present tense disguise is mortal.
The trying times are hastening. Yet here I am
More truly now this abstract act become.

MASTER CAT AND MASTER ME
Do Antoine Ó Máille

The way I see it is that Master
Me is falling out with Servant
Me and understairs is live
With small complaints and clattering.

162

The dust is being too quickly
Feathered off my dear objects.
On the other hand I find myself
Impeded where I want to go.

Even the cat (He has no name.)
Is felinely aware that Master
House's bosom is not what
It used to be. The kitchen door

Swings on its hinges singing on
A foreign pitch. The mice have new
Accents and their little scurries
Have acquired a different grace.

At this time the light is always
Anxious to go away. The mantel
Brasses flicker and Malcolm Mooney's
Walrus tooth gleams yellow.

Who let you in? Who pressed
The cracked Master's cup on you?
I will show you out through
The Master's door to the Servant world.

Dont let Master Cat out.
He has to stay and serve with me.
His Master now must enter
The service of the Master Sea.

THE THERMAL STAIR

For the painter Peter Lanyon killed in a gliding accident 1964

I called today, Peter, and you were away.
I look out over Botallack and over Ding
Dong and Levant and over the jasper sea.

163

Find me a thermal to speak and soar to you from
Over Lanyon Quoit and the circling stones standing
High on the moor over Gurnard's Head where some

Time three foxglove summers ago, you came.
The days are shortening over Little Parc Owles.
The poet or painter steers his life to maim

Himself somehow for the job. His job is Love
Imagined into words or paint to make
An object that will stand and will not move.

Peter, I called and you were away, speaking
Only through what you made and at your best.
Look, there above Botallack, the buzzard riding

The salt updraught slides off the broken air
And out of sight to quarter a new place.
The Celtic sea, the Methodist sea is there.

    You said once in the Engine
    House below Morvah
    That words make their world
    In the same way as the painter's
    Mark surprises him
    Into seeing new.
    Sit here on the sparstone
    In this ruin where
    Once the early beam
    Engine pounded and broke
    The air with industry.

    Now the chuck of daws
    And the listening sea.

    'Shall we go down' you said
    'Before the light goes
    And stand under the old
    Tinworkings around

Morvah and St Just?'
You said 'Here is the sea
Made by alfred wallis
Or any poet or painter's
Eye it encountered.
Or is it better made
By all those vesselled men
Sometime it maintained?
We all make it again.'

Give me your hand, Peter,
To steady me on the word.

Seventy-two by sixty,
Italy hangs on the wall.
A woman stands with a drink
In some polite place
And looks at SARACINESCO
And turns to mention space.
That one if she could
Would ride Artistically
The thermals you once rode.

Peter, the phallic boys
Begin to wink their lights.
Godrevy and the Wolf
Are calling Opening Time.
We'll take the quickest way
The tin singers made.
Climb here where the hand
Will not grasp on air.
And that dark-suited man
Has set the dominoes out
On the Queen's table.
Peter, we'll sit and drink
And go in the sea's roar

To Labrador with wallis
Or rise on Lanyon's stair.

Uneasy, lovable man, give me your painting
Hand to steady me taking the word-road home.
Lanyon, why is it you're earlier away?
Remember me wherever you listen from.
Lanyon, dingdong dingdong from carn to carn.
It seems tonight all Closing bells are tolling
Across the Duchy shire wherever I turn.

I LEAVE THIS AT YOUR EAR
For Nessie Dunsmuir

I leave this at your ear for when you wake,
A creature in its abstract cage asleep.
Your dreams blindfold you by the light they make.

The owl called from the naked-woman tree
As I came down by the Kyle farm to hear
Your house silent by the speaking sea.

I have come late but I have come before
Later with slaked steps from stone to stone
To hope to find you listening for the door.

I stand in the ticking room. My dear, I take
A moth kiss from your breath. The shore gulls cry.
I leave this at your ear for when you wake.

THE DARK DIALOGUES

1

I always meant to only
Language swings away
Further before me.

Language swings away
Before me as I go
With again the night rising
Up to accompany me
And that other fond
Metaphor, the sea.
Images of night
And the sea changing
Should know me well enough.

Wanton with riding lights
And staring eyes, Europa
And her high meadow bull
Fall slowly their way
Behind the blindfold and
Across this more or less
Uncommon place.

And who are you and by
What right do I waylay
You where you go there
Happy enough striking
Your hobnail in the dark?
Believe me I would ask
Forgiveness but who
Would I ask forgiveness from?

I speak across the vast
Dialogues in which we go
To clench my words against

Time or the lack of time
Hoping that for a moment
They will become for me
A place I can think in
And think anything in,
An aside from the monstrous.

And this is no other
Place than where I am,
Here turning between
This word and the next.
Yet somewhere the stones
Are wagging in the dark
And you, whoever you are,
That I am other to,
Stand still by the glint
Of the dyke's sparstone,
Because always language
Is where the people are.

2

Almost I, yes, I hear
Huge in the small hours
A man's step on the stair
Climbing the pipeclayed flights
And then stop still
Under the stairhead gas
At the lonely tenement top.
The broken mantle roars
Or dims to a green murmur.
One door faces another.
Here, this is the door
With the loud grain and the name
Unreadable in brass.
Knock, but a small knock,
The children are asleep.

I sit here at the fire
And the children are there
And in this poem I am,
Whoever elsewhere I am,
Their mother through his mother.
I sit with the gas turned
Down and time knocking
Somewhere through the wall.
Wheesht, children, and sleep
As I break the raker up,
It is only the stranger
Hissing in the grate.
Only to speak and say
Something, little enough,
Not out of want
Nor out of love, to say
Something and to hear
That someone has heard me.
This is the house I married
Into, a room and kitchen
In a grey tenement,
The top flat of the land,
And I hear them breathe and turn
Over in their sleep
As I sit here becoming
Hardly who I know.
I have seen them hide
And seek and cry come out
Come out whoever you are
You're not het I called
And called across the wide
Wapenschaw of water.
But the place moved away
Beyond the reach of any
Word. Only the dark
Dialogues drew their breath.

Ah how bright the mantel
Brass shines over me.
Black-lead at my elbow,
Pipe-clay at my feet.
Wheesht and go to sleep
And grow up but not
To say mother mother
Where are the great games
I grew up quick to play.

3

Now in the third voice
I am their father through
Nothing more than where
I am made by this word
And this word to occur.
Here I am makeshift made
By artifice to fall
Upon a makeshift time.
But I can't see. I can't
See in the bad light
Moving (Is it moving?)
Between your eye and mine.
Who are you and yet
It doesn't matter only
I thought I heard somewhere
Someone else walking.
Where are the others? Why,
If there is any other,
Have they gone so far ahead?
Here where I am held
With the old rainy oak
And Cartsburn and the Otter's
Burn aroar in the dark
I try to pay for my keep.

I speak as well as I can
Trying to teach my ears
To learn to use their eyes
Even only maybe
In the end to observe
The behaviour of silence.
Who is it and why
Do you walk here so late
And how should you know to take
The left or the right fork
Or the way where, as a boy
I used to lie crouched
Deep under the flailing
Boughs of the roaring wood?
Or I lay still
Listening while a branch
Squeaked in the resinous dark
And swaying silences.

Otherwise I go
Only as a shell
Of my former self.
I go with my foot feeling
To find the side of the road,
My head inclined, my ears
Feathered to every wind
Blown between the dykes.
The mist is coming home.
I hear the blind horn
Mourning from the firth.
The big wind blows
Over the shore of my child
Hood in the off-season.
The small wind remurmurs
The fathering tenement
And a boy I knew running

The hide and seeking streets.
Or do these winds
In their forces blow
Between the words only?

I am the shell held
To Time's ear and you
May hear the lonely leagues
Of the kittiwake and the fulmar.

4

Or I am always only
Thinking is this the time
To look elsewhere to turn
Towards what was it
I put myself out
Away from home to meet?
Was it this only? Surely
It is more than these words
See on my side
I went halfway to meet.

And there are other times.
But the times are always
Other and now what I meant
To say or hear or be
Lies hidden where exile
Too easily beckons.
What if the terrible times
Moving away find
Me in the end only
Staying where I am always
Unheard by a fault.

So to begin to return
At last neither early
Nor late and go my way

Somehow home across
This gesture become
Inhabited out of hand.
I stop and listen over
My shoulder and listen back
On language for that step
That seems to fall after
My own step in the dark.

Always must be the lost
Or where we turn, and all
For a sight of the dark again.
The farthest away, the least
To answer back come nearest.

And this place is taking
Its time from us though these
Two people or voices
Are not us nor has
The time they seem to move in
To do with what we think
Our own times are. Even
Where they are is only
This one inhuman place.
Yet somewhere a stone
Speaks and maybe a leaf
In the dark turns over.
And whoever I meant
To think I had met
Turns away further
Before me blinded by
This word and this word.

See how presently
The bull and the girl turn
From what they seemed to say,
And turn there above me

With that star-plotted head
Snorting on silence.
The legend turns. And on
Her starry face descried
Faintly astonishment.
The formal meadow fades
Over the ever-widening
Firth and in their time
That not unnatural pair
Turn slowly home.

This is no other place
Than where I am, between
This word and the next.
Maybe I should expect
To find myself only
Saying that again
Here now at the end.
Yet over the great
Gantries and cantilevers
Of love, a sky, real and
Particular is slowly
Startled into light.

THE DON BROWN ROUTE

Over your head the climbing blue
Sky observes your lonely foot.
Through the lens of language I
Focus on the Don Brown Route.

From where I am, even if I shout,
You will not hear. You climb in slow
Motion on silence on the face
Full of happy, full of woe.

Today is very nothing like
Any other day that once soared
In this place. My lens suddenly
Is crossed with the black of a near bird.

Today is almost without winds
And I can see your fingers brush
Your next hold clean and the sand drift
Fine like the smoke of your own ash.

Through the lens of language each
Act hangs for a long time.
Floated out in the iodine air
Your motion comes to me like home

Ing birds meaning to say something
I should be able to read. Reach
For the hold three feet above your pressing
Cheek bright at the edge of your stretch.

Set your Northern toe-cap in
To where your own weather has set
A ledge of spar like an offered journey
Across the cobbles of your street.

At least I am not putting you off
Through the dumb lens I see you through.
I can't nudge your climbing foot
Or shout out to you what to do.

Yet do not lean too far in
To the father face or it will
Astonish you with a granite kiss
And send you packing over the sill.

If you fall, remember no one will see
You tumbling lonely down. Only
I through this bad focus will see.
Why do you imagine Gravity lonely?

And over your head the climbing blue
Sky observes your lonely foot.
Stopped in the lens of language you
Slowly establish the Don Brown Route.

PRESS BUTTON TO HOLD DESIRED SYMBOL

King William the Fourth's electric One
Armed Bandit rolls its eyes to Heaven.
Churchtown Madron's Garfield Strick
Stands at the moment less than even.

Garfield, pull down the mystic arm
And let the holy cylinders turn.
His wife is stirring jam at home
In a copper pan with damsons in.

Plums, oranges and yellow bells
Bite at the worship of his eye.
A small dog stirs at his feet
Making a woolly soundless cry.

O try again, Garfield Strick.
The electric fruit can drop or fly.
The paradisical orchard goes
Upward with a clicking cry.

Untouched by nature spins the fruit
Of an orchard of magic seed.
Do not disturb. The oracle rolls
Its eyes too fast for him to read.

And stops. King William the Fourth pays out
With a line of clattering oranges.
Garfield turns. His glass shatters
Its shape in our astonished gaze.

In the high air on thin sticks
The blanched rags in the wind blow.
The brass cylinder turns round
Saying I know I know I know.

HILTON ABSTRACT

Roger, whether the tree is made
To speak or stand as a tree should
Lifting its branches over lovers
And moving as the wind moves,
It is the longed-for, loved event,
To be by another aloneness loved.

Hell with this and hell with that
And hell with all the scunnering lot.
This can go and that can go
And leave us with the quick and slow.
And quick and slow are nothing much.
We either touch or do not touch.

Yet the great humilities
Keep us always ill at ease.
The weather moves above us and
The mouse makes its little sound.
Whatever happens happens and
The false hands are moving round.

Hell with this and hell with that.
All that's best is better not.
Yet the great humilities
Keep us always ill at ease,
And in keeping us they go
Through the quick and through the slow.

APPROACHES TO HOW THEY BEHAVE

1

What does it matter if the words
I choose, in the order I choose them in,
Go out into a silence I know
Nothing about, there to be let
In and entertained and charmed
Out of their master's orders? And yet
I would like to see where they go
And how without me they behave.

2

Speaking is difficult and one tries
To be exact and yet not to
Exact the prime intention to death.
On the other hand the appearance of things
Must not be made to mean another
Thing. It is a kind of triumph
To see them and to put them down
As what they are. The inadequacy
Of the living, animal language drives
Us all to metaphor and an attempt
To organize the spaces we think
We have made occur between the words.

3

The bad word and the bad word and
The word which glamours me with some
Quick face it pulls to make me let
It leave me to go across
In roughly your direction, hates
To go out maybe so completely
On another silence not its own.

4

Before I know it they are out
Afloat in the head which freezes them.
Then I suppose I take the best
Away and leave the others arranged
Like floating bergs to sink a convoy.

5

One word says to its mate O
I do not think we go together
Are we doing any good here
Why do we find ourselves put down?
The mate pleased to be spoken to
Looks up from the line below
And says well that doubtful god
Who has us here is far from sure
How we on our own tickle the chin
Of the prince or the dame that lets us in.

6

The dark companion is a star
Very present like a dark poem
Far and unreadable just out
At the edge of this poem floating.
It is not more or less a dark
Companion poem to the poem.

7

Language is expensive if
We want to strut, busked out
Showing our best on silence.
Good Morning. That is a bonny doing
Of verbs you wear with the celandine
Catching the same sun as mine.

You wear your dress like a prince but
A country's prince beyond my ken.
Through the chinks in your lyric coat
My ear catches a royal glimpse
Of fuzzed flesh, unworded body.
Was there something you wanted to say?
I myself dress up in what I can
Afford on the broadway. Underneath
My overcoat of the time's slang
1 am fashionable enough wearing
The grave-clothes of my generous masters.

8

And what are you supposed to say
I asked a new word but it kept mum.
I had secretly admired always
What I thought it was here for.
But I was wrong when I looked it up
Between the painted boards. It said
Something it was never very likely
I could fit in to a poem in my life.

9

The good word said I am not pressed
For time. I have all the foxglove day
And all my user's days to give
You my attention. Shines the red
Fox in the digitalis grove.
Choose me choose me. Guess which
Word I am here calling myself
The best. If you can't fit me in
To lying down here among the fox
Glove towers of the moment, say
I am yours the more you use me. Tomorrow
Same place same time give me a ring.

10

Backwards the poem's just as good.
We human angels as we read
Read back as we gobble the words up.
Allowing the poem to represent
A recognizable landscape
Sprouting green up or letting green
With all its weight of love hang
To gravity's sweet affection,
Arse-versa it is the same object,
Even although the last word seems
To have sung first, or the breakfast lark
Sings up from the bottom of the sea.

11

The poem is not a string of knots
Tied for a meaning of another time
And country, unreadable, found
By chance. The poem is not a henge
Or Easter Island emerged Longnose
Or a tally used by early unknown
Peoples. The words we breathe and puff
Are our utensils down the dream
Into the manhole. Replace the cover.

12

The words are mine. The thoughts are all
Yours as they occur behind
The bat of your vast unseen eyes.
These words are as you see them put
Down on the dead-still page. They have
No ability above their station.
Their station on silence is exact.
What you do with them is nobody's business.

13

Running across the language lightly
This morning in the hangingover
Whistling light from the window, I
Was tripped and caught into the whole
Formal scheme which Art is.
I had only meant to enjoy
Dallying between the imaginary
And imaginary's opposite
With a thought or two up my sleeve.

14

Is the word? Yes Yes. But I hear
A sound without words from another
Person I can't see at my elbow.
A sigh to be proud of. You? Me?

15

Having to construct the silence first
To speak out on I realize
The silence even itself floats
At my ear-side with a character
I have not met before. Hello
Hello I shout but that silence
Floats steady, will not be marked
By an off-hand shout. For some reason
It refuses to be broken now
By what I thought was worth saying.
If I wait a while, if I look out
At the heavy greedy rooks on the wall
It will disperse. Now I construct
A new silence I hope to break.

THE FIFTEEN DEVICES

When who we think we are is suddenly
Flying apart, splintered into
Acts we hardly recognize
As once our kin's curious children,
I find myself turning my head
Round to observe and strangely
Accept expected astonishments
Of myself manifest and yet
Bereft somehow as I float
Out in an old-fashioned slow
Motion in all directions. I hope
A value is there lurking somewhere.

Whether it is the words we try
To hold on to or some other
Suggestion of outsideness at least
Not ourselves, it is a naked
State extremely uncomfortable.

My fifteen devices of shadow and brightness
Are settling in and the Madron
Morning accepts them in their places.
Early early the real as any
Badger in the black wood
Of Madron is somewhere going
His last round, a creature of words
Waiting to be asked to help me
In my impure, too-human purpose.

With me take you. Where shall you find us?
Somewhere here between the prised
Open spaces between the flying
Apart words. For then it was
All the blown, black wobblers
Came over on the first wind

To let me see themselves looking
In from a better high flocking
Organization than mine. They make
Between them a flag flying standing
For their own country. Down the Fore
Street run the young to the school bell.

Shall I pull myself together into
Another place? I can't follow
The little young clusters of thoughts
Running down the summer side.

My fifteen devices in my work
Shop of shadow and brightness have
Their places as they stand ready
To go out to say Hello.

WYNTER AND THE GRAMMARSOW

1

SOUND a long blast
Of silence CUT

Sir Longlegged Liker you
Of the Royal Grammarsow
Under its great slate,
I bow in my disguise
And give you your titles.

SOUND the water organ
Of the Greek CUT

Bryan the Spinner
In endless eddies
Above the weir
Of rushing home.

Fibre-glass swiveller
Over the weaving
Strands of water
In an innocent pool.

Scholar King
Of rare meanders.
Rider of Rivers
Undiscovered.

Nightwalker beside the dykes
Blown like mouthorgans
By the Atlantic wind.

Walker beside the star
Lit fences of Housman.
Black-rod of Ernst's
Beaked politicians.

Masked thinskinned diver
On the Cornish shelf.
Wet-suited Seeker after
The church choir of urchins.

SOUND Beddoes towards us
Saying singing I see
His life as on a map of rivers CUT

2

Bryan the Couth.
Brave of the Sue.
King of the Whirr
Of the Windmill.
Perambulator
Of the Christian Fields.
Charming Monotype.
Failed Prefect.
King of the Blue

Pebbled Peepers.
King of Mon.
Truant to Age.

3

SOUND a Wyntermade
Disturbance of what
We expect light to do.
Hold it Hold it CUT

King the Uncrude. King Aggravator
Of Monkeys. Campion of the Gram
Marsow painting blindly under
Its timeless tons of granite thunder.

Long upperlipped king of the dark vowels.
Charmer of brash northern beasts.
Enthusiast King in the making
Of what your subjects have never seen.

Momaster, Ravenmaster, Caneless
Housemaster of a good family.
Master Ventriloquist of fashioned
Spiders. Doubtful Ringmaster of
The successful circus of your despairs.

4

SOUND MacBryde's Song
And thus spak Willie Peden
As he sat beneath the tree
O will you wear a forgivemenot
And plant a yew for me. CUT

Confronted with what you do I can never
Find anything (not unnaturally)
To say. Of course I try to separate
Any regard for you from the made

186

Object before me. Maybe in a kind
Of way it is legitimate to let
One's self be added to, to be moved
By both at once, by the idea
Of the person, and the object
Adrift stationary in its Art law.
Anyhow I think you must be pretty
Good by the way I think you behave.

SOUND Yours Truly saying with an invisible voice
From the Clydeside welding cradles and the hammering
Nightshift town of Greenock, let's to grips.
Is a chat with me your fancy? Now in the dark
Give me the password. Wince me your grip for O
The times are calling us in and the little babes
Are shouldering arms in the cause of the Future Past.
Are we too old to walk around in the round?
Or have our foxes' throats been bitten through?
I dont really mean to speak to you intimately.
Finish here of Yours Truly. Please please CUT.

    The titles are finished
    It was a way
    Of speaking towards you.

Maybe we could have a word before I go,
As I usually say. I mean there must be some
Way to speak together straighter than this,
As I usually say. There is not a long time
To go between the banks of rubbish and nature
Down to the old beginning of the real sea.

    SOUND Coda of one Raven
    Being a black ghost
    Over the Carn CUT

And that is why I think you think kindly
Of the Grammarsow under its great slate.

The W of Wynter is blown is wisped is faltered
Off to the rivers. Applicable titles are endless.

I leave you now retreating backwards from
The cocked ear of Wynter the King standing
Good-mannered up to let me go and turn
Round in the other direction. I leave the Royal
Grammarsow King under his great slate.

FIVE VISITORS TO MADRON

1

In the small hours on the other side
Of language with my chair drawn
Up to the frightening abstract
Table of silence, taps. A face
Of white feathers turns my head
To suddenly see between the mad
Night astragals her looking in
Or wanted this to happen. She
Monster muse old bag or. Something
Dreamed is yes you're welcome always
Desired to drop in. It was your bleached
Finger on the pane which startled me
Although I half-expected you
But not you as you are but whoever
Would have looked in instead, another
More to my liking, not so true.

He realized it was a mistake. Closing
The door of the tomb afterwards
Secretly he thanked whoever
He could imagine to thank, some quick
Thought up thankable god of the moment.

As slow as distant spray falling
On the nether rocks of a headland never
Encountered but through the eye, the first
Of morning's ghost in blue palely
Hoisted my reluctant lid.
Watch what you say I said and watched
The day I uttered taking shape
To hide me in its bright bosom.

Like struck flints black flocking jack
Daws wheel over the Madron roofs.

3

I am longing not really longing
For what dont tell me let me think.
Or else I have to settle for
That step is that a step outside
At my back a new eddy of air?

And left these words at a loss to know
What form stood watching behind me
Reading us over my shoulder. I said
Now that you have come to stand
There rank-breathed at my elbow I will
Not be put off. This message must
Reach the others without your help.

4

And met the growing gaze willing
To give its time to me to let
Itself exchange discernments
If that surely it said is what
I wanted. Quick panics put out
A field of images round me to

Look back out at it from and not
Be gazed out of all composure.
And found my research ridiculously
Ending forced to wear a mask
Of a held-up colander to peer
Through as the even gaze began
Slowly to abate never having asked
Me if I had recognized an old
Aspect of need there once my own.

Terror-spots itch on my face now.
My mind is busy hanging up
Back in their places imagination's
Clever utensils. I scratch my cheek.

5

When the fifth came I had barely drawn
A breath in to identify who
I newly am in my new old house
In Madron near the slaughterhouse.

The hint was as though a child running
Late for school cried and seemed
To have called my name in the morning
Hurrying and my name's wisp
Elongated. Leaves me here
Nameless at least very without
That name mine ever to be called
In that way different again.

CLUSTERS TRAVELLING OUT

1

Clearly I tap to you clearly
Along the plumbing of the world
I do not know enough, not
Knowing where it ends. I tap
And tap to interrupt silence into
Manmade durations making for this
Moment a dialect for our purpose.
TAPTAP. Are you reading that taptap
I send out to you along
My element? O watch. Here they come
Opening and shutting Communication's
Gates as they approach, History's
Princes with canisters of gas
Crystals to tip and snuff me out
Strangled and knotted with my kind
Under the terrible benevolent roof.

Clearly they try to frighten me
To almost death. I am presuming
You know who I am. To answer please
Tap tap quickly along the nearest
Metal. When you hear from me
Again I will not know you. Whoever
Speaks to you will not be me.
I wonder what I will say.

2

Remember I am here O not else
Where in this quick disguise, this very
Thought that's yours for a moment. I sit
Here behind this tempered mesh.

I think I hear you hearing me.
I think I see you seeing me.
I suppose I am really only about
Two feet away. You must excuse
Me, have I spoken to you before?
I seem to know your face from some
One else I was, that particular
Shadow head on the other side
Of the wire in the VISITORS ROOM.

I am learning to speak here in a way
Which may be useful afterwards.
Slops in hand we shuffle together,
Something to look forward to
Behind the spyhole. Here in our concrete
Soundbox we slide the jargon across
The watching air, a lipless language
Necessarily squashed from the side
To make its point against the rules.
It is our poetry such as it is.

Are you receiving those clusters
I send out travelling? Alas
I have no way of knowing or
If I am overheard here.
Is that (It is.) not what I want?

The slaughterhouse is next door.
Destroy this. They are very strict.

3

Can you see my As and Ys semaphore
Against the afterglow on the slaughterhouse
Roof where I stand on the black ridge
Waving my flagging arms to speak?

4

Corridors have their character. I know well
The ring of government boots on our concrete.
Malcolm's gone now. There's nobody to shout to.
But when they're not about in the morning I shout
HOY HOY HOY and the whole corridor rings
And I listen while my last HOY turns the elbow
With a fading surprised difference of tone and loses
Heart and in dwindling echoes vanishes away.
Each person who comes, their purpose precedes them
In how they walk. You learn to read that.
Sometimes the step's accompanied by metal
Jingling and metrical, filled with invention.
Metal opened and slammed is frightening. I try
To not be the first to speak. There is nothing to say.
Burn this. I do not dislike this place. I like
Being here. They are very kind. It's doing me good.

5

If this place I write from is real then
I must be allegorical. Or maybe
The place and myself are both the one
Side of the allegory and the other
Side is apart and still escaped
Outside. And where do you come in
With your musical key-ring and brilliant
Whistle pitched for the whipped dog?

And stands loving to recover me,
Lobe-skewers clipped to his swelling breast,
His humane-killer draped with a badged
Towel white as snow. And listen,
Ventriloquized for love his words
Gainsay any deep anguish left

For the human animal. O dear night
Cover up my beastly head.

6

Take note of who stands at my elbow listening
To all I say but not to all you hear.
She comes on Wednesdays, just on Wednesdays,
And today I make a Wednesday. On and off
I decide to make her my half-cousin Brigit
Back from the wrack and shingle on the Long Loch.
You yourself need pretend nothing. She
Is only here as an agent. She could not
On her own carry a message to you either
Written or dreamed by word of her perfect mouth.

Look. Because my words are stern and frown
She is somewhere wounded. She goes away. You see
It hasn't been a good Wednesday for her. For you
Has it been a good Wednesday? Or is yours Tuesday?

7

When the birds blow like burnt paper
Over the poorhouse roof and the slaughter
House and all the houses of Madron,
I would like to be out of myself and
About the extra, ordinary world
No matter what disguise it wears
For my sake, in my love.

It would be better than beside the Dnieper,
The Brahmaputra or a green daughter
Tributary of the Amazon.

But first I must empty my shit-bucket
And hope my case (if it can be found)

Will come up soon. I thought I heard
My name whispered on the vine.

Surrounded by howls the double-shifting
Slaughterhouse walls me in. High
On the wall I have my blue square
Through which I see the London-Cairo
Route floating like distant feathers.

I hear their freezing whistles. Reply
Carefully. They are cracking down.
Don't hurry away, I am waiting for
A message to come in now.

IMPLEMENTS IN THEIR PLACES
(1977)

WHAT IS THE LANGUAGE USING US FOR?

What is the language using us for?
Said Malcolm Mooney moving away
Slowly over the white language.
Where am I going said Malcolm Mooney.

Certain experiences seem to not
Want to go in to language maybe
Because of shame or the reader's shame.
Let us observe Malcolm Mooney.

Let us get through the suburbs and drive
Out further just for fun to see
What he will do. Reader, it does
Not matter. He is only going to be

Myself and for you slightly you
Wanting to be another. He fell
He falls (Tenses are everywhere.)
Deep down into a glass jail.

I am in a telephoneless, blue
Green crevasse and I can't get out.
I pay well for my messages
Being hoisted up when you are about.

I suppose you open them under the light
Of midnight of The Dancing Men.
The point is would you ever want
To be down here on the freezing line

199

Reading the words that steam out
Against the ice? Anyhow draw
This folded message up between
The leaning prisms from me below.

Slowly over the white language
Comes Malcolm Mooney the saviour.
My left leg has no feeling.
What is the language using us for?

SECOND POEM

1

What is the language using us for?
It uses us all and in its dark
Of dark actions selections differ.

I am not making a fool of myself
For you. What I am making is
A place for language in my life

Which I want to be a real place
Seeing I have to put up with it
Anyhow. What are Communication's

Mistakes in the magic medium doing
To us? It matters only in
So far as we want to be telling

Each other alive about each other
Alive. I want to be able to speak
And sing and make my soul occur

In front of the best and be respected
For that and even be understood
By the ones I like who are dead.

I would like to speak in front
Of myself with all my ears alive
And find out what it is I want.

2

What is the language using us for?
What shape of words shall put its arms
Round us for more than pleasure?

I met a man in Cartsburn Street
Thrown out of the Cartsburn Vaults.
He shouted Willie and I crossed the street

And met him at the mouth of the Close.
And this was double-breasted Sam,
A far relation on my mother's

West-Irish side. Hello Sam how
Was it you knew me and says he
I heard your voice on The Sweet Brown Knowe.

O was I now I said and Sam said
Maggie would have liked to see you.
I'll see you again I said and said

Sam I'll not keep you and turned
Away over the shortcut across
The midnight railway sidings.

What is the language using us for?
From the prevailing weather or words
Each object hides in a metaphor.

This is the morning. I am out
On a kind of Vlaminck blue-rutted
Road. Willie Wagtail is about.

In from the West a fine smirr
Of rain drifts across the hedge.
I am only out here to walk or

Make this poem up. The hill is
A shining blue macadam top.
I lean my back to the telegraph pole

And the messages hum through my spine.
The beaded wires with their birds
Above me are contacting London.

What is the language using us for?
It uses us all and in its dark
Of dark actions selections differ.

THIRD POEM

1

What is the language using us for?
The King of Whales dearly wanted
To have a word with me about how
I had behaved trying to crash
The Great Barrier. I could not speak
Or answer him easily in the white
Crystal of Art he set me in.

Who is the King of Whales? What is
He like? Well you may ask. He is
A kind of old uncle of mine
And yours mushing across the blind
Ice-cap between us in his furs
Shouting at his delinquent dogs.
What is his purpose? I try to find

Whatever it is is wanted by going
Out of my habits which is my name
To ask him how I can do better.

Tipped from a cake of ice I slid
Into the walrus-barking water
To find. I did not find another
At the end of my cold cry.

2

What is the language using us for?
The sailing men had sailing terms
Which rigged their inner-sailing thoughts
In forecastle and at home among
The kitchen of their kind. Tarry
Old Jack is taken aback at a blow
On the lubber of his domestic sea.

Sam, I had thought of going again
But it's no life. I signed on years
Ago and it wasn't the ship for me.
O leave 'er Johnny leave 'er.
Sam, what readers do we have aboard?
Only the one, Sir. Who is that?
Only myself, Sir, from Cartsburn Street.

3

What is the language using us for?
I don't know. Have the words ever
Made anything of you, near a kind
Of truth you thought you were? Me
Neither. The words like albatrosses
Are only a doubtful touch towards
My going and you lifting your hand

To speak to illustrate an observed
Catastrophe. What is the weather
Using us for where we are ready
With all our language lines aboard?

The beginning wind slaps the canvas.
Are you ready? Are you ready?

IMAGINE A FOREST

Imagine a forest
A real forest.

You are walking in it and it sighs
Round you where you go in a deep
Ballad on the border of a time
You have seemed to walk in before.
It is nightfall and you go through
Trying to find between the twittering
Shades the early starlight edge
Of the open moor land you know.
I have set you here and it is not a dream
I put you through. Go on between
The elephant bark of those beeches
Into that lightening, almost glade.

And he has taken
My word and gone

Through his own Ettrick darkening
Upon himself and he's come across
A glinted knight lying dying
On needles under a high tree.
Ease his visor open gently
To reveal whatever white, encased
Face will ask out at you who
It is you are or if you will
Finish him off. His eyes are open.
Imagine he does not speak. Only
His beard moving against the metal
Signs that he would like to speak.

Imagine a room
Where you are home

Taking your boots off from the wood
In that deep ballad very not
A dream and the fire noisily
Kindling up and breaking its sticks.
Do not imagine I put you there
For nothing. I put you through it
There in that holt of words between
The bearded liveoaks and the beeches
For you to meet a man alone
Slipping out of whatever cause
He thought he lay there dying for.

    Hang up the ballad
    Behind the door.

You are come home but you are about
To not fight hard enough and die
In a no less desolate dark wood
Where a stranger shall never enter.

    Imagine a forest
    A real forest.

UNTIDY DREADFUL TABLE

Lying with no love on the paper
Between the typing hammers I spied
Myself with looking eyes looking
Down to cover me with words.

I won't have it. I know the night
Is late here sitting at my table,
But I am not a boy running
The hide and seeking streets.

I am getting on. My table now
Shuffles its papers out of reach
With last year's letters going yellow
From looking out of the window.

I sit here late and I hammer myself
On to the other side of the paper.
There I jump through all surprises.
The reader and I are making faces.

I am not complaining. Some of the faces
I see are interesting indeed.
Take your own, for example, a fine
Grimace of vessels over the bone.

Of course I see you backwards covered
With words backwards from the other side.
I must tackle my dreadful table
And go on the hide and seeking hill.

A NOTE TO THE DIFFICULT ONE

This morning I am ready if you are,
To hear you speaking in your new language.
I think I am beginning to have nearly
A way of writing down what it is I think
You say. You enunciate very clearly
Terrible words always just beyond me.

I stand in my vocabulary looking out
Through my window of fine water ready
To translate natural occurrences
Into something beyond any idea
Of pleasure. The wisps of April fly
With light messages to the lonely.

This morning I am ready if you are
To speak. The early quick rains
Of Spring are drenching the window-glass.
Here in my words looking out
I see your face speaking flying
In a cloud wanting to say something.

ARE YOU STILL THERE?

I love I love you tucked away
In a corner of my time looking
Out at me for me to put
My arm round you to comfort you.

I love you more than that as well
You know. You know I live now
In Madron with the black, perched beasts
On the shoulder of the gable-end.

The first day of October's bright
Shadows go over the Celtic fields
Coming to see you. I have tucked
You I hope not too far away.

LANGUAGE AH NOW YOU HAVE ME

1

Language ah now you have me. Night-time tongue,
Please speak for me between the social beasts
Which quick assail me. Here I am hiding in
The jungle of mistakes of communication.

I know about jungles. I know about unkempt places
Flying toward me when I am getting ready
To pull myself together and plot the place

To speak from. I am at the jungle face
Which is not easily yours. It is my home
Where pigmies hamstring Jumbo and the pleasure
Monkey is plucked from the tree. How pleased I am
To meet you reading and writing on damp paper
In the rain forest beside the Madron River.

2

Which is my home. The great and small breathers,
Experts of speaking, hang and slowly move
To say something or spring in the steaming air
Down to do the great white hunter for ever.

3

Do not disturb me now. I have to extract
A creature with its eggs between the words.
I have to seize it now, otherwise not only
My vanity will be appalled but my good cat
Will not look at me in the same way.

4

Is not to look. We are the ones hanging
On here and there, the dear word's edge wondering
If we are speaking clearly enough or if
The jungle's acoustics are at fault. Baboon,
My soul, is always ready to relinquish
The safe hold and leap on to nothing at all.
At least I hope so. Language now you have me
Trying to be myself but changed into
The wildebeest pursued or the leo pard
Running at stretch beside the Madron River.

5

Too much. I died. I forgot who I was and sent
My heart back with my bearers. How pleased I am
To find you here beside the Madron River
Wanting to be spoken to. It is my home
Where pigmies hamstring Jumbo and the pleasure
Monkey is plucked from the tree.

TWO POEMS ON ZENNOR HILL

1

Ancient of runes the stone-cut voice
Stands invisible on Zennor Hill.
I climbed here in a morning of mist
Up over a fox's or badger's track
And there is no sound but myself
Breaking last year's drenched bracken.

2

O foxglove on the wall
You meet me nicely today
Leaning your digitalis
Bells toward the house
Bryan Wynterless.

I stand on the high Zennor
Moor with ling and sour
Grass and the loose stone walls
Keeping the weasel's castle.
O foxglove on the wall.

TEN SHOTS OF MISTER SIMPSON

1

Ah Mister Simpson shy spectator
This morning in our November,
Don't run away with the idea
You are you spectating me.

On the contrary from this hide
Under my black cloth I see
You through the lens close enough
For comfort. Yes slightly turn

Your head more to the right and don't
Don't blink your eyes against the rain.
I have I almost have you now.
I want the line of the sea in.

Now I have you too close up.
As a face your face has disappeared.
All I see from my black tent
Is on the shelf of your lower lid
A tear like a travelling rat.

2

The camera nudges him to scream
Silently into its face.
Silently his thought recalls
Across the side of Zennor Hill.

He is here only recalling
Himself being pointed at
By somebody ago and even not
Understanding the language.

I am to do him no harm.
Mister Simpson, stand still.

Look at him standing sillily
For our sake and for the sake
Of preservation. He imagines
Still he is going to be shot.

3

He is as real as you looking
Over my November shoulder.
The sky chimes and the slewing light
Comes over Zennor Hill striking
The white of his escaped head.
His face comes dazzling through the glass
Into my eye imprisoned by Art.
His wife is gone. He has a daughter
Somewhere. Shall I snap him now?
No, you take him and get the number
Now that he's rolled up his sleeves.

4

Mister Simpson Blakean bright
Exile in our Sunday morning,
Stand still get ready jump in your place
Lie down get up don't speak. Number?
Fear not. It is only the high Zennor
Kestrel and I have clicked the shutter.

5

This time I want your face trying
To not remember dear other
Numbers you left, who did not follow
Follow follow you into this kind
Of last home held below the Zennor
Bracken fires and hovering eye.
Move and turn your unpronounceable

Name's head to look at where the horse
Black in its meadow noses the stone.

6

And here I am today below
The hill invisible in mist
In impossible light knocking.
My subject does not expect me.

Mister Simpson, can I with my drenched
Eyes but not with weeping come in?
Five diminishing tureens hang
Answering the fire from the kitchen wall.
There is a dog lying with cataracting
Eyes under a table. The mantel's brasses
Make a bright gloom and in the corner
A narrow Kiev light makes an ikon.

And who would have it in verse but only
Yourself too near having come in only
To look over my shoulder to see
How it is done. You are wrong. You are wrong
Being here, but necessary. Somebody
Else must try to see what I see.

Mister Simpson, turn your face
To get the gold of the fire on it.
Keep still. I have you nearly now.

So I made that. I got in also
A His Master's Voice gramophone,
A jug of Sheepsbit Scabious and
A white-rigged ship bottled sailing
And the mantel-piece in focus with even
A photograph of five young gassed
Nephews and nieces fading brown.

7

Not a cloud, the early wide morning
Has us both in, me looking
And you looking. Come and stand.
Aloft the carn behind you moves
So slowly down to anciently
Remember men looking at men
As uneasily as us. Mister Simpson,
Forgive me. The whole high moor is moving
Down to keep us safe in its gaze
As looking-at-each-other beasts
Who suddenly fly running into
The lens from fearful, opposite sides.
Not a cloud, the early wide morning
Has us both in looking out.

8

Mister Simpson, kneedeep in the drowned
Thistles of not your own country,
What is your category? What number
Did you curl into alone to sleep
The cold away in Hut K
Fifty-five nearest God the Chimney?
Now I have you sighted far
Out of the blackthorn and the wired
Perimeter into this particular
No less imprisoned place. You shall
Emerge here within different
Encirclements in a different time
Where I can ask you to lean easily
Against the young ash at your door
And with your hand touch your face
And look through into my face and into
The gentle reader's deadly face.

9

Today below this buzzard hill
Of real weather manufactured
By me the wisps slide slowly
Over the cottage you stand courageously
Outside of with a spade in your hand.
Pretend the mist has come across
Straight from your own childhood gathering
Berries on a picnic. The mist
Is only yours, I see by your face.
I am charging you nothing, Mister
Simpson. Stand and look easily
Beyond me as you always do.
I have you now and you didn't even
Feel anything but I have killed you.

10

Ah Mister Simpson shy spectator
This morning in our November,
I focus us across the curving
World's edge to put us down
For each other into the ordinary
Weather to be seen together still.
Language, put us down for the last
Time under real Zennor Hill
Before it moves into cloud.

Ah Mister Simpson, Ah Reader, Ah
Myself, our pictures are being taken.
We stand still. Zennor Hill,
Language and light begin to go
To leave us looking at each other.

THE NIGHT CITY

Unmet at Euston in a dream
Of London under Turner's steam
Misting the iron gantries, I
Found myself running away
From Scotland into the golden city.

I ran down Gray's Inn Road and ran
Till I was under a black bridge.
This was me at nineteen
Late at night arriving between
The buildings of the City of London.

And then I (O I have fallen down)
Fell in my dream beside the Bank
Of England's wall to bed, me
With my money belt of Northern ice.
I found Eliot and he said yes

And sprang into a Holmes cab.
Boswell passed me in the fog
Going to visit Whistler who
Was with John Donne who had just seen
Paul Potts shouting on Soho Green.

Midnight. I hear the moon
Light chiming on St Paul's.

The City is empty. Night
Watchmen are drinking their tea.

The Fire had burnt out.
The Plague's pits had closed
And gone into literature.

Between the big buildings
I sat like a flea crouched
In the stopped works of a watch.

ENTER A CLOUD

1

Gently disintegrate me
Said nothing at all.

Is there still time to say
Said I myself lying
In a bower of bramble
Into which I have fallen.

Look through my eyes up
At blue with not anything
We could have ever arranged
Slowly taking place.

Above the spires of the fox
Gloves and above the bracken
Tops with their young heads
Recognising the wind,
The armies of the empty
Blue press me further
Into Zennor Hill.

If I half-close my eyes
The spiked light leaps in
And I am here as near
Happy as I will get
In the sailing afternoon.

2

Enter a cloud. Between
The head of Zennor and
Gurnard's Head the long
Marine horizon makes
A blue wall or is it

A distant table-top
Of the far-off simple sea.

Enter a cloud. O cloud,
I see you entering from
Your west gathering yourself
Together into a white
Headlong. And now you move
And stream out of the Gurnard,
The west corner of my eye.

Enter a cloud. The cloud's
Changing shape is crossing
Slowly only an inch
Above the line of the sea.
Now nearly equidistant
Between Zennor and Gurnard's
Head, an elongated
White anvil is sailing
Not wanting to be a symbol.

3

Said nothing at all.

And proceeds with no idea
Of destination along
The sea bearing changing
Messages. Jean in London,
Lifting a cup, looking
Abstractedly out through
Her Hampstead glass will never
Be caught by your new shape
Above the chimneys. Jean,
Jean, do you not see
This cloud has been thought of
And written on Zennor Hill.

The cloud is going beyond
What I can see or make.
Over up-country maybe
Albert Strick stops and waves
Caught in the middle of teeling
Broccoli for the winter.
The cloud is not there yet.

From Gurnard's Head to Zennor
Head the level line
Crosses my eyes lying
On buzzing Zennor Hill.

The cloud is only a wisp
And gone behind the Head.
It is funny I got the sea's
Horizontal slightly surrealist.
Now when I raise myself
Out of the bracken I see
The long empty blue
Between the fishing Gurnard
And Zennor. It was a cloud
The language at my time's
Disposal made use of.

5

Thank you. And for your applause.
It has been a pleasure. I
Have never enjoyed speaking more.
May I also thank the real ones
Who have made this possible.
First, the cloud itself. And now
Gurnard's Head and Zennor
Head. Also recognise
How I have been helped

By Jean and Madron's Albert
Strick (He is a real man.)
And good words like brambles,
Bower, spiked, fox, anvil, teeling.

The bees you heard are from
A hive owned by my friend
Garfield down there below
In the house by Zennor Church.

The good blue sun is pressing
Me into Zennor Hill.

Gently disintegrate me
Said nothing at all.

GREENOCK AT NIGHT I FIND YOU

1

As for you loud Greenock long ropeworking
Hide and seeking rivetting town of my child
Hood, I know we think of us often mostly
At night. Have you ever desired me back
Into the set-in bed at the top of the land
In One Hope Street? I am myself lying
Half-asleep hearing the rivetting yards
And smelling the bone-works with no home
Work done for Cartsburn School in the morning.

At night. And here I am descending and
The welding lights in the shipyards flower blue
Under my hopeless eyelids as I lie
Sleeping conditioned to hide from happy.

So what did I do? I walked from Hope Street
Down Lyndoch Street between the night's words
To Cartsburn Street and got to the Cartsburn Vaults
With half an hour to go. See, I am back.

3

See, I am back. My father turned and I saw
He had the stick he cut in Sheelhill Glen.
Brigit was there and Hugh and double-breasted
Sam and Malcolm Mooney and Alastair Graham.
They all were there in the Cartsburn Vaults shining
To meet me but I was only remembered.

LOCH THOM

1

Just for the sake of recovering
I walked backward from fifty-six
Quick years of age wanting to see,
And managed not to trip or stumble
To find Loch Thom and turned round
To see the stretch of my childhood
Before me. Here is the loch. The same
Long-beaked cry curls across
The heather-edges of the water held
Between the hills a boyhood's walk
Up from Greenock. It is the morning.

And I am here with my mammy's
Bramble jam scones in my pocket.
The Firth is miles and I have come
Back to find Loch Thom maybe
In this light does not recognise me.

This is a lonely freshwater loch.
No farms on the edge. Only
Heather grouse-moor stretching
Down to Greenock and One Hope
Street or stretching away across
Into the blue moors of Ayrshire.

2

And almost I am back again
Wading the heather down to the edge
To sit. The minnows go by in shoals
Like iron-filings in the shallows.

My mother is dead. My father is dead
And all the trout I used to know
Leaping from their sad rings are dead.

3

I drop my crumbs into the shallow
Weed for the minnows and pinheads.
You see that I will have to rise
And turn round and get back where
My running age will slow for a moment
To let me on. It is a colder
Stretch of water than I remember.

The curlew's cry travelling still
Kills me fairly. In front of me
The grouse flurry and settle. GOBACK
GOBACK GOBACK FAREWELL LOCH THOM.

TO ALEXANDER GRAHAM

Lying asleep walking
Last night I met my father
Who seemed pleased to see me.
He wanted to speak. I saw
His mouth saying something
But the dream had no sound.

We were surrounded by
Laid-up paddle steamers
In The Old Quay in Greenock.
I smelt the tar and the ropes.

It seemed that I was standing
Beside the big iron cannon
The tugs used to tie up to
When I was a boy. I turned
To see Dad standing just
Across the causeway under
That one lamp they keep on.

He recognised me immediately.
I could see that. He was
The handsome, same age
With his good brows as when
He would take me on Sundays
Saying we'll go for a walk.

Dad, what am I doing here?
What is it I am doing now?
Are you proud of me?
Going away, I knew
You wanted to tell me something.

You stopped and almost turned back
To say something. My father,

I try to be the best
In you you give me always.

Lying asleep turning
Round in the quay-lit dark
It was my father standing
As real as life. I smelt
The quay's tar and the ropes.

I think he wanted to speak.
But the dream had no sound.
I think I must have loved him.

SGURR NA GILLEAN MACLEOD

For the Makar & Childer

Dear Makar Norman, here's a letter
Riming nearly to the Scots bone.
I rime it for it helps the thought
To sail across and makes the thought
          Into your Leod heid fly.
I thought I saw your words going
          Over the sea to Skye.

Here I speak from the first of light
On Loch Coruisk's crying shore.
Each bare foot prints the oystercatching
Sand and the ebb is cold streaming
          Itself and creatures by
Between my whole ten toes singing
          Over the sea to Skye.

Norman, you could probably make
This poem better than I can.
Except you are not here. Roll up
Your trews and let the old loch lap
          Your shanks of Poetry.

The bladder-wrack is smelling us
    Over the sea to Skye.

Maybe it doesn't matter what
The poem is doing on its own.
But yet I am a man who rows
This light skiff of words across
    Silence's far cry.
Don't be misled by rime. I row you
    Over the sea to Skye.

Norman, Skye, Norman I shout
Across the early morning loch.
Can you hear me from where I am?
Out on the shining Gaelic calm
    I hear your three names fly.
Look. It is the birds of Macleod
    Over the sea to Skye.

I row. I dip my waterbright blades
Into the loch and into silence
And pull and feather my oars and bright
Beads of the used water of light
    Drip off astern to die
And mix with the little whirling pools
    Over the sea to Skye.

And I am rowing the three of you
Far out now. Norman and Skye
And Norman keep the good skiff trim.
Don't look back where we are going from.
    Sailing these words we fly
Out into the ghost-waved open sea
    Over the sea to Skye.

PRIVATE POEM TO NORMAN MACLEOD

Norman, the same wind
Of gannets and the malt
Whisky is blowing over
To how you are there
In North Carolina.

I hope it brings you a wisp
Of me sitting here
At my writing table.
Do you think we could get on
After that long time
In New York years and years
Ago when Vivienne was alive?

I see you now through
The early Madron morning
With rooks speaking Cornish
And getting into a high
Discussion above Strick's
Trees. My dear Norman,
I don't think we will ever
See each other again
Except through the spaces
We make occur between
The words to each other.

Now your trip is over
And you are back at home.
Of course, here I am
Thinking I want to say
Something into the ghost
Of the presence you have left
Me with between the granite
Of my ego house.

Your visit was a great
Occasion. It is with me now.
I'll always remember you.

2

Early wading on the long
Strand with oyster-catchers
Going peep-peep I looked
Up at the Gaelic Ross
To see a gigantic American
Out of all proportion
Standing against the west
Of Skye making his memoirs
After making his poetry
And genius editing. I
Waded through the Atlantic
Kelp washed up by the west.

And here I stand and I
Would dearly like to have spoken
To Norman Macleod but the gales
That blow in the memory
Change everything round.
I speak from myself now.

3

Macleod. Macleod. The white
Pony of your Zodiac
Trots down here often.
I look at him. He is only
A thought out of a book
You younger made. He's far
Trotted out of his home.
That distance from your boyhood
He nuzzles. Good boy. Good boy.

And after you went back
I thought I could have behaved
Better or was it you.
But it doesn't work like that.

4

Communication is always
On the edge of ridiculous.
Nothing on that, my Beauty.
I walked up Fouste Canyon
With a pack of beans and malt
Whisky and climbed and shouted
Norman   Norman   Norman
Till all the echoes had gone.

In the words there is always
A great greedy space
Ready to engulf the traveller.

Norman, you were not there.

5

Remember the title. A PRIVATE
POEM TO NORMAN MACLEOD.
But this, my boy, is the poem
You paid me five pounds for.
The idea of me making
Those words fly together
In seemingly a private
Letter is just me choosing
An attitude to make a poem.

6

Pembroke gentle and un
Gentle readers, this poem

Is private with me speaking
To Norman Macleod, as private
As any poem is private
With spaces between the words.
The spaces in the poem are yours.
They are the place where you
Can enter as yourself alone
And think anything in.
Macleod. Macleod, say
Hello before we both
Go down the manhole.

JOHANN JOACHIM QUANTZ'S FIVE LESSONS

THE FIRST LESSON

So that each person may quickly find that
Which particularly concerns him, certain metaphors
Convenient to us within the compass of this
Lesson are to be allowed. It is best I sit
Here where I am to speak on the other side
Of language. You, of course, in your own time
And incident (I speak in the small hours.)
Will listen from your side. I am very pleased
We have sought us out. No doubt you have read
My Flute Book. Come. The Guild clock's iron men
Are striking out their few deserted hours
And here from my high window Brueghel's winter
Locks the canal below. I blow my fingers.

THE SECOND LESSON

Good morning, Karl. Sit down. I have been thinking
About your progress and my progress as one
Who teaches you, a young man with talent
And the rarer gift of application. I think

You must now be becoming a musician
Of a certain calibre. It is right maybe
That in our lessons now I should expect
Slight and very polite impatiences
To show in you. Karl, I think it is true,
You are now nearly able to play the flute.

Now we must try higher, aware of the terrible
Shapes of silence sitting outside your ear
Anxious to define you and really love you.
Remember silence is curious about its opposite
Element which you shall learn to represent.

Enough of that. Now stand in the correct position
So that the wood of the floor will come up through you.
Stand, but not too stiff. Keep your elbows down.
Now take a simple breath and make me a shape
Of clear unchained started and finished tones.
Karl, as well as you are able, stop
Your fingers into the breathing apertures
And speak and make the cylinder delight us.

THE THIRD LESSON

Karl, you are late. The traverse flute is not
A study to take lightly. I am cold waiting.
Put one piece of coal in the stove. This lesson
Shall not be prolonged. Right. Stand in your place.

Ready? Blow me a little ladder of sound
From a good stance so that you feel the heavy
Press of the floor coming up through you and
Keeping your pitch and tone in character.

Now that is something, Karl. You are getting on.
Unswell your head. One more piece of coal.
Go on now but remember it must be always
Easy and flowing. Light and shadow must

Be varied but be varied in your mind
Before you hear the eventual return sound.

Play me the dance you made for the barge-master.
Stop stop Karl. Play it as you first thought
Of it in the hot boat-kitchen. That is a pleasure
For me. I can see I am making you good.
Keep the stove red. Hand me the matches. Now
We can see better. Give me a shot at the pipe.
Karl, I can still put on a good flute-mouth
And show you in this high cold room something
You will be famous to have said you heard.

THE FOURTH LESSON

You are early this morning. What we have to do
Today is think of you as a little creator
After the big creator. And it can be argued
You are as necessary, even a composer
Composing in the flesh an attitude
To slay the ears of the gentry. Karl,
I know you find great joy in the great
Composers. But now you can put your lips to
The messages and blow them into sound
And enter and be there as well. You must
Be faithful to who you are speaking from
And yet it is all right. You will be there.

Take your coat off. Sit down. A glass of Bols
Will help us both. I think you are good enough
To not need me anymore. I think you know
You are not only an interpreter.
What you will do is always something else
And they will hear you simultaneously with
The Art you have been given to read. Karl,

I think the Spring is really coming at last.
I see the canal boys working. I realise

I have not asked you to play the flute today.
Come and look. Are the barges not moving?
You must forgive me. I am not myself today.
Be here on Thursday. When you come, bring
Me five herrings. Watch your fingers. Spring
Is apparent but it is still chilblain weather.

THE LAST LESSON

Dear Karl, this morning is our last lesson.
I have been given the opportunity to
Live in a certain person's house and tutor
Him and his daughters on the traverse flute.
Karl, you will be all right. In those recent
Lessons my heart lifted to your playing.

I know. I see you doing well, invited
In a great chamber in front of the gentry. I
Can see them with their dresses settling in
And bored mouths beneath moustaches sizing
You up as you are, a lout from the canal
With big ears but an angel's tread on the flute.

But you will be all right. Stand in your place
Before them. Remember Johann. Begin with good
Nerve and decision. Do not intrude too much
Into the message you carry and put out.

One last thing, Karl, remember when you enter
The joy of those quick high archipelagoes,
To make to keep your finger-stops as light
As feathers but definite. What can I say more?
Do not be sentimental or in your Art.
I will miss you. Do not expect applause.

THE GOBBLED CHILD

To set the scene. It is April
Early with little streams
Of tide running out
Between the kelp and bladders
On the still loch-side.

From the big house behind us
Five-year-old Iain
Comes out to play under
The mewing of terns
And peeping oystercatchers.

His father is up and out
Driving his loud, begulled
Tractor on the high field.
Maggy hums on the green
With a clothes-peg in her teeth.

And Iain with his fair head
Cocked stands listening
To a magic, held shell
And a big beast comes out
Of the loch and gobbles him up.

To set the scene. It is April
Early with little streams
Of tide running out
Between the kelp and bladders
On the still loch-side.

THE LOST MISS CONN

To set the scene. The kirk
Helpers and two elders
Are clearing up from the fête.

Wasps are at the jam.
Miss Conn is going home.

She scorns young MacIvor
And trips into the wood.
Hazel and oak and rowan.
It is not a dark wood
Like the Black Wood of Madron.

Yellow-beak and the jay
Make a happy noise round
Where she treads. She treads
Her way budding gently
Unhappy for MacIvor.

So she was seen to enter
The wood with her young skirt
Flashing. Mr & Mrs
Conn never received her.
Hazel and oak and rowan.

To set the scene. The kirk
Helpers and two elders
Are clearing up from the fête.
Wasps are at the jam.
Miss Conn is going home.

THE MURDERED DRINKER

To set the scene. The night
Wind is rushing the moon
Across the winter road.
A mile away a farm
Blinks its oily eye.

Inside snug MacLellan's
Old Rab, the earth's salt,

Knocks one back for the road.
The pub collie lifts
Its nose as he slams the door.

Rab takes the road. The oak
Wood on his left is flying
Away into itself.
At his right hand the big
Branches of elm flail.

By Rhue Corner he stops
And leans on the buzzing pole
And undeservedly
A sick bough of the storm
Falls and murders him.

To set the scene. The night
Wind is rushing the moon
Across the winter road.
A mile away a farm
Blinks its oily eye.

HOW ARE THE CHILDREN ROBIN
For Robin Skelton

It does not matter how are you how are
The children flying leaving home so early?
The song is lost asleep the blackthorn breaks
Into its white flourish. The poet walks
At all odd times hoping the road is empty.
I mean me walking hoping the road is empty.

Not that I would ever expect to see
Them over the brow of the hill coming
In scarlet anoraks to meet their Dad.
A left, a right, my mad feet trudge the road

Between the busy times. It raineth now
Across the hedges and beneath the bough.

It does not matter let that be a lesson
To cross the fields. Keep off the road. The Black
Wood of Madron with its roof of rooks
Is lost asleep flying into the dusk.
When shall we see the children older returning
Into the treetops? And what are they bringing?

THE STEPPING STONES

I have my yellow boots on to walk
Across the shires where I hide
Away from my true people and all
I can't put easily into my life.

So you will see I am stepping on
The stones between the runnels getting
Nowhere nowhere. It is almost
Embarrassing to be alive alone.

Take my hand and pull me over from
The last stone on to the moss and
The three celandines. Now my dear
Let us go home across the shires.

LINES ON ROGER HILTON'S WATCH

Which I was given because
I loved him and we had
Terrible times together.

O tarnished ticking time
Piece with your bent hand,
You must be used to being

Looked at suddenly
In the middle of the night
When he switched the light on
Beside his bed. I hope
You told him the best time
When he lifted you up
To meet the Hilton gaze.

I lift you up from the mantel
Piece here in my house
Wearing your verdigris.
At least I keep you wound
And put my ear to you
To hear Botallack tick.

You realise your master
Has relinquished you
And gone to lie under
The ground at St Just.

Tell me the time. The time
Is Botallack o'clock.
This is the dead of night.

    He switches the light on
    To find a cigarette
    And pours himself a Teachers.
    He picks me up and holds me
    Near his lonely face
    To see my hands. He thinks
    He is not being watched.

    The images of his dream
    Are still about his face
    As he spits and tries not
    To remember where he was.

I am only a watch
And pray time hastes away.
I think I am running down.

Watch, it is time I wound
You up again. I am
Very much not your dear
Last master but we had
Terrible times together.

THE SECRET NAME

1

Whatever you've come here to get
You've come to the wrong place. It
(I mean your name.) hurries away
Before you in the trees to escape.

I am against you looking in
At what you think is me speaking.
Yet we know I am not against
You looking at me and hearing.

If I had met you earlier walking
With the poetry light better
We might we could have spoken and said
Our names to each other. Under

Neath the boughs of the last black
Bird fluttered frightened in the shade
I think you might be listening. I
Listen in this listening wood.

To tell you the truth I hear almost
Only the sounds I have made myself.
Up over the wood's roof I imagine
The long sigh of Outside goes.

I leave them there for a moment knowing
I make them act you and me.
Under the poem's branches two people
Walk and even the words are shy.

It is only an ordinary wood.
It is the wood out of my window.
Look, the words are going away
Into it now like a black hole.

Five fields away Madron Wood
Is holding words and putting them.
I can hear them there. They move
As a darkness of my family.

3

The terrible, lightest wind in the world
Blows from word to word, from ear
To ear, from name to name, from secret
Name to secret name. You maybe
Did not know you had another
Sound and sign signifying you.

THE FOUND PICTURE

1

Flame and the garden we are together
In it using our secret time up.
We are together in this picture.

It is of the Early Italian School
And not great, a landscape
Maybe illustrating a fable.

We are those two figures barely
Discernible in the pool under
The umbra of the foreground tree.

Or that is how I see it. Nothing
Will move. This is a holy picture
Under its varnish darkening.

2

The Tree of Life unwraps its leaves
And makes its fruit like lightning.
Beyond the river the olive groves.

Beyond the olives musical sounds
Are heard. It is the old, authentic
Angels weeping out of bounds.

3

Observe how the two creatures turn
Slowly toward each other each
In the bare buff and yearning in

Their wordless place. The light years
Have over-varnished them to keep
Them still in their classic secrets.

I slant the canvas. Now look in
To where under the cracking black,
A third creature hides by the spring.

The painted face is faded with light
And the couple are aware of him.
They turn their tufts out of his sight

In this picture's language not
Wanting to be discovered. He
Is not a bad man or a caught

Tom peeping out of his true time.
He is a god making a funny
Face across the world's garden.

See they are fixed they cannot move
Within the landscape of our eyes.
What shall we say out of love

Turning toward each other to hide
In somewhere the breaking garden?
What shall we say to the hiding god?

IMPLEMENTS IN THEIR PLACES

1

Somewhere our belonging particles
Believe in us. If we could only find them.

2

Who calls? Don't fool me. Is it you
Or me or us in a faulty duet
Singing out of a glade in a wood
Which we would never really enter?

3

This time the muse in the guise
Of jailbait pressed against
That cheeky part of me which thinks
It likes to have its own way.
I put her out and made her change
Her coarse disguise but later she came
Into the room looking like an old
Tinopener and went to work on the company.

4

One night after punching the sexual
Clock I sat where I usually sit
Behind my barrier of propped words.
Who's there I shouted. And the face
Whitely flattened itself against
The black night-glass like a white pig
And entered and breathed beside me
Her rank breath of poet's bones.

5

When I was a buoy it seemed
Craft of rare tonnage
Moored to me. Now
Occasionally a skiff
Is tied to me and tugs
At the end of its tether.

6

He has been given a chair in that
Timeless University.
The Chair of Professor of Silence.

7

My father's ego sleeps in my bones
And wakens suddenly to find the son
With words dressed up to kill or at
The least maim for life another
Punter met in the betting yard.

8

He cocked his snoot, settled his cock,
Said goodbye darling to his darling,

Splurged on a taxi, recited the name
Of his host and wondered who would be there
Worthy of being his true self to.
They were out. It was the wrong night.
By underground he returned home
To his reading darling saying darling
Halfway there I realised the night
Would have been nothing without you there.

9

She stepped from the bath, interestedly
Dried herself not allowing herself
To feel or expect too much. She sat
Not naked doing her face thinking
I am a darling but what will they think
When I arrive without my darling.
Moving in her perfumed aura,
Her earrings making no sound,
She greets her hostess with a cheek-kiss
And dagger. Then disentangled
She babys her eyes and sends her gaze
Widening to wander through
The sipping archipelagoes
Of frantic islands. He was there
It was their night. Groomed again
She lets herself in at four with an oiled
Key thinking my handsome darling
Is better than me, able to pull
Our house and the children round him.

10

Out into across
The morning loch burnished
Between us goes the flat
Thrown poem and lands

Takes off and skips One
2, 3, 4, 5, 6, 7, 8, 9,
And ends and sinks under.

11

Mister Montgomerie. Mister Scop.
You, follicles. You, the owl.
Two famous men famous for far
Apart images. POLEEP POLEEP
The owl calls through the olive grove.
I come to her in a set-in bed
In a Greenock tenement. I see
The little circle of brown moles
Round her nipple. Good Montgomerie.

12

I could know you if I wanted to.
You make me not want to.
Why does everybody do that?

13

Down in a business well
In a canyon in lower Manhattan
I glanced up from the shades
To see old dye-haired Phoebus
Swerving appear in his gold
Souped-up convertible.

14

The greedy rooks. The Maw
Of the incongruous deep.
The appetite of the long
Barrelled gun of the sea.
The shrew's consumption.

And me abroad ahunting
Those distant morsels
Admired by man.

15

Raped by his colour slides her delighted
Pupils fondled their life together.
It was the fifty dirty milkbottles
Standing like an army turned their love sour.

16

Failures of love make their ghosts
Which float out from every object
The lovers respectively have ever
Sighed and been alive towards.

17

Sign me my right on the pillow of cloudy night.

18

In my task's husk a whisper said
Drop it It's bad It's bad anyhow.
Because I could not gracefully
Get out of what I was doing, I made
An inner task come to fruit
Invisible to all spectators.

19

The fine edge of the wave expects.
Ireland Scotland England expects.
He She They expect. My dear
Expects. And I am ready to see

How I should not expect to ever
Enfold her. But I do expect.

20

So sleeps and does not sleep
The little language of green glow
Worms by the wall where the mint sprouts.
The tails the tales of love are calling.

21

When you were younger and me hardly
Anything but who is in me still
I had a throat of loving for you
That I can hardly bear can bear.

22

I see it has fluttered to your hand
Drowned and singed. Can you read it?
It kills me. Why do you persist
In holding my message upsidedown?

23

Ho Ho Big West Prevailer,
Your beard brushes the gable
But tonight you make me sleep.

24

It is how one two three each word
Chose itself in its position
Pretending at the same time
They were working for me. Here
They are. Should I have sacked them?

25

At times a rare metaphor's
Fortuitous agents sing
Equally in their right.

26

Nouns are the very devil. Once
When the good nicely chosen verb
Came up which was to very do,
The king noun took the huff and changed
To represent another object.
I was embarrassed but I said something
Else and kept the extravert verb.

27

Only now a wordy ghost
Of once my firmer self I go
Floating across the frozen tundra
Of the lexicon and the dictionary.

28

Commuting by arterial words
Between my home and Cool Cat
Reality, I began to seem
To miss or not want to catch
My road to one or the other. Rimbaud
Knew what to do. Or Nansen letting
His world on the wooden Fram freeze in
To what was going to carry him.

29

These words as I uttered them
Spoke back at me out of spite,

Pretended to not know me
From Adam. Sad to have to infer
Such graft and treachery in the name
Of communication. O it's become
A circus of mountebanks, promiscuous
Highfliers, tantamount to wanting
To be servant to the more interesting angels.

30

Language, constrictor of my soul,
What are you snivelling at? Behave
Better. Take care. It's only through me
You live. Take care. Don't make me mad.

31

How are we doing not very well?
Perhaps the real message gets lost.
Or is it tampered with on the way
By the collective pain of Alive?

32

Member of Topside Jack's trades,
I tie my verse in a true reef
Fast for the purpose of joining.

33

Do not think you have to say
Anything back. But you do
Say something back which I
Hear by the way I speak to you.

34

As I hear so I speak so I am so I think
You must be. O Please Please No.

35

Language, you terrible surrounder
Of everything, what is the good
Of me isolating my few words
In a certain order to send them
Out in a suicide torpedo to hit?
I ride it. I will never know.

36

I movingly to you moving
Move on stillness I pretend
Is common ground forgetting not
Our sly irreconcilabilities.

37

Dammit these words are making faces
At me again. I hope the faces
They make at you have more love.

38

There must be a way to begin to try
Even to having to make up verse
Hoping that the poem's horned head
Looks up over the sad zoo railings
To roar whine bark in the characteristic
Gesture of its unique kind.
Come, my beast, there must be a way
To employ you as the whiskered Art
Object, or great Art-Eater

Licking your tongue into the hill.
The hunter in the language wood
Down wind is only after your skin.
Your food has stretched your neck too
Visible over the municipal hedge.
If I were you (which only I am)
I would not turn my high head
Even to me as your safe keeper.

39

Why should I hang around and yet
Whatever it is I want to say
Delays me. Am I greedier than you?
I linger on to hope to hear
The whale unsounding with a deep
Message about how I have behaved.
Down under in the indigo pressures
He counts the unsteady shriek of my pulse.

40

Kind me (O never never).
I leave you this space
To use as your own.
I think you will find
That using it is more
Impossible than making it.
Here is the space now.
Write an Implement in it.
YOU ....
YOU ....
YOU ....
YOU ....
Do it with your pen.
I will return in a moment

To see what you have done.
Try. Try. No offence meant.

41

I found her listed under Flora
Smudged on a coloured, shining plate
Dogeared and dirty. As for Fauna
We all are that, pelted with anarchy.

42

Your eyes glisten with wet spar.
My lamp dims in your breath. I want
I want out of this underword
But I can't turn round to crawl back.

43

Here now at the Poetry Face
My safety lamp names the muse Mineral.

44

Brushing off my hurts I came across
A thorn of Love deeply imbedded.
My wife lent me her eye-brow tweezers
And the little bad shaft emerged.
It is on the mantel-piece now but O
The ghost of the pain gives me gyp.

45

Tonight late alone, the only
Human awake in the house I go
Out in a foray into my mind
Armed with the language as I know it
To sword-dance in the halls of Angst.

46

By night a star-distinguisher
Looking up through the signed air.
By day an extinguisher of birds
Of silence caught in my impatient
Too-small-meshed poet's net.

47

Under his kilt his master
Led him to play the fool
Over the border and burn
A lady in her tower
In a loud lorry road
In tulipless Holland Park.

48

It is only when the tenant is gone
The shell speaks of the sea.

49

Knock knock. I knock on the drowned cabin
Boy's sea-chest. Yearning Corbiere
Eases up the lid to look out
And ask how is the sea today.

50

I dive to knock on the rusted, tight
Haspt locker of David Jones.
Who looks out? A mixed company.
Kandinsky's luminous worms,
Shelley, Crane and Melville and all
The rest. Who knows? Maybe even Eliot.

51

Hello. It's a pleasure. Is that a knowledge
You wear? You are dressed up today,
Brigit of early shallows of all
My early life wading in pools.
She lifts my words as a shell to hear
The Celtic wild waves learning English.

52

These words as they are (The beasts!)
Will never realize the upper
Hand is mine. They try to come
The tin-man with me. But now (I ask.)
Where do they think what do they think
They are now? The dear upstarts.

53

The word unblemished by the tongue
Of History has still to be got.
You see, Huntly, it is the way
You put it. Said Moray's Earl,
You've spoilt a bonnier face than your ain.
That's what he said when Huntly struck
The Scots iron into his face.

54

Officer myself, I had orders
To stay put, not to advance
On the enemy whose twigs of spring
Waved on their helmets as they less
Leadered than us deployed across
The other side of the ravine of silence.

55

From ventricle to ventricle
A sign of assumed love passes
To keep the organisation going.
Sometimes too hard sometimes too soft
I hear the night and the day mares
Galloping in the tenement top
In Greenock in my child brain.

56

Terrible the indignity of one's self flying
Away from the sleight of one's true hand.
Then it becomes me writing big
On the mirror and putting a moustache on myself.

57

There is no fifty-seven.
It is not here. Only
Freshwater Loch Thom
To paddle your feet in
And the long cry of the curlew.

58

Occasionally it is always night
Then who would hesitate to turn
To hope to see another face
Which is not one's own growing
Out of the heaving world's ship-wall?
From my bunk I prop myself
To look out through the salted glass
And see the school of black killers.
Grampus homes on the Graham tongue.

59

I've had enough said twig Ninety-thousand
Whispering across the swaying world
To twig Ninety-thousand-and-Fifty. This lack
Of communication takes all the sap
Out of me so far out. It is true.
They were on their own out at the edge
Changing their little live angles.
They were as much the tree as the trunk.
They were restless because the trunk
Seemed to never speak to them.
I think they were wrong. I carved my name
On the bark and went away hearing
The rustle of their high discussion.

60

I stand still and the wood marches
Towards me and divides towards
Me not to cover me up strangled
Under its ancient live anchors.
I stand in a ride now. And at
The meeting, dusk-filled end I see
(I wish I saw.) the shy move
Of the wood's god approaching to greet me.

61

You will observe that not one
Of those tree-trunks has our initials
Carved on it or heart or arrow
We could call ours. My dear, I think
We have come in to the wrong wood.

62

In Madron Wood the big cock rook
Says CHYUCK CHYUCK if I may speak
Here on behalf of our cock members,
This year we're building early and some
Of us have muses due to lay.

63

Feeding the dead is necessary.

64

I love you paralysed by me.
I love you made to lie. If you
Love me blink your right eye once.
If you don't love me blink your left.
Why do you flutter your just before
Dying dear two eyes at once?

65

Cretan girl in black, young early
Widow from stark Malia, please have
The last portion and let your mask
Go down on the handkerchief dancing floor.
It's me that's lost. Find me and put
Me into an octopus jar and let me
Be left for the young spectacled
Archaeologist sad in a distant womb.

66

I caught young Kipling in his pelmanic
Kimsgame scribbling on his cuff.
I found he was only counting the beasts
Of empire still abroad in the jungle.

67

Coming back to earth under my own
Name whispered by the under dear,
I extracted with care my dead right arm,
An urchin of pins and needles of love.

68

The earth was never flat. Always
The mind or earth wanderers' choice
Was up or down, a lonely vertical.

69

The long loch was not long enough.
The resident heron rose and went
That long length of water trailing
Its legs in air but couldn't make it.
He decided to stay then and devote
Himself to writing verse with his long
Beak in the shallows of the long loch-side.

70

(Is where you listen from becoming
Numb by the strike of the same key?)
It is our hazard. Heraklion, listen.

71

I can discern at a pinch you
Through the lens of the ouzo glass,
Your face globing this whole Piraeus
Taverna of buzzing plucked wires.
Here we are sitting, we two
In a very deep different country
At this table in the dark.

Inevitable tourists us,
Not in Scotland sitting here
In foreign shadows, bouzouki
Turning us into two others
Across the waiting eating table.
At home in Blantyre if your mother
Looked at the map with a microscope
Her Scotch palate would be appalled
To see us happy in the dark
Fishing the legs of creature eight
Out of the hot quink ink to eat.

72

I am not here. I am not here
At two o'clock in the morning just
For fun. I am not here for something.

73

Of air he knows nor does he speak
To earth. The day is sailing round
His heavenly wings. Daisies and cups
Of butter and dragonflies stop
Their meadow life to look up wondering
How out of what ridiculous season
The wingèd one descends.

74

Somewhere our belonging particles
Believe in us. If we could only find them.

DEAR BRYAN WYNTER

1

This is only a note
To say how sorry I am
You died. You will realise
What a position it puts
Me in. I couldn't really
Have died for you if so
I were inclined. The carn
Foxglove here on the wall
Outside your first house
Leans with me standing
In the Zennor wind.

Anyhow how are things?
Are you still somewhere
With your long legs
And twitching smile under
Your blue hat walking
Across a place? Or am
I greedy to make you up
Again out of memory?
Are you there at all?
I would like to think
You were all right
And not worried about
Monica and the children
And not unhappy or bored.

2

Speaking to you and not
Knowing if you are there
Is not too difficult.
My words are used to that.

Do you want anything?
Where shall I send something?
Rice-wine, meanders, paintings
By your contemporaries?
Or shall I send a kind
Of news of no time
Leaning against the wall
Outside your old house.

The house and the whole moor
Is flying in the mist.

3

I am up. I've washed
The front of my face
And here I stand looking
Out over the top
Half of my bedroom window.
There almost as far
As I can see I see
St Buryan's church tower.
An inch to the left, behind
That dark rise of woods,
Is where you used to lurk.

4

This is only a note
To say I am aware
You are not here. I find
It difficult to go
Beside Housman's star
Lit fences without you.
And nobody will laugh
At my jokes like you.

5

Bryan, I would be obliged
If you would scout things out
For me. Although I am not
Just ready to start out.
I am trying to be better,
Which will make you smile
Under your blue hat.

I know I make a symbol
Of the foxglove on the wall.
It is because it knows you.

from COLLECTED POEMS
(1979)

TO MY WIFE AT MIDNIGHT

1

Are you to say goodnight
And turn away under
The blanket of your delight?

Are you to let me go
Alone to sleep beside you
Into the drifting snow?

Where we each reach,
Sleeping alone together,
Nobody can touch.

Is the cat's window open?
Shall I turn into your back?
And what is to happen?

What is to happen to us
And what is to happen to each
Of us asleep in our places?

2

I mean us both going
Into sleep at our ages
To sleep and get our fairing.

They have all gone home.
Night beasts are coming out.
The black wood of Madron

Is just waking up.
I hear the rain outside
To help me to go to sleep.

Nessie, dont let my soul
Skip and miss a beat
And cause me to fall.

3

Are you asleep I say
Into the back of your neck
For you not to hear me.

Are you asleep? I hear
Your heart under the pillow
Saying my dear my dear

My dear for all it's worth.
Where is the dun's moor
Which began your breath?

4

Ness, to tell you the truth
I am drifting away
Down to fish for the saithe.

Is the cat's window open?
The weather is on my shoulder
And I am drifting down

Into O can you hear me
Among your Dunsmuir Clan?
Are you coming out to play?

Did I behave badly
On the field at Culloden?
I lie sore-wounded now

By all activities, and
The terrible acts of my time
Are only a distant sound.

With responsibility
I am drifting off
Breathing regularly

Into my younger days
To play the games of Greenock
Beside the sugar-house quays.

6

Nessie Dunsmuir, I say
Wheesht wheesht to myself
To help me now to go

Under into somewhere
In the redcoat rain.
Buckle me for the war.

Are you to say goodnight
And kiss me and fasten
My drowsy armour tight?

My dear camp-follower,
Hap the blanket round me
And tuck in a flower.

Maybe from my sleep
In the stoure at Culloden
I'll see you here asleep

In your lonely place.

APPENDIX

UNCOLLECTED AND
MANUSCRIPT POEMS

UNCOLLECTED POEMS (1990)

I AM RICH

I am rich in years
Lived and unlived.

I am rich in tears
Shed and unshed.

I am rich in dreams
Dreamed and undreamed.

The heavens quiver
With laughter and sorrow
Limned in the river
Of now and tomorrow.

HYMN

White is our net but white the sea
That roars between us and the bay.
Haul to the nets. Now comes to me
His word that walked the ancient sea.
    Think us not lost, the sea that roars
    Is but His everlasting doors.

The sky is hidden and the gale
Falls on us with the stoning hail.
Haul to the nets. He hears our cry
And on the sea He walks us by.
    Think us not lost, the falling light
    Is but the shepherd of the night.

The night falls misty on the sea
And blinds the watchers on the quay.
Haul to the nets. So soft I heard
The lovingkindness of His word.
　Think us not lost, the streaming foam
　Is but the blood of Jesu's lamb.

THEN WHO WILL HIDE THE INNOCENT

Then who will hide the innocent
　And who will hide the sly
And who will take the tear out
　Of another's eye?

THE DARK INTENTION

My first intention was at least not this
That darkly gathers over the ground.
The dark discloses us in different ways.

Here in this wood can I be this disguise
Wielding a muffled light without a sound?
My first intention was at least not this.

This dark man strong in spades I have to face.
For I who hide and seek shall not be found.
The dark discloses us in different ways.

The wood is walking round me yet this place
Itself which I have made is still profound.
My first intention was at least not this.

What cracked that stick? Who made that black noise?
The dark is seeing what the blind astound.
The dark discloses us in different ways.

From dark to dark, aloneness to aloneness
I move and hope to move out of the round.
My first intention was at least not this.
The dark discloses us in different ways.

THE SOLDIER CAMPION

For Ishbel, aged 5

Campion so small and brave
Shaking in the Cornish wind
Guard the lady well whose arms
Are bright upon your shield.

When below your hill you see
The banners of an army come
Cry out with your little voice
And growl upon your little drum.

The ragged robin at your side
Shall your gallant sergeant be
And the elver in the pool
Your admiral upon the sea.

Campion red, upon your hill
Shaking in the Cornish gale,
Guard the lady for whose sake
I have written down this tale.

O WHY AM I SO BRIGHT

O why am I so bright
Flying in the night?

Why am I so fair
Flying through the air?

Will you let me in
After all I've done?

You are a good boy
On the fields of joy.

We see you as you go
Across the fields of snow.

We will not let you in.
Never. Never. Never.

IF IT IS ONLY FOR YOU I SPEAK

If it is only for you I speak
Should I stop and turn into
Something more secretly myself?

Was there something you wanted to say?
Tell me the shape however faintly
And I will make a silence for you.

Then you can say in it anything
You want to hear yourself saying
Cut off by words from other words.

I will ride the marches to keep
Your silence a very good place.
It is the only place to speak in.

FALLING INTO THE SEA

Breathing water is easy
If you put your mind to it.
The little difficulty
Of the first breath

Is soon got over. You
Will find everything right.

Keep your eyes open
As you go fighting down
But try to keep it easy
As you meet the green
Skylight rising up
Dying to let you through.

Then you will seem to want
To stand like a sea-horse
In the new suspension.
Dont be frightened. Breathe
Deeply and you will go down
Blowing your silver worlds.

Now you go down turning
Slowly over from fathom
To fathom even remembering
Unexpected small
Corners of the dream
You have been in. Now

What has happened to you?

You have arrived on the sea
Floor and a lady comes out
From the Great Kelp Wood
And gives you some scones and a cup
Of tea and asks you
If you come here often.

FOR JOHN HEATH-STUBBS

I hardly see you nowadays
Being down here on the jetty
Out of town. It is not that
I never think of you. You are
Always around here somewhere.

Of course I meet you here in public
In the pages of your Aquarius.
It is not the best place to talk in.
The pages are bugged but we must make
Do with the sword under the lake.

I have been wanting to ask you how
Your guide god, the little owl,
Is behaving, leading you across
The street of hero ghosts going
Home. Then I saw you sitting

In out of the Celtic rain
In a dark pub in Kildare.
You were speaking to a king from the pig
Market whose brazen helmet lay
Beside him. What did you say?

And who will ride with Heath-Stubbs now
Upon the pages of the world.
Sing me your out of fashion. Literature
With courage is a thousand men.
Shall I meet you with Artorius again?

Another time I saw you tacking
Across Oxford Street in a full
Gale of traffic. You were crewed
Adequately by David Wright
And sailed into The Black Horse.

I hardly see you nowadays.
You hardly see me.
Could I clasp your writing hand
On this ridiculous darkening stage.
John, we are almost of an age.

TO LEONARD CLARK

Dear Leonard what on earth
Are we each doing now?
I know we are both trying
To put down words to say
Something to somebody.

The year is numbered. The wild
Lint blows on the moor
Under the curlew's cry
And here we are, my dear
Proving we are somewhere.

All I am saying is,
Although we have never met,
I've missed you for a while.
Dear Leonard, where are we now
Crouching beneath the bough?

There is no need to answer
As we two ride the year
Hoping to have said
Something to somebody.
The sweet buds cannot wait
For nineteen-seventy-eight.

THE VISIT

How would you like to be killed or are
You in disguise the one to take
Me back? I dont want to go back
As I am now. I'm not dressed
For the sudden wind out of the West.

Also sometimes I get lost.
If I stay on for a bit and try
Upside-down to speak and cry
HELP ME, HELP ME, will anything
Happen? Will I begin to sing?

What a fine get-up you have on,
Mister, if that is your entering name.
How did you get through the window-frame
To stand beside me? I am a simple
Boy from Greenock who could kill

You easily if it was not you.
Please tell me if you come on business.
You are too early. I have to kiss
My dear and another dear and the natural
Objects as well as my writing table.

Goodnight. I will mend the window.
Thank you for giving me time
To kiss the lovely living game.
So he went away
Without having touched me.

He looked at me with courage.
His head was a black orange.

THE ALLIGATOR GIRLS
Remembering John Crowe Ransom

Are you to tell me where my soul is cast
Or in an alligator or a god.

Or would you like to bring the girls at ransom
Over to have a picnic beside the sweet
Clear water. This is the very day for it.
Bring your apricot brandy over. Tell the girls
The mill is off and to come on over
And we'll all put our toes in the sweet river.

An afternoon by the river with two sisters
Is something special. We shouted Gator Gator
And out came May and Bonnie lifting their skirts
Prancing with mock terror out of the shallows
To lovingly berate us. That was when
I worked in America as a young man.

I am told the river had alligators in it.
May and Bonnie are grown up and dead.
But we had some great fun, didnt we?

LOOK AT THE CLOUD
HIS EVENING PLAYING CARDS

Are wisps drifting in from the Atlantic West
For me to look out at when there is nothing
I can draw into myself to make myself
A boy or man of the moment. The little aces
Of cirrus are stopped in the fading afterglow.
How chosen you are to look out of my window.

Look at the aces and the kings and queens
Against the sky floating edgeways making
Horizons fairly true above the real

Horizon. O what a talk to put you into
And you with a new moustache and new breath
Out of Greenock arrived from the Firth.

Look at the boy. He is my brother new
Got up to do the high things of his life.
He doesnt have a moustache but he can see
The beating ghosts of the paddle-steamers crossing
His mind when he shuts his eyes. Kirn
Dunoon, Innellan, Rothesay. How quickly I turn

To catch you not moving. Look at the moon
Sailing across the Firth to put a tear
Into mine and my brother's eyes. Where is
Where is my brother gone, the one with no
Moustache? He is down in the engine-room
Of the ghost steamer taking him home.

I WILL LEND YOU MALCOLM

  I will lend you Malcolm
  Mooney my friend to seem
To take you out to find whatever it is
You need or think you need across the ice.
Deep in the berg there is a freezing office
    With an emerald window
    Waiting to deal with you.

  I will lend you my wooden
  Goggles with slits in
To save your eyes from the literature of the snow.
Take nothing not necessary. Mister Mooney
Will look after you wherever you wish to go.
    Take care of my dogs.
    But Malcolm will do that.

Give them a good crack
An inch above the ear
And there you are holding on and travelling
Out of this poem with the dogs yelping
With joy to go somewhere or to bring
    You further out to find
    Your home in the white wind.

JULY THIRTEENTH MADRON

Getting up this morning nearly
Sixty into a vertical
With dream-stuck eyes kills me.
Not quite, because it is a lovely
    High blue summer day.

Of course I am unkilled and light
Of a very summer July puts brilliant
Shafts into the house. Look, do I have
To step over them or bend beneath
    Drawing in my breath?

Out of each dark night I waken
Up not knowing how I will
Behave. The flying, bright faces
In the dream I came out of
    Are paling out of the love

Of the new butterflying light
Outside my window. In a moment
They will have gone beyond me
Saying for-get-me-not beyond
    Recall. I'll set my hound

Of memory after them some day
To run them down if they are needed
For Art reason or just pure

My soul alone. It is a summer
Day easy to remember.

THE DECEMBER FOX

December whether I like December
Or not, winter has struck the field
And the quick brown fox is ready
To jump as a quick brown fox should
Over the lazy poet running
Across the snow to hide in the wood.

It is the time of the bare thorn
The haw thorn and the black thorn.
Hark hark the perched tree of chirpers
Wakens me up into the white
Morning. I have been hiding busily
Asleep and taking notes of things.

Every good boy deserves favour
And I am a boy growing older
Into the new December. The quick
Red tod runs knowing who he is
Along the hedge-line spilling snow.
I must get up to be jumped over.

THE MUSICAL FARMER

Look at the rain deciding
To swivel over the land.

What nearly a river the lane
Has turned into. Remember
Music and Quartet, the old
Dears of the herd. Look at

Robina wanting to whack
Them up shouting Wara
Warwra and the cows shitting
For spite and not wanting
To get a move on up.

This letter is from the farm.
Nothing much has changed.
Except you will remember
Quintet. She ate something
And died in the Penny Field.

They will remember you,
Those young girls, Harmony,
Buttercup, Enharmonic Change,
Ballad, and good old silly
Largo. They were your pleasure
To milk and they stood for you.

If you came here now they
Would all turn round their chewing
Eyes to remember you.

And how shall we allow the time to go
Across the fields without us?

A PAGE ABOUT MY COUNTRY

1

Quhen Alexander the king wes deid,
That Scotland haid to steyr and leid,
The land sax year, and mayr perfay,
Lay desolat efter hys day.

And that is John Barbour making
'The Bruce'. Dunbar came later, A'

Enermit else as the language
Changed itself from beast to beast.

2

Where am I going to speak tonight
And in what accents? Apprentice me
To Scotland I said under the hammer
Headed crane of Harland and Wolfe
Who were very good to my father keeping
Him on. We did not need to go down
Into the Lyndoch Street soup-kitchen.
I am only telling you. It does not matter.
Dad, are we going to the Big Dam?

Curlew. The curlew cried flying
Crookedly over lonely Loch Thom.

3

Quen I came headlong out to see
The light at the top of the land
At One Hope Street spitting the hairs
Of my mother out, to tell you the truth
I didnt know what to do. The time
Was five oclock the bright nineteenth
Of November nineteen-eighteen.
The time is any time to tell
Whoever you are the truth. I still
Dont know what to do. Scotland?

4

A word meaning an area and
Here I see it flat pressed
On my Mercator writing table.

Look I am looking at my sweet
Country enough to break my heart.

5

MacDiarmid's deid under a mound
O literature making no sound.

And Mars is braw in cramasie.

THE STREET OF KNIVES

In Heraklion in Crete
There is a street of dark
Caves of shops sparking
Steel on stone and men
With mountain moustaches
Plunging red-hot blades
Of knives into water.

Let us go in. Elias,
Down from The White Mountains,
Looks up from the sparks
Of the carborundum wheel.
He is the one who settles
An edge on the tempered blade.

Three workmen in the dark,
Elias, Nikos and a boy.
Nikos is the artist.
He is the one who puts
The metal into a good
Temper. The green water
Sizzles. The sulphur steam
In the dark catches my throat
And I cough and ask the three
Vulcans to have an ouzo with me.

I found the three of them
Were from the same village
High in The White Mountains.

And that is the Street of Knives
In Heraklion in Crete.

THE FIFTH OF MAY

This morning shaving my brain to face the world
I thought of Love and Life and Death and wee
Meg Macintosh who sat in front of me
In school in Greenock blushing at her desk.
I find under the left nostril difficult,
Those partisans of stiff hairs holding out
In their tender glen beneath the rampart of
The nose and my father's long upperlip.

AN ENTERTAINMENT FOR DAVID WRIGHT
ON HIS BEING SIXTY

David, I'm not a kick
Ball player sold to Celtic
Coming to see you only
Because you are sixty.
You being sixty
Is not my concern.
But because I am asked
To say something across
The writing shires of England
To you my dear old friend,
I'm here. I'm here. I'm here.
It's me that's you that's sixty
Speaking across the falling.

I like you fine but this
Writing before people
To a man because he's sixty
Escapes me. We are all
In our own private sixties
Or any simple ages.
David, here I am
Writing into silence
On the twenty-second line
Of a shapeless poem
Of 132 lines.
So I am moving under
All the word's gamut
Of curious beasts to try
To clap your horned head.
Come, my boy, are you there?
Zebra me, I make my snort
Across the golden veldt
To the singing wildebeest.
I well remember that first
Time looking for your place
In Great Ormond Street.
It was a summer morning
And there I was standing
With behind me the high
Tower of children singing
Out of their oilèd wards.
Maybe they were singing
Or some of them were singing.
Catch me catch me cries
The flying towel in the morning.
Can you catch the noise
Twisted within the words
Making no sound to me?
Anvil and stirrup, outside
Sounds of the clink of tied

Implements and utensils
Frightened the Cornish chough.
O what a lonely place.
I hear the tap of my type
Writing machine. I hear
My iambic jaws clicking
Like a Peruvian leaf-eater.
David the falling sun
Stands on Highgate Hill
Looking out for Julian
Coming home from her job.
In the Julian Orde Summer
I remember the bicycles
Of lovers coming home
Laden with blue-bells
From the Highgate woods.
On my elbow listening
I hear your constructed
Secret music humming
Through the old boards
Of my writing table.
Malcolm Mooney would like
The great waving snow
Shining in my window.
It is not snow. It is
The white flourish of the hawthorn.
You realise I am older
By seventy-seven lines.
I am older early
Up this morning grazing
Mistress Muse's pastures.
I am not in pyjamas.
I am a zebra bred
On the Firth of Clyde.
13 6 79 There is not much.
Is there anything there?

The poem is running away
From me. Is something better
Happening to you? Come,
David, I'll take you to
A little place I know
Three days up on the Yang-tse.
Frequenters include
Arthur Waley and Ezra,
Bayonetting Roy and Tse
(What age is Eliot now?).
It's only a put-up hut
By the side of the gorge,
A place for barge people.
And Wright and Graham, children?
What did they do? Because
Mister Wright was sixty
They made their faces all yellow
And put pig-tails on
And big coats and went round
The Ching Kwan rapids
And sat down in the shop.
Children, what did they do?
They asked for Arthur and Ezra
And the white-haired asked after
A countryman called Roy.
We saw them speaking and trying
To make poetry about the river.
You bet, the two of them
Could scoff the noodles. You America?
David, I heard you speaking
To me on a page of The Listener
Trying out your threes.
Fair enough. I can see
Through the words almost
Everything and the host
Of the muse are for me like

The Water Margin heroes
And watch out, David Wright,
The heroes of the Water
Margin are at my side.
Surely you dont want
Me to get Lin Chung
To slice your head off
Like a lonely water-melon.
Good sleight to your hand.

Cheerrrio said the boy.
Cheerio said David Wright.

BEHOLDING THEE

Beholding thee I run away across
The language shouting WOW WOW I BEHOLD THEE
But thee is never there, only the few
Creatures I did not get round to falling
Out with are there. Alas they cannot sing.

Thees are few and far between in any
Country's language. Who am I after? Who
Is thee? How are we getting on today
Beholding our ridiculous disguises?
Look at the red ragworms exchanging kisses.

Guess me my kind. Help me up from the shore.
Unoil my whiskers. What am I going to do
To be slightly patted on the head
By the human elements. In some ways you
Could trim me up to look like nearly a man.

WOW WOW I BEHOLD THEE. Can you hear
My progress? This is me making my way
Across the little darling flounder sand.

Good the thin peep peep of the oyster-catcher.
But let me home to sit in my writing chair.

FROM GIGHA YOUNG

I am not being funny only a little light
In the construction. Shall I put on my blue
Old fancy reading shirt with the turned collar?
This is another morning with the tide
Of Gigha running out tickling our toes.

How do you do it? Why have you changed your name?
Why have you after all always something
To say I need on the strand or in the dark
Daylight of dreaming? You need not answer that.
The language at least helps us to gather shells.

Myself, I do not have to do anything.
I have been everywhere and that is where
I came across you. How shall I enfold

For good safely our first meeting to not
Let mock memory present us to each other
As what we are today.

LOOK AT THE CHILDREN

Look at the children of the world
Looking out at us to say hello
All from their lonely photographs.

Look at the children in their year
Which they know nothing about.
What lovely round big eyes they have.

What's to be done? What's to be done?
The hungry dogs are come to town.
Where have your father and mother gone?

Look at the children of the world
Appearing in the newspapers
Not knowing we are here at all.

The thing is they are beautiful
Because of something maybe not
A mystery all that deep.

Look at them looking out at us
Not knowing we are making an obscene
Use of them. They are all lovely

Enough for us to take home to the soul.
And who would you choose? The difficult one
With the not straight left eye looking?

Look at them. Why are they not seeing us?
The thing is they are beautiful
Not knowing us, in spite of us.

Look at the children of the world
Breaking our hearts but not enough
While we eat our money up.

ALICE WHERE ART THOU

Alice where art thou sings the girl across
The language slipped into a time in Greenock
In was it thirty-three? Hark how through at
The edges of the language in its time
Comes Christine's voice. She was my very first
Girl as a girl grown up walking beside me
After the Kirk on the Whin Hill in the summer.

These are real names. She is alive or dead
Humming whichever way we look at it
Maybe Alice where art thou. She set her mark
On me for ever, a young apprentice to Love.

If you would like to see us through the slow
Camera of the time, there we are
Not speaking hardly touching walking under
The West End sycamores of Greenock dying
Of sheer love. That was me as a boy
Not yet come into the Language which was
To pretend to discover me. I can hear
Her now singing ALICE WHERE ART THOU at
Fifteen and us standing there in the dusk
Inside weeping for love looking between
The railings of the bowling green.

PENZANCE/LONDON

From this point onward we become aware
Of valleys to the sea. Closed as they are
From passengers with intent they fly behind
Lost in their trees. I, myself, beyond
Everything fly lost for ever looking
Out of my window. Was that you I saw
Making love on the embankment among the daisies?
The speed I travel at you would not catch
Me seeing you. Nor would you be put off
What you were doing. You fly away behind
Beyond two bridges into the summer day.

1

Ness, shall we go for a walk?
I'll take you up to the Gulvas
You never really got to.

Put on your lovely yellow
Oilskin to meet the weather.

2

This bit of the road, Ness,
We know well, is different
Continually. Macadam
Has not smoothed it to death.
When the light keeks out, the road
Answers and shines up blue.
I thought we might have seen
Willie Wagtail from earlier.
Nessie, how many steps
Do we take from pole to pole
Going up this hill? I see
Your Blantyre rainy lashes.
The five wires are humming
Every good boy deserves
Favour. We have ascended
Into a mist. And this
Is where we swim the brambles
And catch the path across
The late or early moor
Between us and the Gulvas.

3

Hold on to me and step
Over the world's thorns.

We shall soon be on
The yellow and emerald moss
Of the Penwith moor.
Are you all right beside me?
What's your name and age
As though I did not know.
Are we getting older
At different speeds differently?

4

No, that's not it. The Gulvas
Cannot be seen from here.
Have we left it too late
Maybe the Gulvas is too
Far on a day like this
For us what are our ages
What are our foreign names
What are we doing here
Wet and scratched with the Gulvas
Moving away before us?

5

Let us go back. Reader,
You who have observed
Us at your price from word
To word through the rain,
Dont be put down. I'll come
Again and take you on
The great walk to the Gulvas.
Be well wrapped up against
The high moor and the brambles.

AIMED AT NOBODY
Poems from Notebooks (1993)

PROEM

It does not matter who you are,
It does not matter who I am.

This book has not been purposely
made for any reason.

It has made itself by circumstances.
It is aimed at nobody at all.

It is now left just as an object by me
to be encountered by somebody else.

THE BALLAD OF WILLIE PEDEN

I

Draw your breath on this then
And leave the dogs to bark
For you are fell upon this place
And its tenses are dark.

II

Feather your ears on silence
And watch what you're about
For you will have your say enough
Before the night is out.

III

An act we shall be other to
    Runs on as the dogs bark.
Draw your breath on mine then
    And draw the little cork.

IV

And then the dark disclosed him
    And one wisp of light.
By the light of the glowires small
    Across the ground he went.

V

Whatever time this falls upon,
    Or distantly ago,
These voices that remurmur it
    Are not voices I know.

VI

And silence has disclosed him
    Another element
And he has set that bonny back
    To travel this event.

VII

He came to the quick water then,
    Went that water along.
The wee whistle his breath made
    Was like the finch's song.

VIII

And when he came to the Whin Hill
    And set him at the brae

The whistle in his breath was loud
As you would blow a key.

IX

Draw the little cork for me
For he is pressed sorely,
And he is caught in the right side.
Can that disguise be me?

[THE CIRCUMSTANCES ARE STILL INFINITE]

1

Dear Alan, your Stockport-horned head's not here
Hung between the hart and the Wildebeest.
Zambesi heads and the head-waters of Welsh
Rivers are speaking for us both tonight.
Major Wynne-Jones in the Africa of his years
Knocks on the wall of darkness with a light.
The circumstances are still infinite.

2

Sit in a room of heads. The poems I've made
Are mad in my own lifetime hung for sport
On walls the grammarsow shall soon put down.
Put us into the yard together to talk.
The mind's a betting yard where bets are laid
On creatures we put up into the light.
The circumstances are still infinite.

3

The misty stars are sitting high tonight
In a rocking chair of hills and over Wales
My ear hovers to take a little part.

Stockport puts in its bit to what I write.
The circumstances are still infinite.

SURREALGRAPHS

1

After the rain the delivery trucks
On East 22nd went dead to silence
And slowly somersaulted into
The mauve mist with nothing to tell.
And look they soared to almost nothing
But we can see they are spilling cargoes
Down on us. Watch your heads. They
Rapidly approach down through
The mauve and they are shouting
Watch your heads down there below.
I fall down in the name of the people.
From the crashed cartons sprang
Bones and flesh and hair and became
One man tall and tenor. 'Justice
With courage is a thousand men.'

2

Maiou Maiou my little furry flower.
I hear you have been endangering vessels
Off the Mull of Kintyre. That's all I said
From lying in my bed to the flower
That grows out of the crack in the ceiling.
I went to sleep into the arms
Of the quick first dream but even
At that there I was in a saga
So much pulling at the oars that
The skin might often be seen left

Behind on the wood i.e. on the handle.
Maiou Maiou my little furry flower.

3

Where would you rather be? I do not know.
I have been put down in Crete.
I am in Heraklion standing beside
The sparking shops like square caves.
This is the street of the knife-temperers.
The street is crowded. My dreaming eyes
Are swept clean by moustaches.
No one looks at me because I am here
Only if I wear a devised beast's head.
This mask has curls of red ragworm.
The eyes are cut too wide apart.
My dead mother is sitting in a hive
Of sparks grinding blades and coughing
Sulphur and three men in the shop
Are at their treadles grinding edges
And plunging them into the green barrels.
O what fumes and my nostrils pinched.
Now the four of them are singing
Great moustached songs. Even my mother
Has a moustache. She seems happy.

[ONE GOOD SOUND]

1

One good sound is the sound of nature occurring
At the flayed edge of the idea's ear.
I think today I will fly away. I must
Not say that. I am in my own country
Enough for my own good. I want to stay.
And yet I am on the road hurrying away.

If you ever find me at large again under
The clouds flying like white postmen bearing
No folded messages, please nod your head
And grunt something which will be a sign.
Hurry and speak to me fast. I am being
Chased across the land shouting nothing.

And now the black conveyance drawn by violet
Horses draws up beside me walking to take
Me out of myself shyly wanting to go
Where within me a country has never been.
Good Morning. How do you do. Language
And I enter this eccentric carriage.

I know you cannot follow me but please
Try by example to travel even disguised
Across this part of the country even although
The season is not fashionable. O holidaymaker
On language and its environs, you are now
Entering country where only the words go.

2

I speed along the cambered rain-blue road
Being a flying translator translating
English into English. Chance particulars
Flow past my windows of fine water to fall
To travel forever back. You will observe
The love for their job my wind-screen wipers have.

Where we are going we can hardly see
From here. That hill to the right, that rusted bracken
Inclination of rogue fields and granite
Is lower Zennor Hill. The raven top
Is sailing blind above that in the mist.
We turn off here and up to the right. At least

This is not it. This is only the sound
Of nature occurring at the ear's flayed edge
Where idea begins and language starts
To want to go somewhere, to want to be
Alive in another animal in its particular
Antic. I have fallen down into a colour

Of calling out from rusted, red bracken
Across the loch to you. The morning breathes.
Do you think anybody hears? The sand pipes
Its bivalves into air. And I am read
Like plastic from a picknick on the shore
Keep in a cool place. Shake before you pour.

The point is this is not it and that
And that, those dear hastening particulars
Going past me looking in are not easily
My speaking friends of the day, they come from where
They naturally lurk to speak or not to speak.

THE EIGHTH LETTER

When the word or the word's name
Falls out before us in winter,
Beware of the cunning god
Who crunches across the tense
Fields ready to pretend
To carry this letter between us.

This is the eighth letter
Abridged, of course. The frozen
Spittled messenger lurks
And prowls, anxious to be whistled
To heel to carry the message.
He is better over a distance.

PANGUR

Pangur, my cat (look) jumps,
Foreign to me, at the invisible
Mouse. He is back in my house
Where I am kept from by trying
To speak to you. And why have I
Been put into this ridiculous
Dream because I only wanted
To speak for once thoroughly
To another? Bring in the sea again.

I am not allowed the privilege
Of having Pangur here. At least
The mouse invisible I see.
I could entice it onto my knee
And let it speak for both of us.

MYSELF THE DAY DESIRES

Myself the day desires I thought
So I woke early up and scrubbed
My parts and spirit and went out
As hero to see what I could find.

I walked across and I walked between
Black Madron's trees with my stick
Swishing the nettles of the queen
And I gave the young brambles an extra lick.

And over my desiring head
The morning sky was trailed by others.
So I was out by these words led
Between the hedges and the feathers.

If while I tell you this you want
To interrupt with your some question

Think twice. The dear I am infant
Has started out and he is gone

Is gone on the blue rainlit road
Away and away from what the words call
Anything that I never could
Have as my home at all.

[TO FIND AND FIND]

Let me say we almost see ourselves
Across the half mile of the morning
Loch. There is nobody else here.

Behind me in an eye saw down
Over the bracken from the high hazel
I am a man holding the restless
Stem of a skiff at the loch's edge.

I stand across from you with one
Foot in the loch and see across
The white speckle of your home farm
With all you do that I love in it.

Shall I come across? Can you put me off?
Why should I stand at the thirteenth line
On the loch's edge? It is a real loch
And stretches more than by Art made.

I push out across
The terrible shallows
Across to see who is it
I put my back into
The oars to come across
To see? You will know.
No one else will know,

Who I am crossing
This space to see.

I lean back on the blades and send
Two lines of whirlpools out over
The loch I go to find and find.

[KANDINSKY'S RIBBONS]

Remember it is necessary to be aware
Of every shape, of every kind of silence
That slides past the making ear. Curious
Visiting creatures, don't frighten them off. They are
Your medium from everywhere from even under
The towering pressures of the sea-trench where
The choir of urchins and the sea-stars sing
From their dark ledges and Kandinsky's ribbons
Of weed with yellow follicles lean with the moon.

[FROM THE SLEEPING HOUSE]

Look down from a height on the long
Oystercatching shore of Loch
Long at first light with the tide
Streaming out between the pools
And you will see. Don't breathe
Or frighten me waiting to meet
My dear from the sleeping house coming
Over the shingle with her bare feet.

THE DREDGE

With you present I empty out
The deep-sea dredge. Is there any
Creature which interests you? You
Must watch your feet and put this down
In your life-book and begin

A new curiosity. On this deck
A knot of seaweeds and creatures
Squirms. Kandinsky's micro worms
Are still alive under the weed
To nose out at us two who read.

From the pressures in a kind of jelly
Bag I find I find some other
Lives not unlike what I think
My own life looks like. Your life
Is the red ragworm with the mouth

Gaping shouting why have you taken
Me into a difficult place to play
At what? There was one lost sea
Star clasped on nothing under the yellow
Follicled kelp would not let go.

With you present I sort out
The eatable from the deadly rare.
You have put aside with care
As precious bait to downward wind
Into the fathoms of your kind.

[MORE SHOTS OF MISTER SIMPSON]

[1]

After the rain slewing light
Makes blue the pools between the bull
Rushes and very patient the subject
Stands in his geranium morning
Dressed in his navy-blue best
Outside his cottage in Nancledra.

He stands to be put down. He wants
Some pictures of himself to send
He says over to America.
So we are here, neither of us
For a fee. I see him looking in
At me as a minute passes. His face
Cascades across the eye of the world.
I have him.

That's it, Mister Simpson. You can relax.
But I think I took two faces.
Who was it looking from behind
The black window-glass shouting
With a white face of no sound
Out through the November me
To tell me that the camera
Or myself could not hear?

[2]

Ah Mister Simpson, Mister Me,
Standing under the flying blue
Sky-light of our November under
Zennor Hill, has anything at all
Been done? My cheap camera does not
Allow us nearer. One attempt
For the road and that is finished.

Reader, kestrel, Zennor Hill,
Nephews neices on the mantelpiece,
Unheard voice of master, Mister
Simpson I close up now and turn
Away to go home nearly home.

A DREAM OF CRETE

1

And wakened into sleep to find
Myself diving with ancient speed
Out of newspaper news into
Sincerely yours slowing into
A slow dive descending lonely
Over Malia at night with words
Trailing like bubbles above me from
My slow body falling down
Into Papakouri's grove.

Mother, Mother, I am landing
Myself in an enormous word
Ship down on the silence of Crete.

I have been here before.

Awake observe how underneath
His sleeping lids his eyes belong
To not one of his company.
Can we suppose by their movement
They are watching a place with people
Going to and fro, actual
People who stand and sit and prop
A goat stick in the corner and sit.

2

A dream of remembering between
Words in a crowded dark cave
Taverna and I can't hear any
Single person speak. I can't
See anybody I might know. I can't
Breathe in the bed O I am being
Floated out like a drowned man
Between the men between the buzzing
Instruments to a dark table.

IN CRETE

It is always strange when some other
Voice comes in on the silence we think
Is natural to us, is our home.
I heard. I hear. I long to hear
The Greek owl say his say.

The cry astonished the jug I held
And pierced the room. A cold room
Filled with the January Cretan air.

The Cretan owl has made his voice
And attitude to his own place.
Pleepo pleep. Give me a stopper
To keep the water in to wash
My cheeks imprinted by the guilt
Of not being a peasant. Give
Me, Malamanopolis, another ouzo.

You see here I am lonely in another
Land. I am lonely in another
Full stop period. We are all
Moving or circling what we go around.

To make this scene in a certain fashion
This is how it is. I am sitting
In near darkness looking out from
Myself at foreign people trying
To peer through the dream of Art into
Their polite unbelieving eyes.
It is a Taverna in Malia in Crete.
An ordinary death has taken place.
Bread has been baked for the dead.
Grandfather Paroclasis enters
In the guise of a goat hero
To find Nana his daughter
Speaking to a foreigner
Swimming in the corner chair.
The terrible thing it is all
True and through the ouzo
Glass I can feel him fixing
Me straight. Then Skrates enters and
His Coca Cola son who has been
In the states. I see you three.
You will please allow me to look
At you and your olive daughter
And her husband who has no
Olives but has a mountain moustache.

Why I am here is not the point.
I am the recording tourist hero
Swimming down to stand to walk
In Heraklion in the street of knives.
I am beckoned into the dark
Cave of treadles grinding edges.
Sparks belonging to no time
Are falling down on the floor. Fumes
Of burnt metal enclose two boys

With forced moustaches. I show how later
I tempered steel on Clydeside
And sip Retsina and keep looking
For who it is my slow dive takes
Me down towards. My tourist eyes
See the donkeys with blue beads,
See bible trees in the square,
See a young widow hidden.

[ON THE OTHER SIDE OF LANGUAGE]

Hitherto uncollected I proceed
As a shoal yet like iron filings
Made to beg to the magnet, I
Go in some almost-Victorian direction
Towards my fate, towards my fate.
O what, O what will become of us,
The heroine near to fainting cries.
I do not live in that book tonight
As the owl leaves the tree and takes
His fusilage in a few heavy
Slow flaps down to the little mouse.
The wood is quiet as I wander
Here on the other side of language.
Only a twig from the top floor
Seems to love another audibably.
Leave it. It is only the other
Wind trying to disturb
The formal barrier between
You and I, wherever you
Are listening from, opening up
Your personal package to eat a sandwich.

Here I go on the other side
Of language and the great age

Of language floors me, what an old
Barrier having to do with every-
Thing that has ever been worth
Anything, surrounds me and keeps me cosy,
Tight, or dead if you want that.

Hello. Hia. Are you there? Can you hear
Me through the deafening silence as
It waves over the high towering
Beeches? You are hearing everything
And that, Dear Sir, is your trouble.
What will you do? O do not ask
The poor man on the other side.
I am only trying to get home
And I mean that in my lifetime.
Please keep me from going quickly down
Into the manhole. It's not my style.
Give me a hoot like a red Indian
From the north-west edge of the trees.

[NATURE IS NEVER JOURNALISTIC]

Nature is never journalistic.
It does not tell us to tell how
It is faring now. We still go
All of us in our lanes and roads
Immersed in that which is not us.

In fact last Tuesday afternoon
I locked myself in my coat and closed
The door and threw myself on the mercy
Of rainy December, a new month.
One step two step three step more.

Four step five step I went falling
Into the outofdoors world

311

To give myself a shake to shake
The words I live on up a bit.
I see an old tin can in the hedge.

It is not speaking. Here I am
On Tuesday the   of December
At five o' clock walking the road
Between the whining, beaded hedges
For nothing nothing nothing nothing.

If you would like to contact me
Wait at the telephone pole whose top
Shows just over the misty brink
Of that next hill. Be sure you are
A woman with all a woman's best.

Now as the blinders whistle for dusk
And my simple sophisticated boots
Clip on the road as my metrenome
You should look out for me coming up
Soon to be seen from your side

FILL IN THIS FORM

Your name in capitals. Birth place.
Your mother. Your father. Sex. What
Illnesses have you had. Scars.
Description. Fair. Dark. Height.
Weight. Feet. Member. Moles. Hair.
Is your nose long, short, broken, none?

Do you take after your father? Do you
Take after your mother? Do you take
After a monster somehow composed by
You from an idea of them both? Which
Parent gave you the best of you?

If you have only one parent alive
Which would you choose? If they are both
Dead do you think they would like you
As you are now filling in this form
In the private room. Was your father
Ever a member of the Communist Party?
Was he ever a vegetarian or helped
To fix the acoustics of the Albert Hall?

Have you ever been in any trouble?

[I AM TOLD YOU SPEAK MY LANGUAGE]

Straighten your face. Stand still.
You will not smile or blink your eyes.
These questions I will ask, you you
Will not answer. I will answer.
You are not repeat not to speak.

I have never seen you before but
I know you because I know your kind.
Stand still. You are forbidden to speak.
Have a cigarette. Don't move.
Stop that. Stand still. No tears here.

What are you frightened for? I'm just
Another man. Attention. Stand straight.
Brothers and sisters, have you some?
Your lips wherever they come from must
Not move or quiver a fraction. Silence.

You realise you are keeping me late.
I am told you speak my language although
We are not from the same place. Stop
Making your hands to fists. Step
A pace forward and don't speak.

How did you get yourself into this
Position? Be a man, my boy,
Your mother maybe said. You realise
I am your friend maybe the best
One you will meet. Stand up straight.

ABOUT THE STUFF

O lens of language, how can I focus
My long-sea gun on the white paper
To brown and black and char and startle
It into a speaking flame? The leper
Medium should be black and rise
Into a dazzle bad for the eyes.

Who wants to set the whole hill-side
Bracken foxgloves and playing vixens
On fire? No, only it is I want
To disturb the paper, to burn a sense
Of a changed other person in
On to the white of this public skin.

I have put my ground lens in my pocket.
I did not mean to speak but just
To lie down hidden away on the hill
Above Zennor. But I think I must
Get up out of the humming hill
Side and go down for a conflagrating
Pint of the Tinners' cold ale.

[THIS LITTLE EVENING]

Clawhammered face, hammerheaded
Land-shark of this little evening
Of drinks together afterwards,

314

I don't know how your almond-faced
Wife stands you for a second. Please
Can I freshen your drink? Yes I agree
Cows miss the intellectual impact
A real work has. Take Dianne there
She's more aware of you watching
Her being aware than aware of what
Friell is saying with those spaces.

You would like to take me outside?
I won't go. But maybe Dianne
And I will get our coats and leave
And walk through the dusk of the square
Tenderly and find a taxi
To take us to a place together.

THE HONEY GAME

Lightly the light. Let's try the Honey
Game you and I are best at.
Because I know you are broken
I can put you together again.

Round the house the afternoon
City in an overcoat of light
Swivels to look. I toss the coin.
Who is it shall begin?

So the window of their time
Turned to dusk and looked in.
Dusk being not you or me
Saw only a killed swan.

I see you also as a swan
Very unslain lying there.
Lightly the light, sweet the shame,
Us playing at the honey game.

AS TOLD TO DAVIE DUNSMUIR

Later when the whole thing had blown
Over I ran into her dressed
To kill or maim at least in one
Of the Late Nights at the Town Hall.

I didn't like the one she was with.
A good dancer though. She saw
Me too, sure enough. I saw
Her face before she put her smile

On and turned to him with her hand
Possessive on his padded shoulder
Ready for the last waltz. I thought
Well this is it, I'm out. And yet

When they played The Queen and I got my coat
She must have dumped him because
Well there she was on her own. I said
Can I walk you home? And then without

A word she took my arm and well
That was that, like old times,
Her leaning in on me, her heels
Clacking along in the small hours.

WAITING FOR SNOW

Waiting for snow I look out
At a few scattered rooks blown
Against the pewter sky. Who
Is Hasse? The voice from the deep
Freeze announces a flute concerto.

Waiting for snow I look out
At a few scattered rooks blown

Against the pewter sky, Jemima,
Hold me tight, hold me tight.
Damn you, damn you, Demetrius
Why have you come at this time?

Waiting for snow I look out
At a few scattered rooks blown
Against the pewter sky. Maybe
I should have asked some friends in
To wait. To wait for what?
                               The slow
Cold November dusk grows
Out of Trevayler's waving woods.

[THE PARTICULAR OBJECT]

The particular object must not nearly lose
Its name. In my dear dying light the name
Is – ∪ –. Its hide I'll have and choose
The cured-by Art best areas on my frame.

So late at night I fall to find beside
Me on its side this object not moving.
Your name is – ∪ – beside the Clyde
From which you sprung only Clydeside speaking.

– ∪ –, you dear abstract object
Fastened below the waterline to the Old
Custom House Quay where my father, wrecked,
Took me on Sundays, I stood and stood and called

Down as a boy through the industrial, oily
Water to find you. – ∪ –, please tell
Me now when neither of us can recognise me,
How you are. From here how shall I call?

317

Many a time at night I fall to find
You still under the water over the quay's
Edge half out of sleep. Then I pretend
To say your name to put us at our ease.

Maybe it is a pity to make you so dramatic.
You are not that at all. But did you hear me
When I called down from the quay-side to ask
Your name? My – ∪ –. My – ∪ –.

[MALCOLM MOONEY'S FIGMENT]

Why I can be articulate and
Dream at the same time does not matter.
I have the licence. Greenock also
Has its deserved licence to speak
To me, its child, dreaming to meet it
Here late in the oily firth night.

Always when I stop saying hello
And lie down to sleep I know I have
A small dried up Greenock under my pillow.
Malcolm and what he stands for sips
His hurried last and as I pass
His silhouette shows through RAB NOOLAS.

What shall I do, me trying
To speak to Greenock like a person?
I know my infant, childhood, youth,
Sweet town not at all, only
I happen to be Malcolm Mooney's
Figment rocked on Malcolm's knees.

THE GREENOCK DIALOGUES

I

O Greenock, Greenock, I never will
Get back to you. But here I am,
The boy made good into a ghost
Which I will send along your streets
Tonight as the busy nightshifts
Hammer and spark their welding lights.

I pull this skiff I made myself
Across the almost midnight firth
Between Greenock and Kilkreggan.
My blades as they feather discard
The bright drops and the poor word
Which will always drown unheard.

Ah the little whirlpools go
Curling away for a moment back
Into my wake. Brigit. Cousin
Brigit Mooney, are you still there
On the Old Custom House shore?
You need not answer that, my dear.

And she is there with all the wisps
And murmers in their far disguise.
Brigit, help with the boat up
Up over the shingle to the high
Tide mark. You've hardly changed, only
A little through the word's eye.

Take my hand this new night
And we'll go up to Cartsburn Street.
My poor father frightened to go
Down the manhole might be in.
Burns' Mary sleeps fine in
Inverkip Street far from Afton.

And here's the close, Brigit. My mother
Did those stairs a thousand times.
The top-flat door, my father's name
Scrived by his own hand in brass.
We stand here scrived on the silence
Under the hissing stairhead gas.

II

I (Who shall I be?) call across
The shore-side where like iron filings
The beasts of the tide are taken through
Their slow whirls between the words.
Where are you now, dear half-cousin
Brigit with your sandprints filling
In the Western, oystercatching morning?

This is a real place as far
As I am concerned. Come down over
The high-tide bladder-wrack and step
Over the gunwale of our good skiff.
I lean back on the bright blades
To move us out on language over
The loch in the morning, iodine air.

Abstract beasts in a morning mirror
By memory teased very far
Out of their origins. Where where
Shall I take us as the little whirl
Pools leave the blade and die back?
The house is shrinking. Yeats' hazel
Wood writes in a dwindling style.

From where I pull and feather I see
You dearly pulled towards me yet
Not moving nearer as we both
Move out over the burnished loch.
Move with the boat and keep us trim.

320

If it is a love we have, then it
Is only making it now, Brigit.

III

I am not trying to hide
Anything anything anything.
My half-cousin Brigit
With me rowed over the loch
And we pulled the skiff up
Up over the bladder
Wrack of the high tide
And climbed the Soor Duik ladder.

Ben Narnain is as good
A shape as any Ben
And I liked Ben Narnain
And half-cousin Brigit.
Remember she was only half
A cousin and not het.
These words play us both
About that time yet.

All this is far too
Innocently said.
I write this down to get her
Somewhere between the words.
You yourself can contribute
Somewhere between the words
If it does you any good.
I know what I climb towards.

Is that not (Will you say?)
Is that not right, Brigit?
With your naked feet printing
The oystercatching sand?
Shall I come back to Scotland,
My ear seeking the sound

Of what your words on the long
Loch have put in my mind.

After the bracken the open
Bare scree and the water
Ouzel and looking down
At the long loch. It was
I suppose fine but nothing
Now as the wind blows
Across the edge of Narnain
And the Soor Duik burn flows.

IV

There are various ways to try to speak
And this is one. Cousin Brigit,
Sit steady. Keep us trim
And I will pull us out over
The early morning firth between
Kilkreggan and Greenock. I'll put my blades
Easily with all my sleight into
My home waters not to distort
The surface from its natural sound.

Behind your head, where I can see,
The sleeping warrior lies along
The Arran hills. Steady, Brigit,
If you would ride the clinkered skiff
And see the little whirlpools scooped
Into their quick life and go
Sailing away astern. O help
To keep me headed into the fair
And loud forest of high derricks
And welding lights blue in the sun.

Whoever you are you are; keep
Us trimmed and easy as we go
Gliding at each stroke through

The oily shipbuilding approaches.
We are here to listen. We are here
To hear the town in the disguise
My memory puts on it. Brigit
Is with me. Her I know. I put
Her in between the lines to love
And be alive in particulars.

Brigit, dear broken-song-tongued bag,
I'll not be jilted again. I see
You younger now this morning, urged
Towards me as I put my back
Into the oars and as I lean
Towards you feathering the dripping blades,
I think almost you are more mine
Than his who was before. Remember
Your name is Brigit Mooney, kin
To Malcolm in his slowly moving
Ultramarine cell of ice.

Brigit, take me with you and who
Ever it is who reads himself into
Our presence here in this doubtful
Curious gesture. Come, step over
The gunwale. I think, it seems we're here
On the dirty pebbles of my home
Town Greenock where somewhere Burns' Mary
Sleeps and John Galt's ghosts go
Still in the annals of their parish

[FROM DARK DIALOGUES]

How they spoke, the make
Shift father and mother
Here between the poor
Shift of words or

Her shy were willing ways
Towards legend turned
Into a great bull
That the sky learned.

The man I pretend
To think I am walked
Listening in the dark
Talking to who he liked.

I hope I do not write
Only for those few
Others like myself
Poets maimed for the job.

I had to choose this way
This branks, this clamp, this iron
Impediment to keep the tongue
On its toes so to speak.

[SON, OR WHO YOU ARE]

Son, or who you are, knocking
With your word at the late door
What have you come back to say?
And hush and don't let your clever
Word knock too loud. You'll wake
More than a poetry boy can chew.
With your forefinger fish the key
Up from my side of the door
And turn the old lock easily
And do not wake your mother, though
It is not likely the way time
Whispers and waves across us all.

[WHAT'S THE NEWS?]

What's the news, my bold
Retreater from the wars?
Play it on your fife
And rest your stump a bit.
You are the fork and knife
That ate the storm and strife.

Play your fife and I
Will bring you chitterlins.
He comes under the lamp
And I will make the words.
Settle your tender stump
Out of the night's damp.

Elizabeth, move the pot
Over nearer the fire.
Rob Kerr (at least a part
of him) has come back.
He's back to his own airt.
Bring that flannel shirt.

Hurry, Elizabeth, and bring
Maggie and Sheila out.
Old Maggie knows him well.
Tell Shaun and make him bring
His father's varnished fiddle.
Rob Kerr's come over the hill.

I'll pull the little cork.
And Shaun, fiddle easy.
Young Sheila, swing him gently
As the night goes, the night
Humming from the sea.
Rob Kerr's come home to stay.

THE BRIDGE

Ah yes, you've caught me sitting alone
So early up this morning crossing
My bridges before I'll ever come
To those particular bridges. Never,
In fact, will those bridges flying
Ahead of me like carrots of wrath
Be stepped out on by me. Other
Swaying spans I'll find myself on
Before I know it, a personal dream
Yang tse kiang growling under
Me as I hesitate and look over
The yellow roar to wonder if ever
That slant-eyed bosom will take me in.

[I WRITE AS I SPEAK]

I write as I speak. Peculiar
Images ask me to take them in
To stay to be used. This morning
I am easily walking over
The high moor above Zennor

Ready to be killed by anything.
I walk under the lark and who
Should I see approaching over
The sour grasses but you round
The carn across the red ground.

Hello. You are a new one.
Do you see me saying that?
So they approached, two people
With faces they believed in having,
To stand together and say something.

Zennor Hill is a hill I can
Take or leave. But this morning
Under the endearing lark
It is a bit different because
I am by Art changing its ways.

So we approached too near
To hear or see each Zennor other.
He is nodding back trying to mean
Something I might have been.

[HERE BEHIND THE ALPHABET]

Hello, then, you at the front, yes you
With the puzzled blinkers. If you like
I'll make arrangements for you to sit
Here with me on the other side
Of language for a spell. In a way
You'll see it from the inside and as
The quick stations of silence slide
Past our ears, we might, I might
Slip you a message to take back.

Sit here with me in my bugsnug home.
There outside the window go
The flying shapes of silence always
Inviting me, the crossword lonely
Fiend to fill them in. Shouting
Is useless. It only frightens off
The necessary beasts I begin
To have an affection for. Silence
Is the boundary of every cry, the medium
Which gives the cry a shape to speak.

And what do you think tonight sitting
With me beyond all possibilities

Of communication? Your friends proceeding
In daydreams down their corridors
With cigarettes or weeping may
Wonder, for a second between lifting
A cup and putting it down, where
You are at this time, at this word
You give a meaning to. You are
With me here behind the alphabet
Silence has raked and chosen us from.

[x]

Let us have no nonesense.
This is a real place.
Between the words the blizzard fires
Its arrows at my face.

Yet the language is having us on,
Is making cods of us.
That big wave took us two points off.
I'll pull the spokes for us.

In ice like flies in amber stands
Let us say, the cabin boy
Out of the Jeannette. Corbiere
Would speak so well about this boy.

He is frozen with every word
He spoke within Time's Gorgon cave.

[SEND ME A NOTE]

Send me a note. Blow me a little ladder
Of various tones and pitches against the day
And I will know how you are. Open your ear to the sly

Shapes of silence which will slide past
But, remember, they are your meat, the medium which
We have in common. Don't frighten them off.
They will allow a shape for you to speak
Within and even add to what you say
Because you chose them as you chose them. Yet
Your intention moving between that will be ready
To deviate from its nature at the last
Minute to something else. You must listen
As well as you are able when you strike
Your fingers into the breathing apertures and
Make speak the holy cylinder of sound.

THE WORD'S NAME

When the word or the word's name
Falls out before us in Winter
To look at the tense fields
Or look up at the curving
Flock or rooks like iron
Filings making the sky
Another thing. Then.

I walked out on the iron
Frost of the road with almost
My dear and the low orange
Sun tinted her cheek.
It is always the right time
For everything. Although
The climate of this literary
Place freezes my balls,
I can steer her in
Under the young birch-wood
Over the crunching ground

And begin a not
Too literary conversation.

The rooks of Madron over
Hear only the rustle
Of my almost dear
And me lying below
The brittle skyline tops
Of the red dead bracken.

Here in the word's name
I am surrounded again
By that Winter place
Where my almost dear
Looked up over my shoulder
With blindly open eyes.

The talking rooks across
The white Winter put
Their noisy flying language.
Are you there are you there are you there,
My literary, almost dear?

[IF IT IS ONLY FOR YOU I SPEAK]

If it is only for you I speak
Should I specially turn into
A something vulgar else? And now

In my writing kitchen I see
You smile by the way you listen
Across the cat. If you see me

Here among my bright objects
Of sorry and happiness
On this Sunday morning

I will give you a kiss of cold
Abstract untensils. I am
At last only a ghost wanting

The ghost of unknown lips pressing
On mine. And this is not your place.

FIVE VERSES BEGINNING WITH THE WORD LANGUAGE

1

Language ah now you have me. Night-time tongue,
Please speak for me between the social beasts
Which quick assail me. Here I am hiding in
The jungle of mistakes of communication.

I know about jungles. I know about unkempt places
Flying toward me when I am getting ready
To pull myself together and plot the place
I speak from. I am at the jungle face

Which is my home where great and small breathers,
Experts of speaking, hang and slowly move
To say something or spring in the steaming air
Down to do the great white hunter for ever.

2

Language, but not with words, cool me down
And swipe those flies away. Why I entered
The uniform and rain-forest of my fathers
I will never know. This is a place that isn't
The place for dying in. I find myself
Wanting to ask my mother to wipe the flies
Away. But I am frightened she should see
My shot-up face here on the paddy field.

Language is when the speaker kills himself
In a gesture of communication and finds
Himself even then unheard. Or language is
What people hear when they are unspoken to.
It is always the wagging of an abstract
Tongue which reaches the ear. Come down again
Into the jungle metaphor with your whiskers
Alive and ready and I will see you all right.

4

Language is my very home where pygmies
Hamstring jumbo and the young pleasure monkey
Is plucked from the tree. Do not be frightened.
You are only here to be entertained and make
Something of yourself which is not true. O,
Excuse me, do you write poetry yourself?
But I know you do. Here we are among
The great cats of stature in their literary
Camouflage and all I can do is lay
My head on the paper trying to speak and then
Shift over to have my jungle-wounded head
Easy against the flank of the yellow leopard.

5

Language, I know you don't like words very much.
And yet I have to use you and be used.
I have always tried to destroy you. I hear
You now in the humming, buzzing, ticking under
Growth. Language, we have come a long way
From Ba-Ba. Reader, would you like to enter
But you have entered already, into here
Which is not really your place. There are no tusks
In (yours or mine) jumbo's graveyard. The jungle

Of words is changing and the monsoon rains
Are drenching me and drenching my uniform
Which you don't recognise. The flies are busy
Where my eyes were. Why does the language shine
Such great heat on my face. O yours truly.

THE CONSCRIPT GOES

I

Having fallen not knowing,
By what force put down or for
What reason, the young fellow raises
His dreaming bloody head. The fox
Glove towers and the whiskered rye
He sees between just. He sees
His mother wading through the field
In a uniform of the other side.
Urine and blood speak through
The warmth of his comfortable pain.

His fingers open towards her but
He is alone, only a high
International lark sings
'Hark Hark my boy among the rye.'

II

Far at home, the home he always
Was impatient of, his mother
Is making jam in a copper pan.
His mongrel he knows well lies down
To whine and knock his tail on once
The card-table's leg. Upstairs
His young sister Jean takes
A long time to get ready

To meet her boy she isn't sure
She loves or even likes or whether
To let him do everything today.

III

It is my mother wading through
The broken rye and I can see
Her plain, entering my good eye.

The approaching mother bush shocks
His fading guilt. The pain has gone.
As his parochial head nestles
Into the springing field he quite
Accurately sees a high sky-trail
Dispersing slowly to the west.

IV

Father and Mother I am not here.
They stir me with a wooden spoon.
I fell. I seemed to fall. I thought
You wanted to speak to me and I turned
For a second away from what I was doing.
I am frightened of flies. Surely
You must maybe want to speak to me.

Do you think I have done something bad?
Who is right and who is wrong?
The stalks of rye rustle and
A terrible fly is on my cheek.
You know you know I am calling you.
I'll wink my good eye once for yes
And twice for no, although the lid
Is weighing a ton and not even
My pinky moves when I want it to.

Lark, my high bright whistler
And friend, are you still exploring
Your blue place where you see me from?
Where I am lying is any where
Near you all. Pencil and slate
Has a funny smell I can smell now
In Kelvin's School just up the road.
The girl who sat in front of me,
Her name was Janet. She liked me.

VI

Dad O Mum, I know I'm cheeky.
I will be a better boy. I'll try
Better this time. You'll see you'll see.
My new suit out of Pointers?
Is it ready safe, hanging there?
Mother I didn't like it I mean
I'll be glad to get back away.
Mum, will you put me into the kitchen
To see your bright mantel-brasses
And keep the dog from licking my neck
And keep the flies off my face.
Mother, I am not well.

SLAUGHTERHOUSE

Hung on the hooks the voices scream

Nightwatching here I go my rounds
Among those voices as they hang
And drip blood in the sweet drains.
I landed this job by stealth,
For free meat and the sake of my health.

Bang at the door or I'll not hear,
With calves at the back waiting their turn.
Whoever you are, it's worth a visit.
The watchman's clock is no great company
And I'll take you round for a small fee.

I've always wanted to live in a slaughter
House of my own and take my tea
Between my rounds with the clock in harness
Hung on the wall beside the stove.
The slaughter-house is a house of Love.

[THE PRISONER]

He opened his mouth to speak
With all the best, loved
Modulations of Man.
Out came monkeys, mews,
Whale-speech, rabies-bark,
Rebec-tunes, orgasm-cries,
Blown blades of grass between
The thumbs of boyhood, cries
Of fear blown like a key
Put up to the lips, measured
Shrills from telephones
In empty rooms, screams
Of a falling pin, gnashing
Of the teeth of a rose,
Trembling of chords stretched
Across the dark window
Of his anxious prison.

[MY LONG HOME LOCH]

My long home
Loch is still
Lying between
Hills in my mind.
In memory
Reflections slow
Ly move and change
And elongate

Into gigantic
Wisps alive
In their own right.
Loch Long lies
Held still between
Hills after
My words write
On the long water.

AS BRILLIANCE FELL

As brilliance fell I girded me with voice.

But always all words waste from inward out
And I who was fastened to that furious choice
Turned out to hear myself as a contrary shout.

As the night signed I made making my house.

Yet always all words waste and alter into
A formal ruin lesser than that voice
So clenched in prison in my mortal tree.

At final night I perished into words.

And always all words ill-devise the tongue
That at poor best must sing the beast it guards.
As his blood sang the poem-imprisoned king

Sang me more than myself and made the whole
Descended house of night my house excel.

[AND I WOULD BE A SOLDIER WITH A GUN]

And I would be a soldier with a gun
The moment that my politician smiled
And said, 'we'll marshall every mother's son
I'll show the blighters how our roof is tiled.'
And yet I would not hate the men I killed
Because my country would not tell me why
We fought and who this murdering had willed.
But I would pass all books and music by
And turn from hills and glens and leave the mist
Of mountains where the grass is red and go
Where bodies stink. Their names will grace the list
Of some dull mound of granite and they'll know
That they have bought the glory for their land,

BUT DAMN THE DRUMS OF YON RECRUITING BAND.

TO ND

No two can meet the way that we have met,
Completely, like the marriage of fused stars
That streak their meteord lights each into each
And shuddering to the life of leaping light
Start down the sky charged to a double blaze.

No two can come the ways that we have come,
Like silver moonlight creeping over stones
On stream-banks, lighting every crystal vein
To Beauty's sadness. No, they have no dreams
To break the steady darkness of their night.

FOURTH SONNET

Sometimes the whisky-balanced miner sings
On Saturday's bustop swinging in the night
Brings through his pit-hoarse voice his lea-rig heart
And lifts from slag his fierce young poet's head.
Sometimes a tear starts from the evervoid
Threading from soul to time through time to soul.
And this love-kernel tear of Burns has forked
Out from the star-soul-splintering fields of time
And found this pit-shift-guarded centre prince.
Crumble the coal bent hours. The heart is here
Breaking in trees of song between the slags
Rearing through spectrum voids in grains of time.
Sometimes the whisky-balanced miner sings
And brings through his dark voice his lea-rig heart.

LETTER X

My dear so many times
My dear, more than this is
Is nothing to the high
Silences unhailed
That surge around us all
Ways wearing us away.
It is easily said
You lie somewhere there
Elegantly under
Unrehearsed possibilities
Of language turning and
Turning with the slow

342

Drift of the stellar stoure.
Yet I turn a little
Towards where you may be
My dear, seeing the started
Poem grow bolder out
Of the corner of my eye.
And this becomes almost
A place where those two
We loved as once stand
On either side of language
To watch. And so even
That is something if nothing
More than making from
The behaviour of silence
Maybe the slow gathering
Way at night over
The unhailed water held
Still for a moment within
These words becoming
Our obstacle in common.

from A DREAM OF CRETE

1

And wakened into dream to find
Myself falling with ancient speed
Slowly through the dark dividing
At my headlong approach. The Malia
Plain of heroic ghosts floats
Its floor up to discover me.

Mother I have tripped and fallen
Out of the sleep I know into
Crete at night with some words
Trailing in worlds above me from

My making tons. Why did you let
Me out of you both to land here
Not knowing? Like a new war-friend
I land and tumble over and tuck
My notebook safe ready to kill
Reality by my literature.

Here I am trying to brush the sleep
Off my Hope Street Greenock chin
And lying looking up between
Now I know they are olive trees.

I have been here before have I
Been here before? The olive grove
Trees above me speaking down ask
Who are you how do you spell your name?

I try to introduce myself
I try to speak what I think is
My home tongue. I had hoped
Not attempting the least edge
Of that language, my dream's creatures
Would shelter me and be interested.

And that is what has happened. All
I have done now is to put on
A mask of features of imagined love
And look, see, they steer me into
Not a cave but the plucked wires
Of the taverna of Nickos Poulis.

from WITH THE DULLE GRIET IN CANADA

1

     ...and less articulate
Which I was well aware of and
Griet or Margot or Mad Margaret
Sipped her breath at eighteen
Thousand feet and so we roared
To land in Calgary, Canada.

Bruegel had given us a note
To cover every difficulty
Taking Margaret to Canada.

Going through the people at Calgary
I was slightly drunk. So was she
But she swam through with her dark glasses
Perched on her seeking Flemish
Nose and not a Calgarian soul
Speired who she was. They should have known
Her walking leaning forward as Bruegel
Made her ready to do battle
With the new world. She had taken me
On this long journey flying across
The Atlantic from devils to devils
New breaking out terrible Uneuropean
Broken eggs with new creatures avid
To punish us. How pleased we are
To meet you I said for us both
And we found ourselves in an Inn
Of no mean dimensions. She polished
Her helmet, took off her armour, powdered
Her Netherlands nose and went to sleep.

     Hush. She was not my choice
     To companion me across
     The big grey lonely waste

To say my piece here.
Yet when I see her face
Let out of Bruegel's beasts
With her staff by her side
And a wee bit whisky and ice
Still in the glass in her hand
In this room we are booked
Into in the Highlander Motel,
I think I can see her point.
I think I can go to sleep
Now tonight in Calgary
And be a poet in the morning.

2

Pieter Bruegel the Elder
Has got me here waking up
To be a poet in Calgary.
I am being taken care of.
That covers everything
Except love and, of course
Margaret. Hush. Dont look.
The warrior is sitting
Up in bed pretending
To not see me. She
Is looking at the television
And burnishing her armour.
It is all new to her,
The poor soul, the infant
From Bruegel's element.
Maggie, I am frightened
At doing my poetry tomorrow.
Do you think they will like it?
Jock (She calls me Jock.),
If they dont see your worth
I'll put them to the sword.

'There seems, in fact, no doubt
That to Bruegel's contemporaries
The central figure of his painting
Appeared no other than a virago
At large.' To tell you the truth
I didnt know where to look.

3

A human head reversed
Scurries away on an arm.
Fat toads jump from bed
To bed from me to her and
The whole room is darkening.
Outside I see the blizzard
Of arrows passing the window.
I shout Featherston Skelton
Sylvia Nessie Vivienne
George Wood Pieter. The phone
Rings like a shrill dispeller
And the room is turned into
A morning room in the Highlander's
Motel with a shy girl
Flemish cleaning her teeth
Beautiful in the bathroom.
She can do that you see.

5

Three a.m. I think maybe
I've drunk too much and Maggie
Hasnt come in. What is
She doing? I hope she isnt
Abroad in that rig-out
Breugel painted her in
Frightening the Indians
And Art students to death.

Shall I go to sleep
Without her coming in?
To tell you the truth if she came
In in one of her sweet
Disguises I would say
Maggie forget your Breugel
Birth and come in to bed.
She can, if she choses
Be Florence Nightingale
Or Puchawhanta or the Blond
Bombshell or Nessie Vivienne
Ruth Elizabeth Sylvia Margaret
Jean Sarah Star or anybody's
Dear imagined on the pillow.
But O she is not really
The right woman for me.
I am putting off the light.

6

Margaret you bitch. Youve left it late.
Put on your helmet. The plane goes
Over the Rockies in less than an hour.

I made her pack her case so fast.
Fish with hands and feet, beehives,
A hollow live owl filled with choirs
Of people looking out singing Indian
Folk-songs, a dog-fish from beyond
The Netherlands dyke, Johann Quantz's
Traverse flute, Edinburgh Castle's
Mons Meg, a barrel on legs with a human
Face, two creatures locked in spasm,
A slain knight with a stream of sausages
Coming out from under his visor, oose,
A candle, a dried cunt, an eary wig,
An address book, lipstick, a bar of chocolate,

Three coathangers, slips, panties,
False eyelashes, pessaries, herion grass
Whips dirty postcards comic-papers roller
Skates pasties vibrators beatles jelly-beans
Theorums Aristotles syndrums rebecs
Humdrums diseases anthraxes sea-urchins
Sculpters painters poets ballydancers
Lesbians homosaxons hermaphrodities
And good ordinary men of our time,
All reduced and miniaturised
By her spell to be packed in. Right
Run for the taxi to the flying machine.

11

Qwhen that the castell o forfar
And all the towris tumlit var
Doon tae the erd I straightened up
And put my face on and spolk well
To all the people. Imagine me
In a great hall waiting till the last
Coughs have settled. Suddenly I am
Presented by the silence of Canadian young
Good people. WOW WOW. O what shall I say
Across the the space to people with un-
Known values and secret pleasures buzzing
Within their faces as they sit? Ho Ho
I say in my heart thinking O I have
Come a long way from 1, Hope Street
In Greenock. To hear my own voice
    Sending out words I made myself
A while ago I listen to myself
Speaking beautifully and between
Each word the space of lonliness
Is ready to bite me. I saw in a way
Those tiers of listening faces changing

Round for a time. The words as I made
Them surely disturbed a few even
At the back. A sad thing never to know
What has happened in the centres sitting
All in their seats, rows of solitary
Different faces wanting to be fed.

14

However, surely you know her face
And style, the Dulle Griet. The bitch
Tries beside me to represent
An old surrealist Europe. She
Rushes me back to saskatoon
Where I arrive with my wide eyes
Open on my birthday. By this time
I am a bit battered by circumstances
But good in the kernal of my soul.
I go through not being frisked for
My thoughts and Margaret this time
Visible comes behind me almost
A child with her Bruegel helmet
Helmet and necessarries concealed
In a fashionable hat-box. Meg,
I know those people. Do your best
And dont let them be calling you
Sour Tongued Margot. The times
Are not our own and shake the hand
Of ...... Reader
Of this account, I am alone
In the waste with some indication
Of man which terrifies me.

16

I go to do my reading. My friend
Meets me and takes me in his car.

350

I am ready I am ready. I have drunk
Myself to almost death. I say
Silently The teeth the lips the tip
Of the tongue. The car goes on through
Always new buildings. I try
The Leith police dismisseth us but
I see I am no good. Thank God
That line does not occur. I see
We are getting there. I wish
Indians with their rights would thunder
Down on ponies and save me their pale
Faced friend and take me away. I
Refrain from biting the cyacide and
Think of my far-off dear. I have
No buttercup in my lapel and we enter
The presincts of the college. What
Would you do if you were me no need
To answer that. I would like to have
My mother and father with me seeing this
My reading on my birthday in Saskatoon.
I am here. And the reading ran like this.

Notes

Details of first publication following poem titles are, in most cases, drawn from the valuable bibliography in Lopez, *PWSG*. For abbreviations of book titles, see Bibliography, page 381.

THE SEVEN JOURNEYS (1944)
This was the first of Graham's collections to be written, but was not published till two years after *CWG*.

'The Narrator' *Life and Letters*, vol. 36, February 1943.

'The First Journey' *Life and Letters*, vol. 39, December 1943. Not included in *CP*.

'The Second Journey' *Poetry Quarterly*, vol. 5, no. 3, Autumn 1943. Not included in *CP*.

'The Third Journey' *Poetry (London)*, vol. 2, no. 7, October 1942. Not included in *CP*.
> *Scholar of seas*: compare the lines in 'The Nightfishing' about the 'poor sea-scholar'.

'The Fourth Journey' *Life and Letters*, vol. 39, December 1943. Not included in *CP*.
> *Keels of glaciers*: an image that recurs in 'Malcolm Mooney's Land'.
> *Elizabethan turtled air*: Graham seems to have regarded Elizabethan pastoral poetry as an archetype of the artifice of poetry in general (hence the name and description of Elizabeth, the 'furry ... queen/ of Malcolm Mooney's Land' in that poem). 'Turtled' alludes to the shell-like barrier separating such art from reality as well as to the 'turtles' (turtle-doves) often mentioned in Elizabethan poems. 'Air' is also a punning allusion to songs.
> *Philomel*: a woman transformed into a nightingale in a Greek myth also alluded to by Eliot in 'The Waste Land'.
> *Madrigals*: a typical Graham creative malapropism.

'The Fifth Journey' *7J*, 1944. Not included in *CP*.

'The Sixth Journey' *7J*, 1944. Not included in *CP*.

'The Seventh Journey' *7J*, 1944. Not included in *CP*.
> *Cage without grievance*: this phrase provided the title of Graham's next collection.

CAGE WITHOUT GRIEVANCE (1942)
Most of the poems in *CWG* have no title. In *CP*, the first line is used as the title, and I have followed this convention for poems that were not included in *CP*.

'Over the Apparatus of the Spring is Drawn' *CWG*, 1942.
'Of the Resonant Rumour of Sun, Impulse of Summer' First published as
'Who, with a Pen' in *Poetry (London)*, vol. 2, no. 8, November 1942.
  Love-me-not: a coinage based on forget-me-not and the she-loves-me-she-
  loves-me-not game played when, e.g., blowing the 'silken floaters' of a
  dandelion head.
'O Gentle Queen of the Afternoon' First published as 'O Gentle Queen' in
  Poetry (London), vol. 2, no. 8, November 1942.
'As If in an Instant Parapets of Plants' *CWG*, 1942.
'1st Letter' *CWG*, 1942. Not included in *CP*.
'Here next the Chair I Was when Winter Went' *CWG*, 1942.
'There was when Morning Fell' *CWG*, 1942.
'Say that in Lovers with Stones for Family' *CWG*, 1942.
'This Fond Event My Origin Knows Well' *CWG*, 1942.
'Let Me Measure My Prayer with Sleep' *CWG*, 1942.
'Endure no Conflict. Crosses are Keepsakes' *CWG*, 1942. Not included in *CP*.
'To Girls at the Turn of Night Love Goes on Knocking' *CWG*, 1942. Not
  included in *CP*.
'No, Listen, for This I Tell' *CWG*, 1942.
  We fall down darkness in a line of words: this phrase became a favourite of
  Graham's, and is repeated in several of his letters. See, for example, his letter
  to Roger Hilton of 31 October 1968 (*NFM*).
'2nd Letter' *CWG*, 1942. Not included in *CP*.
'I No More Real than Evil in My Roof' *Poetry (London)*, vol. 2, no. 8,
  November 1942.

2ND POEMS (1945)
'2ND also means "To Nessie Dunsmuir," my wife.' Graham, in a letter to Peter
  Moldon, 4 May 1979 (*NFM*).

'Explanation of a Map' *Angry Penguins Broadsheet*, c. 1944.
'Soon to be Distances' *Poetry (London)*, vol. 2, no. 7, October 1942.
'The Serving Inhabiters' *Life and Letters*, vol. 36, February 1943.
  The serving distance: a phrase Graham used later in 'The Nightfishing'. It
  seems to refer to the distance necessary to poetic communication.
'Next My Spade's Going' *Horizon*, vol. 7, no. 37, January 1943. Not included in
  CP.
'His Companions Buried Him' *Poetry Scotland*, no. 1, 1943.
  Graham described the title as 'a phrase which seemed to me to occur again
  and again in accounts of exploration and man's struggle against the
  elements'. (Annotated typescript in the University Libraries, State University
  of New York at Buffalo.)

Furry queen: The phrase, with its echo of Spenser's *The Faerie Queene*, recurs in 'Malcolm Mooney's Land'.

'The Name Like a River' *Sailing To-Morrow's Seas*, ed. by Maurice Lindsay (London: Fortune Press, 1944).

'Allow Silk Birds that See' *Life and Letters*, vol. 40, no. 79, March 1944.
 The poem is a word-acrostic – the first word of each line spells out a message.

'Many without Elegy' *2P*, 1945.

'The Bright Building' *Poetry Folios*, Autumn 1943. Not included in *CP*.

'A Letter More Likely to Myself' *2P*, 1945. Not included in *CP*.

'My Glass Word Tells of Itself' *Poetry Quarterly*, vol. 4, no. 4, Winter 1942. Not included in *CP*.

'The Dual Privilege' *2P*, 1945. Not included in *CP*.
 In whose darks/ We burn bright in: though this poem contains deliberate violations of grammar, this is presumably a simple oversight.

'Continual Sea and Air' *Life and Letters*, vol. 39, December 1943.

'Warning Not Prayer Enough' *Sailing To-Morrow's Seas*. Not included in *CP*.
 Sclims the starling lether: see Glossary. Graham quotes the children's rhyme as follows (letter to Sven Berlin, 12 March 1949, in *NFM*):
 Sclim the lether, sclim the lether. High, high, high
 Up to the top of the bonnie blue sky.
 Dr Brown's a very good man.
 He teaches children all he can.
 First to read and then to write
 Then eery airy ory.

'The Narrator' from *7J* is inserted at this point in *2P* and *CP*. It can be found here in its original position.

'The Crowd of Birds and Children' *Poetry Scotland*, no. 1, 1943.

'By Law of Exile' *Poetry Quarterly*, vol. 5, no. 3, Autumn 1943.

'The Halftelling Sight' *2P*, 1945.

'Except Nessie Dunsmuir' *Horizon*, vol. 7, no. 37, January 1943.
 The title and some phrases in the poem refer to the children's song 'Water water wallflower', also referred to in 'Letter II'.

'At Her Beck and Miracle' *2P*, 1945. Not included in *CP*.

'One is One' *2P*, 1945. Not included in *CP*.
 The title alludes to the folksong 'Green Grow the Rushes-O'.

'Remarkable Report by Some Poetic Agents' *Poetry Scotland*, no. 1, 1943.

'The Day and Night Craftsmen' *Poetry Quarterly*, vol. 7, no. 2, 1945. Not included in *CP*.

THE WHITE THRESHOLD (1949)

'Since All My Steps Taken' *Poetry Quarterly*, vol. 7, no. 4, Winter 1945.

'Listen. Put on Morning' *Quarterly Review of Literature*, vol. 3, no. 4, 1947.

Corner boys. 'Men from 17 to 100 who usually stood at the corner of our streets.' WSG in a letter to David Wright (*NFM*).

The sister Mary: An allusion to a children's skipping rhyme.

Sugar docks: 'The docks where raw sugar is unloaded for refining in the Greenock refineries.' WSG to David Wright (see above).

'Lying in Corn' *Life and Letters*, vol. 48, March 1946. Not included in *CP*.

'My Final Bread' *Jazz Forum*, no. 2, September 1946. Not included in *CP*.

Fergus-driven breaker: a reference to Yeats's poem, 'Who Goes with Fergus?'

'With All Many Men Laid Down in the Burial Heart' *Windmill*, vol. 2, no. 5, 1946. Not included in *CP*.

'The Hill of Intrusion' *Voices*, no. 126, Summer 1946.

'The Search by a Town' *Chronos*, vol. 1, no. 3, 1948.

'The Children of Greenock' *Poetry Quarterly*, vol. 10, no. 2, Summer 1948.

'The Children of Lanarkshire' *Poetry Scotland*, no. 2, 1945.

To put it springtime: Graham explains this phrase in a letter to William Montgomerie (*NFM*), as a variant of 'to put it mildly', an example of his 'conscious use of clichéforms'.

Gloworm: the eccentric spelling, which makes the noun into a portmanteau instead of a mere compound, is characteristic of Graham's occasional attempts to 'disturb the language' by tampering with the structure of words. Compare 'lamblood' in 'The White Threshold', and his splitting of words such as 'home/Ing' ('The Don Brown Route').

'The Lost Other' *New Poetry*, no. 2, 1946.

'To a Tear' *Contemporary Poetry*, vol. 7, no. 3, 1947. Not included in *CP*.

'Two Love Poems' *WT*, 1949.

Glowormed: see note to 'The Children of Lanarkshire'.

'Other Guilts as Far' *Poetry (Chicago)*, vol. 69, March 1947.

'The Birthright Twins Outrun' First published in this form in *WT*, 1949. With an additional second section, it appeared as 'The Common and Private River' in *Windmill*, vol. 2, no. 7, 1947. Not included in *CP*.

'Shian Bay' *Life and Letters*, vol. 48, March 1946.

'Gigha' *WT*, 1949.

'Men Sign the Sea' *Accent*, vol. 8, no. 3, 1949.

'Night's Fall Unlocks the Dirge of the Sea' *Windmill*, vol. 2, no. 5, 1946.

'At Whose Sheltering Shall the Day Sea' *Poetry Quarterly*, vol. 10, no. 1, 1948.

'Three Poems of Drowning' *Now*, no. 7, February 1947.

'Michael's Sea-Lamb before My Breath this Day' *WT*, 1949. Not included in *CP*.

'The Voyages of Alfred Wallis' *Life and Letters*, vol. 48, no. 103, March 1946.

Boatfilled arms: as in 'The Nightfishing', the embracing sea-walls of a man-made harbour.

His poor house: the Madron workhouse where Wallis died.

'*Over the jasper sea*': an allusion to the hymn 'Safe in the arms of Jesus' by Fanny Crosby.

'The Bright Midnight' *Poetry Quarterly*, vol. 9, no. 3, Autumn 1947.

'Definition of My House' *Poetry Scotland*, no. 3, July 1946. Not included in *CP*.

'Definition of My Brother' *Poetry Scotland*, no. 3, July 1946.
My Brother: Alastair Graham. (See People, p. 377).

'At that Bright Cry Set on the Heart's Headwaters' *WT*, 1949. Not included in *CP*.

'For the Inmost Lost' *Quarterly Review of Literature*, vol. 3, no. 4, 1947. Not included in *CP*.

'The White Threshold' First published in full in *Sewanee Review*, vol. 56, no. 4, 1948.
1. *All ways*: a deliberate splitting of the word to create additional meanings.
Seabraes: a coinage, meaning hillsides of the sea.
Lamblood: compare 'Glowormed' in 'Two Love Poems'.
Caaing thresher: thresher is the name of a species of shark, but Graham may be using the word here to refer to a whale threshing the water. A caaing whale is a pilot whale often taken by caaing or driving ashore. (Scots.)
Hundred weights: see note on 'all ways' above.
Morven maiden: 'The Maiden of Morven' is a traditional Scottish song.
3. *Arkyard*: a conflation of the Clydeside shipyards and the theme of the Flood.
Tom Bowling: character in a song by Charles Dibdin (1745–1814).
The fox: many of Aesop's fables feature a fox, whose cunning is sometimes rewarded, sometimes punished.
4. *The foggy dew*: probably, given Graham's use of 'The Smashing of the Van' in 'The Broad Close', a reference to the Irish Republican song 'Foggy Dew' by Cathal O'Doyle rather than any of the other songs that use the same phrase.
Kevin's song: perhaps another Irish Republican song, 'Kevin Barry'.

'Three Letters' *Hudson Review*, vol. 1, no; 4, Winter 1949.

'To My Father'. '*The Bonny Earl o' Moray*': Scots ballad also referred to in 'Implements in Their Places'.

THE NIGHTFISHING (1955)

'The Nightfishing' *Botteghe Oscure*, vol. 8, November 1951. In the following notes, references to Section 3 include stanza numbers.
1. *The present opens its arms*: throughout the poem, 'arms' connotes the embracing sea-walls of a man-made harbour, as in 'The Voyages of Alfred Wallis': 'waved into boatfilled arms'.
2. *My bundle*: the placenta.

3. The place names in this section have a Scottish flavour, suggesting that Graham was thinking of a voyage beginning in the Firth of Clyde, and moving out past the islands.

3.7 *The fixed and flying signs*: constellations.

3.18 *My ghostly ... articulated*: in a letter of this period, Graham used the phrase 'ghostly constant' to describe the continuity of identity in a world of flux. (Letter to Sven Berlin in the National Library of Scotland.)

3.19 *Tensile light*: a borrowing, perhaps unconscious, from Pound's 'Canto LXXIV, one of *The Pisan Cantos*, published in Britain in July 1949.

3.26 *Blackbacks*: a coinage suggesting the great blackbacked gull, here applied to waves.

3.29 *Clip*: a pun on its archaic meaning, 'to kiss'.

A mull: the word seems to be being used in several of its senses here: 'against our going' implies that the sea blocks them like a promontory; 'unfastened' implies that it is wrapped round them like a fabric; and 'curdled' suggests a brew like hot wine.

3.35 *Tenting*: seems to be a coinage, meaning 'forming a tent'.

Black Rosses ... Skeer: there are several landmarks whose names include the word Ross on the coast of Dumfries and Galloway. *Ros* is Gaelic for a promontory. *Skeer* also appears in the names of several islands. Graham remarks in a note on the poem (University of Victoria archive) that it is 'the name of a sharp-toothed rock about two miles off-shore'. In one draft (National Library of Canada), he uses the plural, 'The Skeers', suggesting that he was trying to invent a convincing fictional name rather than referring to a real place.

4. *The serving distance*: a phrase Graham had used in 'The Serving Inhabiters'. It seems to refer to the distance necessary to poetic communication.

'Letter I: Welcome then anytime' *NF*, 1955.

'Letter II: Burned in this element' First published in different form in *Merlin (Paris)*, no. 3, 1953, and in *Lines Review*, no. 3, Summer 1953.

Water ... again: a children's play-rhyme, in which the name is changed to fit one of the participants.

'Letter III: As Mooney's calls Time' *Hudson Review*, vol. 7, no. 2, Summer 1954.

Mooney's: clearly in the 'Seven Letters' the bar is referred to, though they later introduce a real Mooney as the landlord. (See People)

'Letter IV: Night winked and endeared' *NF*, 1955.

Then what ... bowers: Original.

'Letter V: Lie where you fell' *NF*, 1955.

Dumb founded: the splitting of the word is deliberate.

'Letter VI: A day the wind was hardly' *NF*, 1955.

'Letter VII: Blind tide emblazoning' *NF*, 1955.

'The Broad Close' *Botteghe Oscure*, vol. 9, 1954.

Bluenose, sperm: Wordplay combining the names of whales ('blue' and 'sperm') with 'bluenose' (see Glossary) and sperm in its literal sense.

Bad knee: Graham had injured a knee falling from a roof in 1950.

The Smashing of the Van: Irish republican song.

Wit and weapons: from *The Lay of Sigrdrifa*, part of the *Volsung Saga*: 'Both wit and weapons/ Well must the king have.'

'Baldy Bane' *Nimbus*, vol. 2, no. 3, Autumn 1954.

The title is from a children's rhyme: 'What's ma name? Baldy Bane. What's your other? Ask ma mither.' Graham in a letter to Ronnie and Henriette Duncan, 9 December 1978 (*NFM*).

Bowbender. Graham explains: 'Old wooden roof beams used to be "bowbent" – bent in the shape of a bow ... Here the immediate connotations are – I am the man who can bend the big bow – The Ulysses who can bend the woman like a bow.' (Letter to Alan Clodd, 16 November 1954 in *NFM*.)

Kate Dalrymple: a Scottish song by William Watt (1792–?).

Pas de bas: a highland dance.

Can you ... shirt: a traditional song, often used as a beginners' piano exercise.

The glint ... caught: reference to the great pilchard-shoals which once sustained an industry in Cornwall. Their silver gleam was watched for from the cliffs every year.

Causewayside: not a street in Greenock – either fictional or a reference to the one in Edinburgh.

Fingal: a hyperbolic expression for vastness. The reference is to Fingal's Cave on Staffa in the Hebrides.

MALCOLM MOONEY'S LAND (1970)

'Malcolm Mooney's Land' *Poetry (Chicago)*, vol. 108, no. 6, 1966.

Malcolm Mooney's Land: the name is a parody of Frantz Josef Land where Nansen's Arctic expedition finished up. The setting is, like Franz Josef Land, an island in the frozen Arctic ocean. The poem draws heavily on Nansen's account of his voyage in his book *Farthest North*.

1. *Cranes*: perhaps an allusion to the American poet Hart Crane (1899–1932), whose 'North Labrador' is a classic poetic treatment of the Arctic.

The boy: Mooney's son.

2. *A ruff*: a thread of Elizabethan imagery is generated by the name of Mooney's wife. Graham seems to have regarded Elizabethan poetry as typifying poetic artifice in general (compare 'The Fourth Journey' with its 'sweet Elizabethan turtled air').

My impediment: Graham frequently refers to himself as 'impedimented' or

'maimed' (see, for example, 'The Thermal Stair') by his artistic vocation.
A fox: Nansen records that his thermometer was stolen by foxes.
The telephone ... *a blue crevasse*: Graham commented in the *Poetry Book Society Bulletin* (Spring 1970): 'I am always very aware that my poem is not a telephone call. The poet only speaks one way. He hears nothing back. His words are not conditioned by a real ear replying from the other side.'
Compare the 'telephoneless, blue/ Green crevasse' of 'What is the Language Using Us for?'
Word-louse: a 'translation' of his pun on 'grammarsow'. (See Glossary.)
3. *My friend* ... *owls*: Lopez suggests this friend may be the blind poet John Heath-Stubbs (see 'For John Heath-Stubbs'). The artist Tony O'Malley is another possibility. However, Graham himself shows an obsession with owls in the Cretan poems and elsewhere.
4. *This tent of a place*: the stanzas of this section are arranged in the form of a tent.
5. *My furry queen*: a play on Spenser's *The Faerie Queene*, and hence another Elizabethan reference. The same punning allusion occurs in 'His Companions Buried Him'.
Yet not mistake ... *real thing*: Elizabeth's presence is a hallucination, like that of the third explorer in Part V of Eliot's 'The Waste Land'.
The foolish voices ... *lamps*: a reference to the parable of the Wise and Foolish Virgins (Matthew 25. 1–13.)
'The Beast in the Space' *Poetry (Chicago)*, vol. 110, no. 1, 1967.
'The Lying Dear' *MML*, 1970.
The poem is echoed in Implement 67.
'Yours Truly' *MML*, 1970.
Listen ... *Listen*: The ending of 'Letter VII'.
'Dear Who I Mean' *MML*, 1970.
Wrecked dragon ... *five high singing wires*: A kite caught in the telegraph wires. The five wires also suggest a musical stave.
'The Constructed Space' *Poetry (Chicago)*, vol. 93, no. 1, October 1958.
Graham wrote of this poem to Alan Clodd, 9 February 1955, 'It is meant to be as "abstract" as I can make it, unvisual in its images and suggesting no place or atmosphere' (*NFM*).
'Master Cat and Master Me' *Malahat Review*, no. 10, April 1969.
The epigraph translates as 'For Antony [Tony] O'Malley' (Irish Gaelic).
'The Thermal Stair' *MML*, 1970. Read by Graham in a television programme about Peter Lanyon broadcast on Westward Television in October 1968.
Lanyon's semi-abstract work was inspired by the west Cornish landscape (including its industrial heritage) especially as seen from his glider.
Thermal Stair: rising current of warm air used by glider pilots in their ascent. The phrase is the title of a painting by Lanyon, now in the Tate St Ives.

Botallack, Ding Dong, Levant: sites of disused tin mines in west Cornwall.
Jasper sea: see note to 'The Voyages of Alfred Wallis'.
Lanyon Quoit: a prehistoric dolmen near Lanyon Farm, Madron.
Little Parc Owles: house near St Ives where Lanyon lived.
Engine house: conspicuous above-ground feature of a tin mine.
Morvah: site of another west Cornish tin mine.
alfred wallis: the lack of capitalization evokes Wallis's own semiliterate writing.
SARACINESCO: a painting by Lanyon, now in the Tate St Ives. Graham habitually capitalized titles.
Godrevy and the Wolf: Godrevy and Wolf Rock are lighthouses off the Cornish coast.
The tin singers: Cornish tin-miners singing on their way to or from work.
The Queen's: Lanyon used to play dominoes at The Queen's Hotel, St Ives.
Labrador: the subject of paintings by Wallis.
'I Leave This at Your Ear' *MML*, 1970.
Naked-woman tree: A tree near the Grahams' home which had the image of a naked woman scratched into the bark.
Kyle: This Scottish feature combines with the Cornish 'naked-woman tree' to form a fictitious setting.
'The Dark Dialogues' *Botteghe Oscure*, vol. 23, Spring 1959.
1. *Europa*: Europa was seduced by Zeus in the form of a bull and carried over the sea to Crete. The bull was transformed into the constellation Taurus.
3. *Cartsburn ... Otter's/ Burn*: Cartsburn is a stream in Greenock, now underground. I have been unable to trace the Otter's Burn; Graham may be alluding to the anonymous poem 'The Battle of Otterburn'. The forest landscape of this section is largely symbolic.
'The Don Brown Route' *MML*, 1970.
'Press Button to Hold Desired Symbol' *MML*, 1970.
'Hilton Abstract' *The New Statesman and Nation*, 5 January 1957.
'Approaches to How They Behave' *MML*, 1970.
'The Fifteen Devices' *Malahat Review*, no. 10, April 1969.
The Fifteen Devices: the fifteen sections of 'Approaches to How They Behave'. Compare the terminology of other poems, '*Implements* in Their Places' and '*Clusters* Travelling Out'.
With me take you: this rearrangement of a familiar phrase is typical of the wordplay Graham was using to generate ideas in his writing exercises around this time.
Fore/ Street: the main street in Madron.
'Wynter and the Grammarsow' *MML*, 1970.
Meanders A favourite theme of Wynter's paintings.

Star ... Housman: From Poem LII of *A Shropshire Lad* ('Far in a western brookland'):

> There, by the starlit fences,
> The wanderer halts and hears
> My soul that lingers sighing
> About the glimmering weirs.

Masked thinskinned diver: Wynter was an amateur diver.

I see ... rivers: From Thomas Lovell Beddoes's play *Death's Jest Book*.

Sue: Wynter's first wife, Susan Lethbridge.

Mon: Monica Wynter, the artist's second wife.

Campion: a play on the name of a wild flower, the scarlet campion, common in Cornwall. See 'The Soldier Campion'.

Momaster: a reference to Wynter's dog, Mo.

Willie Peden: see 'The Ballad of Willie Peden'.

'Johann Joachim Quantz's First Lesson' is inserted at this point in *MML* and *CP*.

'Five Visitors to Madron' *The Listener*, 22 June 1967.

Slaughterhouse: The Madron slaughterhouse was a short distance from Graham's home. In an earlier incarnation, it had been the poorhouse in which Alfred Wallis died.

'Clusters Travelling Out' *Poetry (Chicago)*, vol. 112, no. 3, 1968.

Clusters: A term Graham used for the spontaneous prose paragraphs he was writing at this time, which helped to generate ideas for many of the later poems.

2. *Slaughterhouse*: see note to 'Five Visitors to Madron'.

IMPLEMENTS IN THEIR PLACES (1977)

'What is the Language Using Us for?' *Malahat Review*, no. 32, October 1974.

'First Poem' *Telephoneless, blue/ Green crevasse*: compare section 1 of 'Malcolm Mooney's Land'.

Messages: A pun on its Scots meaning of 'shopping'.

'Second Poem' 2. *The Sweet Brown Knowe*: 'The Maid of the Sweet Brown Knowe', an anonymous Irish song.

'Third Poem' 2. *O leave 'er Johnny leave 'er*: the refrain of a sea shanty.

'Imagine a Forest' *Malahat Review*, no. 17, January 1971.

Ettrick: the reference is to James Hogg ('The Ettrick Shepherd'), whose novel *The Private Memoirs and Confessions of a Justified Sinner* (1816) has a *doppelgänger* theme.

Liveoak: presumably Graham chose this American tree for the connotations of the name.

'Untidy Dreadful Table' *IITP*, 1977.

'A Note to the Difficult One' *Akros*, vol. 9, no. 27, April 1975.

'Are You Still There?' *The Listener*, 8 January 1976.

Black, perched beasts ... gable end: perhaps a reference to the rooks and crows perching on the cottage roof.

'Language Ah Now You Have Me' *Stand*, vol. 17, no. 1, 1976.

Leo pard: a deliberate division of the word into its etymological constituents, meaning 'lion' and 'panther'.

'Two Poems on Zennor Hill' *IITP*, 1977.

'Ten Shots of Mister Simpson' *London Magazine*, vol. 11, no. 6, 1972.

'The Night City' *The Listener*, 8 January 1976.

'Enter a Cloud' *Malahat Review*, no. 33, January 1975.

Table-top: possibly an allusion to Graham's 1946 essay 'Notes on a Poetry of Release' (reprinted in *NFM*), in which he argues that the attempt to make poetry out of human feelings rather than words is as impossible as making 'a table out of water'.

Fishing Gurnard: Gurnard's Head is so called because of its resemblance to the fish of that name. There may also be the suggestion that it extends into the sea like a rod and line.

'Greenock at Night I Find You' *IITP*, 1977.

'Loch Thom' First published, in different form, in *Malahat Review*, no. 39, July 1976.

GOBACK/ GOBACK GOBACK: a verbal representation of the clicking call of the grouse.

'To Alexander Graham' *Malahat Review*, no. 33, January 1975.

'Sgurr na Gillean Macleod' *Pembroke Magazine*, no. 5, 1974.

The MacLeods, one of whose branches is named Norman, are one of the principal clans on Skye. Macleod named his son Norman, and his daughter Skye.

Over the sea to Skye: quoted from the refrain of 'The Skye Boat Song' by Sir Harold Boulton, which commemorates the escape of Bonnie Prince Charlie to Skye after the Battle of Culloden.

'Private Poem to Norman Macleod' *Pembroke Magazine*, no. 5, 1974.

Gaelic Ross: probably the district of north-west Scotland. *Ros* is Gaelic for a promontory.

The white/ Pony of your Zodiac: an obscure reference.

Good boy: a phrase Graham regularly used to his cat, but then adapted for addressing others, even his wife. (John Haffenden, interview with Graham, *Poetry Review*, 76, no. 1–2.)

'Johann Joachim Quantz's Five Lessons'

'Johann Joachim Quantz's First Lesson' was first published in *Malahat Review*, no. 10, April 1969, and reprinted in *MML*, 1970. 'Johann Joachim Quantz's Fourth Lesson' was first published in *The Times Literary Supplement*, 11 October 1974, and revised before inclusion in *IITP*.

'The First Lesson'. *My Flute Book*: Johann Joachim Quantz, *On Playing the Flute* (1752), which is echoed by several phrases in the poem.

'The Third Lesson'. *Traverse flute*: the correct name for a flute of this period.

'The Last Lesson'. *Archipelagoes*: a deliberate variation on the word 'arpeggios', or perhaps 'appoggiaturas', which are referred to frequently in Quantz's book. See Graham's letter to Fraser Steel of 8 March 1977 (*NFM*) for the light it throws on both 'traverse' and 'archipelagoes'.

'The Gobbled Child' *Aquarius*, no. 7, 1974.

'The Lost Miss Conn' *IITP*, 1977.

'The Murdered Drinker' *Aquarius*, no. 7, 1974.

'How Are the Children Robin' *PN Review*, vol. 4, no. 2, 1977.

'The Stepping Stones' *IITP*, 1977.

'Lines on Roger Hilton's Watch' *Malahat Review*, no. 39, July 1976.

Botallack: the village where Hilton lived.

'The Secret Name' *Malahat Review*, no. 27, July 1973.

Secret Name: Robert Graves, in *The White Goddess*, a book that greatly influenced Graham, notes that 'in ancient times, once a god's name had been discovered, the enemies of his people could do destructive magic against them with it.'

Hurries away ... to escape: this passage may be a reminiscence of the wood where things have no names in Lewis Carroll's *Through the Looking Glass*. The fawn which Alice meets there runs away when they leave the wood and it realizes its own identity and that of the child accompanying it.

'The Found Picture' *PN Review*, vol. 4, no. 4, 1977.

'Implements in Their Places' First published, in different form, in *Malahat Review*, no. 17, July 1972.

11. *Scop*: the Scops owl, a resident of south-eastern Europe, appears in several draft poems of the early 1970s with a Cretan setting. Lopez notes that it is named after the natural historian Giovanni Antonio Scopoli. Graham visited Crete twice, in 1964 and 1977. His many attempts to write about it suggest that he saw in it exotic parallels to his childhood memories of Greenock.

Follicles: the follicles around a woman's nipples, studied by the physician William Montgomery.

POLEEP: Graham's representation, also used in the Cretan poems, of the Scops owl's whistling call. The significance of the word there, not apparent in the present poem, is that it is an anagram of 'PEOPLE'.

13. *Phoebus*: god of the sun.

40. *Never never*: a pun on the slang term for hire purchase.

53. *Huntly, Moray*: the reference is to the killing of James Stewart, 2nd Earl of Murray, or Moray, by George Gordon, 1st marquess of Huntley, or Huntly, in 1592, subject of the Scots ballad 'The Bonny Earl of Moray'.

66. *pelmanic ... Kimsgame*: Pelmanism and Kim's Game, the latter

described by Rudyard Kipling in his novel *Kim* (1901), are both memory games.

67. A recapitulation of 'The Lying Dear'.

70. *Numb ... same key*: Lopez suggests this may be a reference to the alliterating Ls in the previous section.

Heraklion: Anticipates the Greek imagery of the next section.

'Dear Bryan Wynter' *IITP*, 1977.

Meanders: A favourite theme of Wynter's paintings.

Housman's star/ Lit fences: see note to 'Wynter and the Grammarsow'.

Trying to be better: 'Try to be better', or 'TTBB', was a motto of Graham's.

COLLECTED POEMS (1979)

'To My Wife at Midnight' *PN Review*, vol. 4, no. 4, 1977.

Dun's moor: a play on his wife's maiden name, Dunsmuir.

Culloden: battle in which the Hanoverian (redcoat) army of the Duke of Cumberland defeated Bonnie Prince Charlie at Drummossie Moor, near Inverness (16 April 1746).

Sugar-house quays: the quays used by sugar factories.

APPENDIX: UNCOLLECTED AND MANUSCRIPT POEMS

UNCOLLECTED POEMS (1990)

'I am Rich' *UP*, 1990. Written *c.* 1939.

'Hymn' *The Cornish Review*, no. 2 (Summer 1949). Graham notes that his 'Hymn' is to be sung to the tune of 'Eternal Father of Mankind' by J.B. Dykes.

'Then Who Will Hide the Innocent' *Promenade*, no. 65 (1955).

'The Dark Intention' *New Statesman and Nation*, 18 September 1954.

'The Soldier Campion' *New Statesman and Nation*, 27 October 1956.

'O Why am I So Bright' *UP*, 1990. Dated 9 June 1976.

'If It is Only for You I Speak' *UP*, 1990. Dated 30 May 1977.

'Falling into the Sea' *Observer Magazine*, 20 November 1977.

'For John Heath-Stubbs' *Aquarius*, no. 10 (1978).

And who ... Heath-Stubbs now: an allusion to Yeats's poem 'Who Goes with Fergus?'.

Artorius: King Arthur, eponymous hero of Heath-Stubbs's epic poem (1973).

'To Leonard Clark' *UP*, 1990. Dated December 1977.

'The Visit' *PN Review*, vol. 6, no. 2, 1979.

'The Alligator Girls' *PN Review*, vol. 6, no. 2, 1979.

Graham must have met John Crowe Ransom on one of his two visits to the US, in 1947-8 or 1951-2.

Beside the sweet/ Clear water: this phrase, and the setting of the poem itself allude to Ransom's poem 'Vision by Sweetwater'.

'Look at the Cloud his Evening Playing Cards' *UP*, 1990. Dated 8 May 1978.
'I Will Lend You Malcolm' *PN Review*, vol. 6, no. 2, 1979.
'July Thirteenth Madron' *UP*, 1990. Dated 15 July 1978.
'The December Fox' *UP*, 1990. Dated 20 August 1978.
'The Musical Farmer' *PN Review*, vol. 6, no. 6, 1980.
'A Page about My Country' *Aquarius*, no. 10, 1979.

> *Quhen Alexander ... hys day*: a reminiscence or deliberate distortion of the 'Lament For King Alexander III' by Andrew of Wyntoun (1350?–1420?):
>> Quhen Alysander oure kyng was dede,
>> That Scotland led in luve and le,
>> Away wes sons of ale and brede,
>> Of wyne and wax, of gamyn and gle;
>
> *A'/ Enermit*: A reminiscence of Dunbar's 'Lament for the Makers', in which knights are described as 'anarmit [armed] under helme and scheild'.
> *Harland and Wolfe*: Harland and Wolff, the famous Belfast shipbuilding firm, which also had works on Clydeside.
> *The Big Dam*: Probably Murdieston Dam in the centre of Greenock.
> *Mars ... cramasie*: from MacDiarmid's poem 'The Bonnie Broukit Bairn' (where the last word is spelled *crammasy*).

'The Street of Knives' *PN Review*, vol. 6, no. 6, 1980.

> For the significance of Crete, see note to 'Implements in Their Places, section 11.
> Compare [In the Street of Knives] from *AAN*, below.

'The Fifth of May' *PN Review*, vol. 6, no. 6, 1980.
'An Entertainment for David Wright on His Being Sixty' *UP*, 1990. Dated 13 June 1979.

> *The flying towel*: in his article 'W. S. Graham in the Forties' (*ER*) Wright tells how Graham explained to him the importance of washing towels, with the remark, 'First catch your towel.'
> *Roy*: Wright's compatriot, the poet Roy Campbell (1901–57).
> *Tse*: a Chinese twist on the intitials of T.S. Eliot.
> *Threes*: three-stress lines, a speciality of Graham's, as used in the present poem.
> *The Water/ Margin*: either the classic Chinese novel or the television adventure series based on it, which was shown in Britain in the late 1970s.

'Beholding Thee' *UP*, 1990. Dated 24 August 1979.

> WOW ... THEE: Graham used many variations on this phrase in his letters: 'WOW WOW is only to signify I feel I've said too little in too many words.' (Letter to Fraser Steel, 8 March 1977, in *NFM*.)

'From Gigha Young' *Malahat Review*, no. 55, July 1980.
'Look at the Children' *Malahat Review*, no. 55, July 1980.

'Alice Where Art Thou' *PN Review*, vol. 6, no. 6, 1980.
 Alice ... thou: a nineteenth-century American popular song.
'Penzance/London' *UP*, 1990. Dated 5 October 1980.
'A Walk to the Gulvas' *UP*, 1990. Written *c*.1980.
 The Gulvas: Graham's version of the Galvers, the hills Carn Galver and Little
 Galver in west Cornwall (perhaps influenced by the village name Gulval).

AIMED AT NOBODY: POEMS FROM NOTEBOOKS (1993)
All these poems were first published in *AAN*. Square brackets indicate a title
given by Skelton and Blackwood rather than Graham himself.

'Proem' *c*.1973.
'The Ballad of Willie Peden' *c*.1952.
 A companion piece to 'The Broad Close' and 'Baldy Bane'.
[The Circumstances Are Still Infinite] *c*.1970.
 Alan: Alan Lowndes. (See People)
'Surrealgraphs' 11 November 1975.
[One Good Sound] *c*.1972.
'The Eighth Letter' *c*.1970.
 Compare 'Dear Who I Mean', in *MML*.
 The eighth letter: in other words, a sequel to 'Seven Letters'.
'Pangur' *c*.1970.
 Pangur: a reference to the anonymous Irish poem 'Pangur Ban'.
'Myself the Day Desires' Dated 26 October 1969.
[To Find and Find] *c*.1970.
[Kandinsky's Ribbons] *c*.1967.
[From the Sleeping House] *c*.1970.
'The Dredge' Dated 5 October 1971.
[More Shots of Mister Simpson] Dated 3 May 1971.
'A Dream of Crete' *c*.1970.
 For the significance of Crete, see note to 'Implements in Their Places, section
 11.
 Compare the *Aquarius* version of 'A Dream of Crete', below.
'In Crete' *c*.1969.
[In the Street of Knives] *c*.1972.
 Compare 'The Street of Knives' from *UP*, above.
[On the Other Side of Language] *c*.1965.
 Audibably: a deliberate wordplay.
[Nature Is Never Journalistic] Dated 11 December 1969.
'Fill In This Form' Dated 5 May 1971.
[I Am Told You Speak My Language] Dated 23 October 1970.
'About the Stuff' Dated 30 October 1968.
 Tinners': The Tinners' Arms, a pub in Zennor.

[This Little Evening] *c*.1971.

'The Honey Game' Dated 5 August 1970.

'As Told to Davie Dunsmuir' Dated 5 February 1966.

'Waiting for Snow' *c*.1970.

[The Particular Object] Dated 8 October 1971.

    – ∪ –: Skelton and Blackwood erroneously transcribe the metrical symbol for an unstressed syllable as a lowercase letter U. In a note on the MS, Skelton speculated that Graham's hieroglyphics might represent the word 'Mum'. There are, however, many Graham MSS covered with similar signs, which prove that they are scansion marks, using the old-fashioned symbol – to represent a stressed syllable (now usually written ´). Sounding the particular object's name as 'dum de dum' restores the pentameter rhythm of the lines, eg: 'Your name? My dum de dum. My dum de dum.'

[Malcolm Mooney's Figment] *c*.1968.

'The Greenock Dialogues' *c*.1970.

    I. *Burns' Mary*: Mary Campbell was buried in the old West Highland Churchyard in Greenock and in 1920 reinterred in the Greenock Cemetery. Graham's claim that she lies in the Old Burial Ground in Inverkip Street, where John Galt is buried, is an error.

    Afton: the reference is to Burns's poem 'Sweet Afton': 'My Mary's asleep by thy murmuring stream,/ Flow gently, sweet Afton, disturb not her dream.'

    II. *A real place . . . the loch*: the setting has changed from the Firth of Clyde of the first section to a more abstract Scottish landscape.

    Yeats' hazel/ Wood: in 'The Song of Wandering Aengus'.

    IV. The setting reverts to that of the first section.

    The sleeping warrior: a hill of this name on Arran is visible from the Firth of Clyde.

[From Dark Dialogues] *c*.1958.

[Son, or Who You Are] *c*.1974.

[What's the News?] *c*.1968.

'The Bridge' *c*.1970.

[I Write as I Speak] Dated 14 May 1972.

[Here Behind the Alphabet] *c*.1974.

[X] Dated 9 August 1968.

[Send Me a Note] *c*.1967.

    Compare 'Johann Joachim Quantz's Five Lessons', above.

[The Word's Name] *c*.1967.

    Compare 'Dear Who I Mean', above.

[If it is Only for You I Speak] *c*.1972.

[Five Verses Beginning with the Word Language] *c*.1974.

    An early version of 'Language Ah Now You Have Me'. Skelton and Blackwood quote a note from Graham on another MS: '. . . this poem sprung from me trying to write about a soldier dying on the Paddy fields of Vietnam of a belly-wound and the flies at his face and wanting his mother and not knowing what he was fighting for.' Compare also 'The Conscript Goes', below.

'The Conscript Goes' Dated 25 August 1968.

'Hark ... rye': Not from a real song, though it borrows from the famous song in Shakespeare's *Cymbeline* and from Burns's 'Coming through the Rye'.

Pointers: an undertaker in Greenock.

'Slaughterhouse' Dated 5 October 1969.

Another poem referring to the Madron slaughterhouse near Graham's home. See note to 'Five Visitors to Madron'.

[The Prisoner] Dated 12 September 1970.

[My Long Home Loch] Dated 23 March 1967.

from SELECTED POEMS (1996)

'As Brilliance Fell' *Stand*, no. 8, 1954.

OTHER UNCOLLECTED AND NOTEBOOK POEMS

[And I Would Be a Soldier with a Gun] Dated September 1937.

'To ND' Dated November 1939.

'Fourth Sonnet' *Poetry (London)*, no. 7, October/November 1942.

'Letter X' *Encounter*, vol. 10, no. 1, January 1958.

from: 'A Dream Of Crete' *Aquarius*, no. 6 (1973).

For the significance of Crete, see note to 'Implements in Their Places', section 11.

from 'With the Dulle Griet in Canada'

The unfinished and unpublished 'With the Dulle Griet in Canada' describes a reading tour of Canada by Graham in 1973. These extracts were first published in *CS*. See Michael and Margaret Snow, 'With the Dulle Griet in Canada' (*CS*).

Dulle Griet: or 'Mad Meg', a painting by Bruegel.

'There seems ... At large': This quotation is probably invented, though Leonard Rosoman, in an essay on 'Mad Meg' which Graham used, refers to her as a 'virago'. Leonard Rosoman, *Bruegel's 'Mad Meg'*, Painters on Painting Series (London: Cassell, 1969).

Puchawhanta: presumably a variation on Pocahontas.

Mons Meg: a siege gun in Edinburgh Castle.

Theorums: the spelling matches 'syndrums' and 'humdrums'.

WOW WOW: see note to 'Beholding Thee'.

Cyacide: probably intended as a portmanteau of *cyanide* and *suicide*.

Glossary

Airt A direction or locality. (Scots)
Astragal A glazing bar in a window
Athanor An alchemical furnace
Baillie An alderman. (Scots)
Ben A mountain. (Scots Gaelic)
Bing A slag-heap. (Scots)
Binnacle The case containing a ship's compass. (Nautical)
Birl To twist or spin. (Scots)
Blaeberry Bilberry. (Scots)
Bluenose A puritanical person. (Scots)
Bothy A small hut. (Scots)
Branks A scold's bridle. (Scots)
Bright As a verb, apparently a coinage in the sense *to polish*
Caa To drive. (Scots)
Calyx The outer covering of a flower
Cardinals The four principal points of the compass
Chairoplane Fairground ride of the merry-go-round type
Chirpers A fishermen's nickname for herring, derived from the sound made by
   their collapsing air-bladders as they are hauled out
Churchtown Cornish term for a village having a church
Close Alley leading to the inner courtyard of a Scottish tenement building
Comber A long, curling wave
Cramasie Crimson. (Scots)
Creel A wicker basket used by anglers to hold fish
The Dancing Men The *aurora borealis*
Deserves A noun coined from the verb, with a suggestion of *reserves*
Ding The sound of a bell or similar metallic object being struck
Drouth Thirst
Dulse A kind of seaweed
Felsite A light-coloured volcanic rock
Flamen An ancient Roman priest. (Latin)
Flense To strip blubber and/or skin from a whale
Found A ring of stones or brushwood on which a haystack is built.
   (Scots)
Gean A species of cherry. (Scots)
Gowan A daisy. (Scots)
Graith Apparatus or accoutrements. (Scots)

Grammarsow Graham's deliberate misspelling of *grammersow*, a Cornish dialect word for a woodlouse

Grampus An orca or killer whale

Hake in the throat A sore or dry throat. (Scots)

Het 'It' or 'He' in a children's game of tag or 'tig'. (Scots)

Hoodie A hooded crow. (Scots)

Hoster A soldier, one of a host. (Scots)

Inish An island. (Irish)

Jackeasy Indifferent, easy-going, offhand. (Scots)

Jible To talk nonsense or babble drunkenly. (Scots)

Keek To peep. (Scots)

Keeling Traversing with a keel, sailing

Kern A sheaf, technically, the last one reaped at the harvest

Kingforked Apparently a coinage. The meaning is obscure

Knowe A knoll or hill. (Scots/Irish)

Kyle A narrow channel between two islands or between an island and the mainland. (Scots)

Land A tenement building. (Scots)

Lead (Pronounced *leed*.) A fissure in the pack ice of polar seas

Lea-rig A strip of grass left untilled in a ploughed field. (Scots)

Lintroot Flax-root. (Scots)

Linty Linnet. (Scots)

Liveoak An evergreen tree found in North America

Lochan A small loch. (Scots)

Lyn A waterfall. (Scots)

Lythed Full of pollack. Graham's coinage from 'lythe', Scots word for the Atlantic pollack. (See *Saithe*)

Makar Poet. (Scots)

Mavis Thrush. (Poetic)

Meander The winding course of a stream or river

Messages Shopping. (Scots)

Milt The sperm of fish

Minch Common noun derived by Graham from the proper noun (see *Places*): a channel

Needfire Luminescence, as of decaying wood

Nighthead Graham's pun on *knighthead*, a timber supporting the inner end of the bowsprit on a sailing ship. (Nautical)

Peever A flat stone used in the game of hopscotch, from which Graham derives the past participle *peevered*. (Scots)

Pinhead A tadpole. (Scots)

Playrope A skipping rope. (Scots)

Quern A handmill for grinding corn

Rhinn Common noun derived by Graham from the proper noun (see *Places*): a rocky promontory

Saithe The Atlantic pollack, a fish. (Scots)

Sclim the lether To climb the ladder, also a children's game, and rhyme. (Scots)

Screeve In shipyards, a scored dimension line or to score a dimension line on steel

Scrived Inscribed

Scunnering Loathsome. (Scots)

Set-in bed A bed set into the thickness of a wall in a Scottish tenement. (Scots)

Shallop A vessel used for sailing in shallow water

Sheepsbit The sheepsbit scabious, a flower

Sheldrake Male of a species of duck, having a greenish-black head

Shirred (Of cloth.) Gathered into decorative rows by parallel stitching

Siding Leaning

Signs Frequently used by Graham in the sense of constellations

Skelp A slap, to slap. (Scots)

Smirr Light rain. (Scots)

Smither A fragment. (Scots)

Sneck A latch. (Scots)

Sparstone A pale or translucent mineral

Speir To ask. (Scots)

Stoor To rise in clouds, as dust or smoke. (Scots)

Stoure Dust, tumult. (Scots)

Stranger A fluttering piece of ash in the fire

Strath A wide river-valley. (Scots)

Swither To waver or fidget. (Scots)

Taliped A person with a clubfoot

Teel To till or cultivate. (Scots)

Tig The children's game of tag. (Scots)

Tod A fox. (Scots)

Venust Beautiful. (Obsolete)

Wakerife Wakeful. (Scots)

Waly A cry of lamentation. (Scots)

Wapenschaw A muster of armed men. (Scots)

Watercombs Probably a portmanteau of 'water' and 'catacombs'

Wheesht Hush. (Scots)

Whinfire A fire caused by the annual burning of gorse, or whin, on moorland. (Scots)

Worm The spiral tube of a still

Yella-yite A yellowhammer, but Graham explains (letter to Alan Clodd, 16 November 1954, in *NFM*) that it is an 'insulting expression meaning cowardly' (Scots)

People

John Barbour Scottish poet (?–1395)

Brigit A fictional character, referred to in, e.g.,'The Greenock Dialogues', as the poet's 'half-cousin' and childhood sweetheart. Her name may derive, as Lopez suggests, from an Irish goddess mentioned in Graves's *The White Goddess*

Don Brown English artist and teacher (1930–), and friend of Graham

Brueghel Pieter Brueghel the Elder (1525?–1569), Flemish artist

Burns' Mary Mary Campbell ('Highland Mary', 1763–86)

Leonard Clark British poet (1905–81)

Corbière Tristan Corbière, French poet (1845–75)

Hart Crane American poet (1899–1932)

Dunbar William Dunbar, Scottish poet (1460?–1513?)

Nessie Dunsmuir (Ness) Agnes Kilpatrick Dunsmuir Graham, the poet's wife (1909–99)

Featherston Bill Featherston, Canadian artist and teacher (1927–), a friend of Graham

Friell Brian Friel, Irish playwright (1929–)

John Galt Scottish novelist (1779–1839), resident in Greenock, author of *Annals of the Parish* (1821)

Alastair Graham The poet's younger brother (1926–2001)

Alexander Graham The poet's father (1884–1954)

Hasse Johann Adolf Hasse, German composer (1699–1783), whose works include concertos for flute

John Heath-Stubbs British poet (1918–), partially blind for most of his life and totally blind since 1978

Roger Hilton St Ives artist (1911–75), and close friend of Graham

David Jones Welsh poet and artist (1895–1974)

Kandinsky Wassily Kandinsky, Russian artist (1866–1944)

Karl A fictional character, pupil of Johann Joachim Quantz

Peter Lanyon St Ives artist (1918–64)

Lin Chung Hero of the Chinese novel *The Water Margin*, and the television series based on it

Alan Lowndes British artist (1921–78)

MacBryde Robert MacBryde, Scottish artist (1913–66), and friend of Graham

MacDiarmid Hugh MacDiarmid, pseudonym of Christopher Murray Grieve, Scottish poet (1892–1978)

Norman Macleod American poet (1906–85) who edited the *Pembroke Magazine*

from Pembroke State University, North Carolina, where he was poet-in-residence

Malcolm Mooney The fictional hero of 'Malcolm Mooney's Land' and 'What is the Language Using Us for?' According to Lopez, the name derives from a chain of bars owned by Guinness

Michael St Michael the Archangel, patron saint of mariners

Montgomerie William Fetherston-Haugh Montgomery (1797–1859), physician who described the changes in the follicles surrounding the nipples in the early stages of pregnancy

Nansen Fridtjof Nansen, Norwegian explorer and diplomat (1861–1930), whose expedition to the Arctic in 1888–9 on his ship the *Fram* and on foot was a source of inspiration to Graham

Tony O'Malley Irish artist and friend of Graham (1913–2003)

Julian Orde Actress and poet, girlfriend of Graham (1917–74)

Paul Potts Canadian poet and autobiographer (1911–90) who frequented the same Soho pubs as Graham in the 1940s

Johann Joachim Quantz German flautist and composer (1697–1773)

John Crowe Ransom US poet and critic (1888–1974)

Roy Roy Campbell, South African poet (1901–57)

Shony A Celtic sea-god

Robin Skelton British-born Canadian poet and scholar (1925–97), editor of *Malahat Review*

Albert Strick, Garfield Strick Neighbours of Graham in Madron

Vivienne Vivienne Koch, American writer and critic (1914–61), who was Norman Macleod's second wife and became Graham's lover in the late 1940s

Vlaminck Maurice de Vlaminck, French artist (1876–1958)

Alfred Wallis Cornish sailor and naive artist (1855–1942)

George Wood Curator of Alberta College of Art at the time of Graham's visit to Canada

David Wright South African poet (1920–94), resident in Britain for most of his life

Bryan Wynter St Ives artist (1915–75), a close friend of Graham

Places

Afton River in Ayrshire
Ben Cruachen Ben Cruachan, mountain in Argyll and Bute
Black Rosses 'Ross' or 'Ros' has been variously associated with coastal rocks
    and promontories off Scotland, Ireland and Cornwall
Blantyre Town in Lanarkshire, birthplace of Nessie Dunsmuir Graham
Botallack The village in the west of Cornwall where Hilton lived
Bothwell Town in Lanarkshire
Broad Close Street in Greenock
Calder River in south-west Scotland
Cartsburn Street, Cartsburn Vaults Street and pub in Greenock, near Graham's
    old home in Hope Street
Dechmont Village and hill in West Lothian, Scotland
Dunoon Town seven miles west of Greenock
Ettrick Village in the Scottish Borders, birthplace of James Hogg ('The Ettrick
    Shepherd')
Fouste Canyon Possibly Faust Canyon, Utah
Gareloch Loch in Argyll and Bute
Gigha Island off the west coast of Scotland
Goatfell Mountain on the Isle of Arran
Greenock The Clydeside town where Graham grew up
The Gulvas The Galvers, the hills Carn Galver and Little Galver in west
    Cornwall
Gurnard's Head Promontory in west Cornwall
Hamilton Town in Lanarkshire
Heraklion Town in Crete
Hope Street One, Hope Street, Greenock, was where Graham was born and
    spent his childhood
Innellan Village on the Firth of Clyde, Argyll and Bute
Inverkip Street In Greenock
Jura Island off the west coast of Scotland
Kestle Village near Mevagissey in Cornwall
Kilkreggan Kilcreggan, town on the Firth of Clyde, roughly opposite Greenock
Kinmore Village in County Fermanagh, Northern Ireland
Kintyre Promontory in south-west Scotland
Kirn North-east extension of the town of Dunoon
Kirriemuir Town in Angus, Scotland
Loch Coruisk Loch in the Cuillin Hills on the Isle of Skye

Loch Long Loch whose entry is visible across the Clyde from Greenock
Loch Thom Reservoir in Inverclyde, near Greenock
Lyndoch Street Lynedoch Street in Greenock
Madron The Cornish village where Graham lived from 1967 to his death in 1986
Malia Town on the north-east coast of Crete
Mor Light A lighthouse. *Mor* is both the Cornish for 'sea' and the Scots Gaelic for 'big' or 'lofty'
Nancledra A village in south-west Cornwall, near Madron
Narnain Ben Narnain is one of a group of mountains known as the Arrochar Alps situated at the head of Loch Long
Old Custom House A large classical style building (1817), the former centre for Greenock's extensive overseas trade
Penwith The western peninsula of Cornwall
Piraeus The port of Athens, often mentioned in Graham's Cretan poems as the embarkation point for a journey to Crete
Rhinns The Rhinns of Galloway, a rocky promontory of south-west Scotland
Rhue Corner Near Ullapool in the Scottish Highlands
Ross District of north-west Scotland, opposite the Isle of Skye
Rothesay Town on the Isle of Bute
St Buryan Village in west Cornwall
St Just Small town in west Cornwall
Sgurr nan Gillian, Sgurr na Gillean Sgurr nan Gillean, 'The Peak of the Young Men' in the Cuillin Hills on Skye
Sheelhill Glen Shielhill Glen, a wooded valley near Loch Thom
Shian Bay On the Island of Jura
Skeer From the Gaelic *sgeir*, an isolated sea rock, rarely submerged
Skerry Vore Skerryvore, a lighthouse off the coast of Orkney
Soor Duik Soor Dook, 'Sour Milk', the stream descending from Ben Narnain to Loch Long (Gaelic name *Allt a'Bhalachain*, the Buttermilk Burn)
Tara Seat of ancient Irish kings, referred to in Thomas Moore's poem 'The Harp that Once through Tara's Halls'
Trevayler Trevaylor House and estate one mile east of Madron
Whin Hill Steep hill on the outskirts of Greenock, marking the edge of an extensive area of moorland close to Graham's childhood home
White Mountains In western Crete
Yang tse kiang Yangtze Kiang, the Yangtze river, China
Zennor Village in the west of Cornwall
Zennor Head A promontory near Zennor

Bibliography

The abbreviations in brackets are those used in the Notes to refer to the book concerned.

BOOKS BY W. S. GRAHAM (in order of publication)

Cage Without Grievance, Glasgow: Parton Press, 1942 (*CWG*)
The Seven Journeys, Glasgow: William MacLellan, 1944 (*7J*)
2ND *Poems*, London: Nicholson and Watson, 1945 (*2P*)
The White Threshold, London: Faber and Faber, 1949 (*WT*)
The Nightfishing, London: Faber and Faber, 1955 (*NF*)
Malcolm Mooney's Land, London: Faber and Faber, 1970 (*MML*)
Implements in Their Places, London: Faber and Faber, 1977 (*IITP*)
Collected Poems 1942–1977, London: Faber and Faber, 1979 (*CP*)
Selected Poems, New York: Ecco Press, 1980
Uncollected Poems, Warwick: Greville Press, 1990 (*UP*)
Aimed at Nobody: Poems from Notebooks, ed. Margaret Blackwood and Robin Skelton, London, Faber and Faber, 1993 (*AAN*)
Selected Poems, London: Faber and Faber, 1996
W. S. Graham Selected by Nessie Dunsmuir, Warwick: Greville Press, 1998
The Nightfisherman: Selected Letters of W. S. Graham, ed. Michael and Margaret Snow, Manchester: Carcanet, 1999 (*NFM*)

WORKS ABOUT W. S. GRAHAM

Duncan, Ronnie, and Davidson, Jonathan, *The Constructed Space: A Celebration of W. S. Graham*, Lincoln: Jackson's Arm, 1994 (*CS*)
Francis, Matthew, *Where the People Are: Language and Community in the Poetry of W. S. Graham*, Cambridge: Salt, forthcoming
Lopez, Tony, *The Poetry of W. S. Graham*, Edinburgh, Edinburgh University Press, 1989 (*PWSG*)
Pite, Ralph, and Jones, Hester, (eds.), *W. S. Graham: A Selection of Essays*, Liverpool: University of Liverpool Press, forthcoming

Aquarius, no. 25/26 (George Barker/W. S. Graham Issue, 2002)
Edinburgh Review, no. 75 (W. S. Graham Issue, February 1987) (*ER*)

Index of Titles

Index of First Lines

386

Remember it is necessary to be aware, 304
Right break your tooth on faith. Climb up the sea, 20
Roger, whether the tree is made, 177

Say that in lovers with stones for family, 23
Send me a note. Blow me a little ladder, 328
Shrill the fife, kettle the drum, 145
Shut up. Shut up. There's nobody here, 157
Since all my steps taken, 59
Since once (livelong the day) my prayer measured, 78
Smiling locked round with calling that she is, 50
So does the sea, 45
So that each person may quickly find that, 228
Sometimes the whisky-balanced miner sings, 342
Somewhere our belonging particles, 240
Son, or who you are, knocking, 324
Soon to be distances locked sound, 34
SOUND a long blast, 184
Straighten your face. Stand still, 313

Tear shed on the soon cracking roof, 78
That firewood pale with salt and burning green, 82
Then holier than innocence, like ten infant commandments, 41
Then who will hide the innocent, 270
There are no certain miles in ice-invented vales, 7
There was from March 3rd to April 3rd the appearance of reality, 53
There was when morning fell, 22
This fond event my origin knows well, 23
This is only a note, 258
This morning I am ready if you are, 206
This morning shaving my brain to face the world, 284
This step sails who an ocean crossed, 64
Time and again a Mayscape's botany shapes, 11

To girls at the turn of night love goes on knocking, 26
To make this scene in a certain fashion, 309
To put it springtime the green shepherd, 69
To set the scene. It is April, 232
To set the scene. The kirk, 232
To set the scene. The night, 233
Today, Tuesday, I decided to move on, 153
Towards that other, the dim, the one queen, 52

Under (not ground but the mind's), 100
Unmet at Euston in a dream, 215

Very gently struck, 105

Waiting for snow I look out, 316
The way I see it is that Master, 162
Welcome then anytime. Fare, 121
What does it matter if the words, 178
What is the language using us for?, 199
Whatever you've come here to get, 237
What's the news, my bold, 325
When the word or the word's name, 301, 329
When who we think we are is suddenly, 183
Which I was given because, 235
White is our net but white the sea, 269
Why I can be articulate and, 318
Why so notbright, the comets and magpies rocket?, 49
With all many men laid down in the burial heart, 62
With you present I empty out, 305
Wonder struck one inhabitant of me, 35
Workmen on the unleashed drowning floors, what can, 84
Worldhauled, he's grounded on God's great bank, 87
Writing this so quietly writes of itself 43

Yes as alike as entirely, 99
Your name in capitals. Birth place, 312